D1214850

Consumer price indices

An ILO manual

Ralph Turvey

with contributions by

D. J. Sellwood, Bohdan J. Szulc, H. W. J. Donkers et al., M. A. Marret, L. C. Clements et al., Thomas J. Woodhouse and Kathleen M. Hanson

International Labour Office Geneva

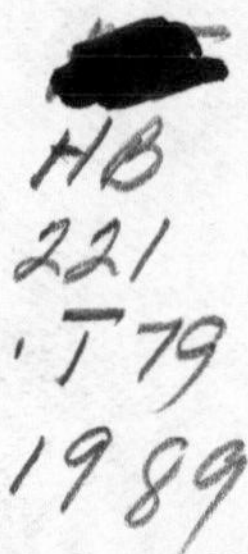

ISBN 92-2-106436-0

First published 1989

ILO publications can be obtained through major booksellers or ILO local offices in many countries, or direct from ILO Publications, International Labour Office, CH-1211 Geneva 22, Switzerland. A catalogue or list of new publications will be sent free of charge from the above address.

Printed in Switzerland IRL

Preface

In this manual I have tried to make widely available the wisdom and experience of the experts. I have neither tried nor wanted to be original, although no doubt some personal ideas and prejudices have crept in; it would have been less fun to write if they had not.

I have endeavoured to make this manual self-contained. Many of the readers at whom it is aimed will not have access to libraries, and in any case there is not much published material on the practical aspects of index construction; I wish that there were more.

This book contains very little about sample design, though in almost all countries this is directly relevant, both because of the use of household expenditure surveys as a prime source of data for weighting and because of the use of dwelling surveys for the collection of rental data. However, the design and conduct of such surveys is really a separate topic. On this subject the reader is referred to the separate manual to be published by the National Household Survey Capability Programme of the United Nations Statistical Office: *Technical studies on income and expenditure surveys.*

Conversations and correspondence with the experts from national statistical offices have provided most of the material I have used – and have been very enjoyable. Many of them have given me copies of internal technical memoranda, manuals and worksheets which, though none are reproduced here, have all been useful.

In particular, I owe a great deal to the participants in the two seminars on consumer price indices held in 1981 and 1986, organised jointly by the ILO and the European Conference of Statisticians, and to those delegates to the Fourteenth International Conference of Labour Statisticians in October 1987 who participated in the committee which produced the resolution on consumer price indices (reproduced in Appendix 1). Many of these people have also helped me in conversations on other occasions, by providing working papers and by sending extensive written comments on earlier drafts of this manual; I am especially grateful to Hugues Picard, Jean-Paul Baraille and Marie-France Bobin; Don Sellwood and Martin Hargreaves; Gunnar Stolpe, Göthe Isacsson and Hugo Johanneson; S. Guckes; Barbara Slater, Arthur Ridgeway, Bohdan Szulc and Andrew Baldwin, and Colin Clements.

I am indebted to Jack Triplett for the "What is the question?" approach [1] and to Peter Steiner for the distinction between what are here called acquisition, use and payment.[2] A draft work by Joel Popkin was also helpful.

---

[1] "Escalation measures: What is the answer? What is the question?", in *Price level measurement* (Minister of Supply and Services, Ottawa, Canada, 1983).

[2] "Consumer durables in an index of consumer prices", in *Government price statistics* (Joint Economic Committee, Congress of the United States, Jan. 1961).

Mme Khin Khin Glauser, one of my colleagues in the ILO Bureau of Statistics, has been indefatigable in assisting me with the collection and analysis of information about national practices in index compilation and in various editorial tasks. My ILO colleague Ralf Hussmanns, and Laszlo Drechsler of the United Nations Statistical Office, both contributed many useful comments on the second draft.

In short, so much help has been so willingly given by so many people towards this book that I can almost say that if it contains errors they are hardly my fault!

As with other endeavours pursued during a period of our 30 happy years together, the work on this manual started with the support and encouragement of my wife. Alas, she did not live to see it completed, so I can only dedicate it, with love, to her memory.

Ralph Turvey,
Director,
Labour Information and Statistics Department, ILO.
February 1989

Contents

Appendices

(reprinted from the ILO *Bulletin of Labour Statistics*)

Figures

Boxes

Introduction

1

The purpose of this manual

This manual is aimed at practising statisticians who have to construct or revise a consumer price index (CPI). It reflects the international resolution on the subject, reprinted in Appendix 1, but goes beyond it in discussing matters of detail which could not be covered in such a brief document.

It is also designed to help the users of consumer price indices, including students of economics, who need to learn about the problems and limitations of these indices. Finally, it is addressed to governments which need to know about the resources required by their statisticians to produce a reliable index.

The manual deals with the practice of consumer price index numbers and does not attempt to survey the academic literature on the subject. Much of that extensive and fascinating literature is irrelevant for the purposes of this manual. One reason is that no compiler of a consumer price index, whether it be monthly or quarterly, can hope to obtain new weights more than once a year at the most, and the data used to compute new weights always refer to the past rather than to the present, whereas much of the literature deals with other types of index. In any case, there is no point in providing references to publications that are available only in large specialised libraries, and the manual is intended to be self-contained. For this reason it includes in Appendices 2 to 8 a number of articles reprinted from the *ILO Bulletin of Labour Statistics*. The text draws upon them to some extent but by no means summarises them completely. Those readers who feel the need for a more academic treatment should turn to the late Professor R. G. D. Allen's book *Index numbers in theory and practice* (London, Macmillan, 1975) which, however, does not profess to deal with the operational aspects of weighting, collecting and computing.

The reader may notice that two topics, the treatment of owner-occupied dwellings and of seasonally available items, are dealt with at apparently disproportionate length in the following pages. This reflects the fact that far from there being any unique best practice for incorporating these items into an index, there are several alternative methods for dealing with them whose relevance and nature demands a fairly extensive discussion. More generally, the space devoted to different subjects cannot be taken as a measure of their relative importance.

The terminology used in this manual

This section provides definitions of the most important terms relating to consumer price indices that are used in the manual.

Consumption. All goods and services that are acquired, used or paid for by households, but not for business purposes and not for the acquisition of wealth. Thus the purchase of intermediate goods and services and investment in all forms of assets are both excluded.

Item, composite item and elementary aggregate. These three related terms are explained in figure 1. The term "item" is used loosely to mean any good or service included in the expenditure covered by the index. The term "composite item" is used more precisely to signify the most detailed level of aggregation of consumption for which weights can be estimated. If a breakdown of the consumption of a composite item by region or type of outlet is not available and cannot be estimated, then that composite item constitutes an elementary aggregate. But if such a further breakdown can be made, then the composite item is decomposed into a number of elementary aggregates. These are the most detailed levels of expenditure by item, by region and by outlet type for which weights are used. For example, butter sold in the northern region in supermarkets might constitute an elementary aggregate. But if no breakdown by type of outlet is available, it would consist of all butter sales in the northern region.

Weight. The relative expenditure or consumption share of an elementary aggregate, or sometimes of its component parts, estimated from available data.

Specification. The description of a representative item which is provided by the central office to the price collectors. It may be printed on the form used for price collection or provided in a separate list. More detailed descriptions of the particular varieties selected by the collectors within the specification provided will normally be reported by them on the price collection forms.

Representative item, variety. In most cases, prices cannot be obtained for all items constituting an elementary aggregate. Those items selected to represent it, for which specifications are provided to the price collectors, are called "representative items". In most cases, the specification of a representative item will cover a number of "varieties", so that one or more of them must be precisely identified in each outlet for pricing. For example, if a group of domestic appliances sold in department stores in the capital city constitutes an elementary aggregate, a particular type of vacuum cleaner might be specified as a representative item and the price obtained in a particular store would then be for a variety described in more detailed terms so as to be narrowed down to a particular brand and model.

Price, relative. Ratio of a single price at a given point in time to the corresponding price in a previous period.

Index base period. The period for which the index is set to 100.

Price reference period. The period (or date) whose prices are used as denominators in calculating price relatives.

Weight reference period. The period covered by the expenditure statistics used to calculate weights.

Elementary aggregate index. An index constructed from price data, often with no specific weighting of its components, for one or more representative items, often for a specified outlet type and/or region.

Group index. An index for a major group of items, e.g. clothing, being a weighted average of the elementary aggregate indices within the group.

All-items index. The consumer price index, when it is necessary to distinguish it from its components. It is a weighted average of all elementary aggregate indices and of all group indices.

Figure 1. Terminology relating to consumer price indices

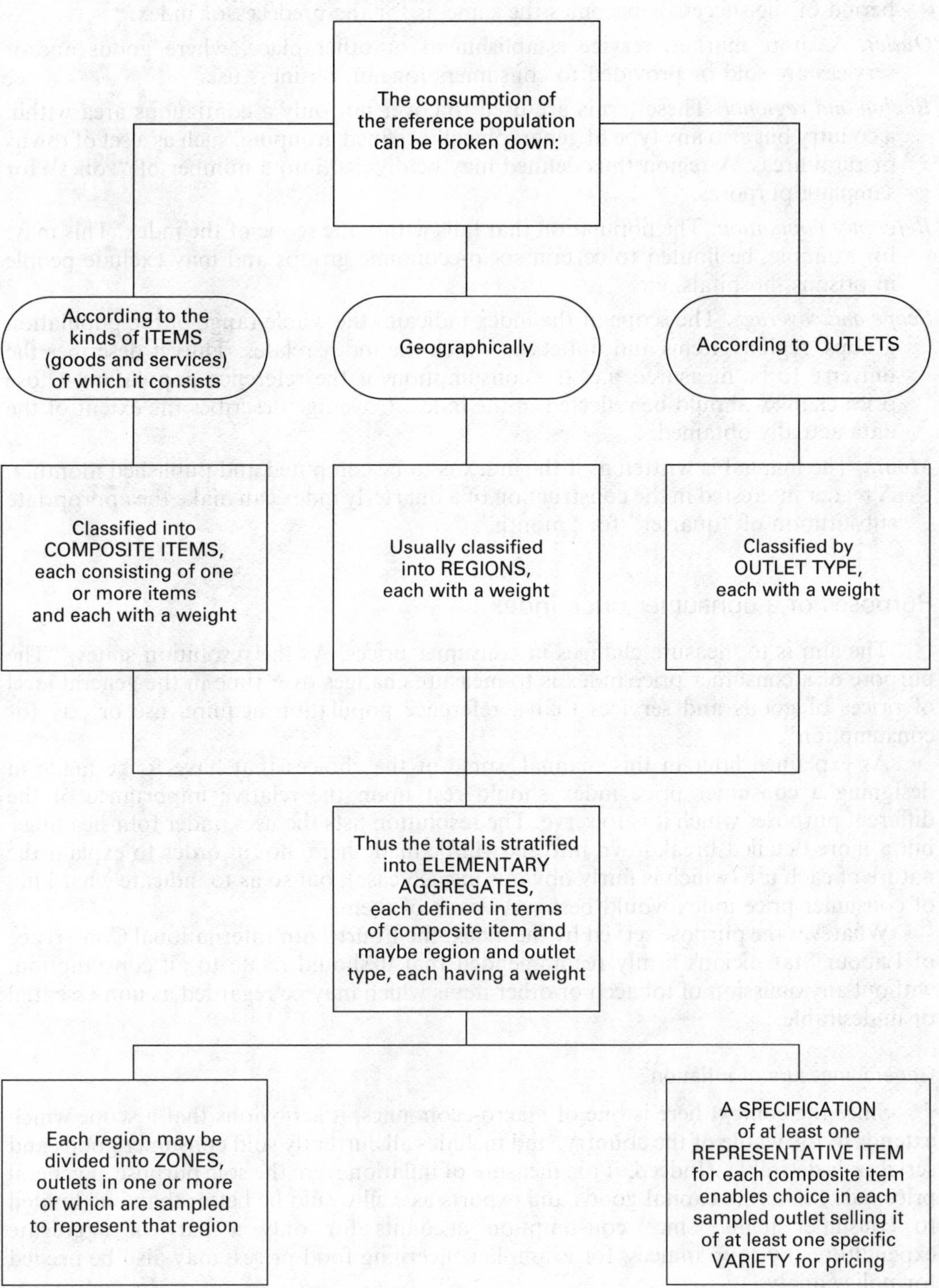

Chain and link. A chain index consists of a series of successive indices, each linked (spliced) to its predecessor. Linking consists of multiplying the values of the successor index by the value of its predecessor in an overlap period, so that the index base period of the successor becomes the same as for the predecessor index.

Outlet. A shop, market, service establishment or other place, where goods and/or services are sold or provided to consumers for non-business use.

Region and regional. These terms are used to cover not only a contiguous area within a country but also any type of geographically defined grouping, such as a set of towns or rural areas. A region thus defined may be divided into a number of "zones" for sampling purposes.

Reference population. The population that falls within the scope of the index. This may, for example, be limited to certain socio-economic groups and may exclude people in prisons, hospitals, etc.

Scope and coverage. The scope of the index indicates the whole range of the population groups, regions, items and outlets to which the index relates. Thus it describes the universe to be measured, i.e. the consumption of the reference population whose price changes should be reflected in the index. Coverage describes the extent of the data actually obtained.

Month. The manual is written as if the index is to be computed and published monthly. A reader interested in the construction of a quarterly index can make the appropriate substitution of "quarter" for "month".

Purposes of a consumer price index

The aim is to measure changes in consumer prices. As the resolution states, "The purpose of a consumer price index is to measure changes over time in the general level of prices of goods and services that a reference population acquire, use or pay for consumption".

As explained later in this manual, some of the choices that have to be made in designing a consumer price index should rest upon the relative importance of the different purposes which it is to serve. The resolution lists the uses under four headings, but a more detailed breakdown into six will be made here, not in order to explain the nature of each use (which is fairly obvious in each case), but so as to indicate what kind of consumer price index would best serve each of them.

Whatever the purpose served by the index, the Fourteenth International Conference of Labour Statisticians firmly recommended that it should relate to all consumption, without any omission of tobacco or other items which may be regarded as non-essential or undesirable.

General measure of inflation

Since the context here is one of macro-economics, it is obvious that a scope which extends to the whole of the country, and includes all currently sold consumer goods and services, is desirable. (Indeed, if the measure of inflation were the sole purpose, a general price index covering capital goods and exports as well would be better than one limited to consumer items, since consumption accounts for only a part of aggregate expenditures.) Group indices, for example concerning food prices, may also be needed for policy analysis.

As inflation is generally viewed as relating to market transactions, imputed items are best omitted. Similarly, since increases in prices and in interest rates have different causes and different effects, and since interest-rate policy sometimes aims at controlling inflation, it may be a good idea to measure them separately, excluding interest rates from a general measure of inflation.

The same consideration also applies to taxes (or at least tax changes), though the technical problems of excluding them are greater. Thus if there is a shift from direct to indirect taxation, or vice versa, it may be considered that the resulting change in prices is different in nature from other changes and should be excluded from the index, or at least estimated as a particular component of changes in it. The same view may be taken with regard to some of the other uses of the index discussed next. For instance, it may be decided that a rise in prices reflecting an increase in indirect taxation which is offset by a fall in direct taxes does not warrant an increase in indexed incomes.

Indexation by government

If taxes, fines or fees levied by government are tied to the consumer price index, the aim is presumably to adjust them so as to maintain the burden upon the people paying them constant in real terms. By "real burden" we understand the amount of goods and services that the people who pay these taxes, and so on, might have bought with the money if they had not had to hand it over to the government. So the question is: Which "people" and which "goods and services"?

The use of a consumer price index for indexing state pensions is important and widespread, the aim being to preserve their purchasing power over the goods and services on which they are spent. Certain other transfer payments by government, together with certain payments fixed by the courts, such as alimony, are similarly indexed.

Prices and wage and salary adjustment in contracts

Indexation of wages and salaries in contracts of employment presumably avoids the need to renegotiate the contracts when prices rise. So the question is: Which prices are deemed relevant by employers and employees when negotiating wages and salaries? The obvious general answer is that they consist of the prices paid by those employees whose wages and salaries are indexed.

Indexation of prices in contracts for the supply of goods and services by firms is also common. The consumer prices most relevant (or least irrelevant) for this purpose will vary from case to case. In many cases it will appear that a wage index or a materials price index would be more appropriate. Even when it is consumer prices that are relevant, the indexation may apply to purchases on which no tax is paid, so that the consumer price index including indirect taxes should not be used.

Current cost accounting

The revaluation of fixed assets and stocks for accounting purposes obviously requires indices of fixed asset prices and of input and output prices. Hence the consumer price index should be used for inflation accounting *only* if no more relevant reliable and frequently published price indices exist. But this still leaves open such questions as whether changes in indirect taxes, rents and interest rates are relevant to current cost accounting.

National accounting deflation

Component sub-indices of the consumer price index will almost certainly be used by the national income statisticians for obtaining constant-price estimates of consumption expenditure. They obviously want the whole country to be covered. Otherwise, the needs of the national income statisticians should not have much influence on the design of the published consumer price index. The selections of elementary aggregate indices that are combined to yield sub-indices used by the national income statisticians for deflation do not have to be identical with those combined into the published consumer price index group indices. The national accounting treatment of some items can very well differ from treatment appropriate to a consumer price index, as discussed below.

Retail sales deflation

Published group indices used for this purpose should clearly have the same scope as the turnover figures which they are used to deflate.

The nature of a consumer price index

A sample estimate

The index is estimated as a weighted average of elementary aggregate indices, preferably defined in terms of a three-dimensional stratification of items, regions and types of outlets. Formula (1) in box 1 expresses this, and the formulae that follow it explain the different ways of calculating unweighted elementary aggregate indices.

When the reference period for the consumption basket, the prices used for valuing it to obtain weights and the prices used in calculating the price relatives all coincide, then the index is a Laspeyres index. It measures the ratio of the current cost of the reference period basket to its reference period cost. Thus, it can be *defined* in terms of revaluing the physical quantities in the basket, though it is *calculated* as a weighted average of elementary aggregate indices, using expenditures and prices (in practice, a sample of prices), not physical quantities.

But few consumer price indices are in fact pure Laspeyres indices. The period for which expenditures are measured to obtain weights usually precedes the price reference period, and the weights may be calculated using a revaluation of these expenditures to the prices of another period, which may or may not be the same as the price reference period. Thus, for example, weights could be the shares in what the 1990 basket would have cost at 1991 prices (each 1990 expenditure being multiplied by the appropriate 1991/1990 price relative or sub-index), while the price reference period could be January 1992. Such complications are examined in the chapter on computation. Meanwhile, the simple distinctions between *(a)* the period to which the expenditure data used for calculating weights relate, i.e. the weight reference period, *(b)* the price reference period and *(c)* the index base period, which may or may not coincide with *(b)*, should be borne in mind.

The computation of the estimate necessitates, inter alia, a choice of: the reference group; the concepts of price and expenditure; the expenditure items covered; the stratification into elementary aggregates; the method of weighting them; and the method of sample estimation of these component elementary aggregate indices.

It is, however, not just a straightforward sampling problem which is involved in making the estimate. The universe of consumer transactions changes through time as old shops are closed down and new ones opened and as old purchase items become unobtainable and new ones appear. So the estimation process involves not only sampling but also the substitution within the sample of new outlets and items for old ones. Substitution as well as the initial sampling therefore requires discussion.

Relation to consumption deflator

The consumption deflator in the national accounts, whether it is calculated as a separate index or is implicit, is the ratio of the final consumption expenditure of households at current prices to its value at constant (price reference period) prices. Component sub-indices of the consumer price index are normally used by national income accountants for deflating components of this private consumption expenditure

Box 1. Index number formulae

A consumer price index is a weighted sum of the indices for all elementary aggregates

$$\mathrm{CPI}_{t/0} = \sum_{a=1..e} I^a_{t/0} \cdot w^a \qquad (1)$$

where the $I^a_{t/0}$ are these indices for period t with a price reference period of 0, and the w^a, which sum to unity, are the shares of each elementary aggregate, **a**, in weight reference period expenditure.

With *n* prices P^c, an elementary aggregate index can be calculated in three ways, assuming that no weights are available:

Relative of arithmetic mean prices

$$\frac{\sum_{c=1..n} \frac{P^c_t}{n}}{\sum_{c=1..n} \frac{P^c_0}{n}} = \frac{\sum_{c=1..n} P^c_t}{\sum_{c=1..n} P^c_0} \qquad (2)$$

Arithmetic mean of relative prices

$$\frac{\sum_{c=1..n} \frac{P^c_t}{P^c_0}}{n} \qquad (3)$$

Geometric mean of relative prices = Relative of geometric means of prices

$$\sqrt[n]{\prod_{c=1..n} \frac{P^c_t}{P^c_0}} = \frac{\sqrt[n]{\prod_{c=1..n} P^c_t}}{\sqrt[n]{\prod_{c=1..n} P^c_0}} \qquad (4)$$

(2) can be computed by chaining period to period relatives of arithmetic mean prices:

$$\frac{\sum_{c=1..n} P^c_1}{\sum_{c=1..n} P^c_0} \cdot \frac{\sum_{c=1..n} P^c_2}{\sum_{c=1..n} P^c_1} \cdot \ldots \cdot \frac{\sum_{c=1..n} P^c_{t-1}}{\sum_{c=1..n} P^c_{t-2}} \cdot \frac{\sum_{c=1..n} P^c_t}{\sum_{c=1..n} P^c_{t-1}}$$

(4) can be computed similarly as:

$$\frac{\sqrt[n]{\prod_{c=1..n} P^c_1}}{\sqrt[n]{\prod_{c=1..n} P^c_0}} \cdot \frac{\sqrt[n]{\prod_{c=1..n} P^c_2}}{\sqrt[n]{\prod_{c=1..n} P^c_1}} \cdot \ldots \cdot \frac{\sqrt[n]{\prod_{c=1..n} P^c_{t-1}}}{\sqrt[n]{\prod_{c=1..n} P^c_{t-2}}} \cdot \frac{\sqrt[n]{\prod_{c=1..n} P^c_t}}{\sqrt[n]{\prod_{c=1..n} P^c_{t-1}}}$$

(3) *cannot* be computed similarly.

It follows that if elementary aggregate indices are calculated as in (2) or (4), (1) is equivalent to:

$$\mathrm{CPI}_{t/0} = \sum_{a=1..e} [I^a_{t-1/0} \cdot w^a] \cdot I^a_{t/t-1} \qquad (5)$$

Note that:

$$\mathrm{CPI}_{t/0} \neq \mathrm{CPI}_{t-1/0} \cdot \sum_{a=1..e} [I^a_{t-1/0} \cdot w^a]$$

in order to obtain the constant-price estimates of these components. But even when this is done with most of the components, the consumer price index and the implicit deflator can differ significantly for the following reasons:

(1) The treatment of owner-occupied housing in the consumer price index may differ from that in the national accounts, where consumption expenditure is taken to include imputed rents.

(2) Similarly, there may be differences of approach in the treatment of certain other items, such as health expenditure, insurance, consumer credit and income in kind. There may also be differences in the treatment of subsidies.

(3) Weights may differ because of differences in scope. For example, a consumer price index may relate to the consumption of urban workers rather than to total consumption.

(4) Weights may also differ because the implicit deflator is a current-weighted index while the consumer price index is not. Hence, even when the price reference period is the same for both indices and even when all other things are equal, the two indices will differ. While the consumer price index for any two points of time can be used to compare two costs of the same reference period basket, the current-weighted comparisons provided by the implicit deflator relate only the current period cost to the price reference period cost of the current basket, so that implicit deflator comparisons between any other pair of periods will confuse compositional change (weight shifts) with price changes. Unfortunately, non-statisticians do sometimes use such comparisons of the implicit deflator for other pairs of periods as a measure of pure price change between them.

Some major choices which depend upon the purpose of the index 2

There are a number of issues in the design of a consumer price index where there is no unique best way of doing things. They are issues where different questions may yield different answers. Hence choices should be made by considering the relative importance of the different questions. There is no single best practice; there are several. To choose between them, the statistician must consult the users and consider their needs.

This does not mean that the relative utility of answering different questions should be the sole determinant of the choices made. Suppose that question A is more important than questions B and C. Even so, it may be sensible to select the method which directly answers question C because its answer will clearly not diverge much from that which would be yielded by the method which answers A, while it is easier or cheaper to compile or more readily comprehensible by users of the index.

Given the need to weigh up such divergent considerations, it is important to recognise them all in taking a decision. Thus it is not a good idea, for example, to ask simply: "What is the best treatment of owner-occupied housing?" Instead, it is better to:

— start by examining, for each use of the consumer price index, which of the various possible questions about the cost of owner-occupation is the most relevant;
— then consider which of the answers may in practice come close to the answers to other questions;
— examine the relative cost and complexity of producing the different answers; and
— consider how well they are likely to be understood by the users.

The relative importance of different needs and the relative weight to be given to various practical considerations will vary with national circumstances. If inflation is especially rapid, for example, seasonal correction may be both more difficult and less useful, while the problem of dealing with prices which are measured and/or paid only a few times a year becomes more acute.

More generally, there are various types of choice to be made in designing a consumer price index, and this chapter deals with only one, namely choices which primarily depend upon the purposes to be served by the index. Other types of choice are not given separate treatment but arise throughout succeeding chapters. One is the obvious trade-off between cost and quality: consumer price indices cost money and their quality can be improved if more resources are devoted to them. Thus with given resources, such choices arise, for example, as whether to devote more effort to field supervision at the expense of central work on the formulation and updating of specifications, or whether to increase the frequency of price collection while restricting geographical coverage. Then there are even more technical choices, such as whether to improve price sampling by the introduction of probabilistic sampling, which would increase the number of discontinuities in price observations, requiring more quality adjustments to be made. (Sampling shortcomings are less likely to produce cumulative errors than are imperfections in quality adjustments.) These are further examples of choices, the need for which is raised in subsequent chapters, and which must be made in the light of national circumstances.

The scope of the index

Geographical scope

Whether a consumer price index is to cover all regions of the country or only part of it is an important issue, but there is not much to say about it in general terms. On the one hand, an index which covers only part of the country may be cheaper and administratively easier to compile, especially when communications within the country are poor. On the other hand, some uses of the consumer price index require the whole country to fall within the scope of the index. If it does not, then the question of whether wider geographical coverage would make much difference arises, i.e. it has to be asked whether prices in different regions move in parallel.

A limitation to urban areas is fairly common. The justification is essentially the practical one that they often account for the majority of consumers and, even more, for the bulk of consumer expenditure, that price collection in rural areas is expensive and that price movements (though not necessarily price levels) are similar to those in urban areas.

Sales in a region or purchases by its residents?

The households within any region may make some of their purchases outside that region and some of the household purchases made within the region may be made by households resident outside the region. In either case, there will be a difference between observing the prices paid within the region and the prices paid by residents of the region. This raises questions concerning both the purposes of the index, the subject of this chapter, and about the sampling aspects of index construction, discussed in a later chapter.

One question is independent of whether the index covers the whole country or only some regions of it. It is whether or not an index includes expenditure abroad. Even when residents' direct purchases across a frontier are unimportant, their holiday expenditure abroad may be considerable.

Similarly, it has to be asked whether an index relating to sales within the geographical region or regions covered includes sales to the residents of other countries. The issue is obviously important in countries which receive a large number of tourists. Except, perhaps, for hotels, sales to visitors and the prices charged to them cannot be distinguished from other sales.

The other question arises when regional sub-indices are produced. If they are computed merely as one step in the calculation of the overall index, the issue is a practical one of regional weighting by regional sales versus weighting by purchases of residents and of sampling outlets according to where they, or where their customers, are located. But if regional sub-indices are to be published and used, it has to be decided as a matter of principle whether they are to relate to prices charged within the region or to prices paid by residents of the region. One cannot ask which of these is "correct"; the question is what one wants to measure. The two alternative questions and, perhaps, the two corresponding answers may differ considerably in cases where an urban or metropolitan region is distinguished and where many people who live outside it carry out some of their major purchases there, especially of clothes and consumer durables.

An obvious practical point that deserves mention is that the "sales in the region" approach can use any regional sales data that may exist, while the "residents of region" approach cannot.

The reference population

It may be decided to exclude the top and/or the bottom income group (defined in terms of fractiles of the income distribution, rather than in absolute monetary terms). One reason, referred to below, may be that their expenditure patterns are thought to be very different from those of the rest of the population (possibly even justifying a separate index) and another may be that the purposes served by the index do not require their inclusion.

It may also be decided to leave out some of the institutional population, because the purposes served by the index do not require their inclusion (or for the practical reason that data on their consumption patterns are difficult to obtain). The institutional population includes, for example, people living in hospitals, barracks, hostels, boarding-houses, monasteries, prisons and ships.

In some cases, the main purpose served by the index may require that its scope be defined in terms of the groups that are included rather than as all consumers with specified exclusions. Thus if the regulation or evaluation of wages and salaries is the dominant purpose, it would be appropriate to define the reference population as employee households, that is to say households which obtain the bulk of their incomes from wages and salaries.

Separate indices for different reference populations, such as wage-earners or pensioners, may be useful depending upon the uses to which the consumer price index is put.

Sometimes separate expenditure data are available for a specific population group such as pensioners, but no separate data are available concerning the prices they pay, i.e. concerning their regional distribution or the outlets from which they make their purchases. In such a case it is tempting to use the one set of price data available, with a special set of weights, to produce what is described as a separate index for pensioners. But with prices not collected separately and the weighting of different outlet types and regions not estimated separately, such a separate index implicitly assumes that any differences between pensioners and other consumers as to where they spend their money or as to the appropriate choice of representative items have negligible effects. If the assumption is reasonable, it should be made explicitly; if it is not, the separate index should not be published.

Which expenditure items should be omitted?

The aim is to cover all the expenditure of households on goods and services which are acquired, used or paid for, but not for business purposes and not for investment, i.e. not for the acquisition of assets. Given this aim, it is apparent that savings, life insurance and pension fund contributions and financial investments are *not* included. Taxes are included only when they are inescapably linked with consumption of items for which the household can choose whether or not to consume.

This general definition needs to be supplemented by considering a few special issues of principle. (The main practical difficulty which arises is to distinguish and omit business purchases when the data used in calculating expenditure weights are sales data or include household survey data obtained from self-employed people.)

Membership fees and gifts

If some members of the target population pay subscriptions or make gifts to charitable organisations, the money finances consumption by these organisations and this consumption of non-profit-making organisations is usually regarded as outside the scope of a consumer price index. But if they pay subscriptions to a club which provides them with some kind of service, the expenditure can be regarded as part of their consumption and apt for inclusion in the index.

Second-hand purchases

For some purposes, such as the evaluation of the purchasing power of money received by consumers as a group and indexation, transactions internal to the group (i.e. between households) are not relevant. Another way of expressing this is to say that, while second-hand purchases use up money, second-hand sales for cash add to it; similarly, trade-ins help to pay for other consumption and should thus also be counted as negative receipts. When the value of the target population's second-hand sales (including trade-ins) does not differ very much from the total value of its second-hand purchases and/or when prices are very difficult to obtain for second-hand goods, it may be practical to assume that they cancel each other out.

Second-hand dealers in a wide variety of goods are, however, important in many developing countries, so households may well spend more on second-hand purchases than they receive from second-hand sales. Indeed, some developing countries are net importers of second-hand goods. The omission of second-hand goods from the index would then be unfortunate.

In developed countries the same will hold for cars. If it is feasible to collect second-hand car prices, it will be appropriate to include the reference population's net purchases of cars in the index. Net purchases of second-hand cars by households from the business sector are fairly large in some countries and, apart from this, sales to second-hand dealers will have a lower value than purchases from them on account of the dealers' margins. Hence the appropriate weight for second-hand cars is the value of net purchases from the business sector plus the aggregate of dealers' margins on the cars that they buy from and resell to households. In calculating this second component, trade-ins should count as part of sales of second-hand cars by households. If so, the weight given to new cars should not include any deduction for the value of trade-ins.

Illegal prices and consumption

Statisticians are concerned with facts. If the purpose of the consumer price index is best served by the inclusion of black or free market prices paid by consumers, then the only good reason for excluding them can be that they are quantitatively unimportant. If they are important, then it should be possible to measure them.

Own-account production and income in kind

No one doubts that for a number of purposes the addition of the imputed value of any own-account production and of any income in kind should be added to a measure of money income or consumption to obtain a measure of total income or consumption. It may also be useful to include a measure of the value of government services provided free. If a deflator for such a total measure is required, then this deflator should obviously include the imputed prices of these imputed values. But when the sales to be deflated or the incomes to be deflated, evaluated or determined include no value imputations, then the price index should not include them either. Hence, whether or not to include imputed items should depend on what is the most important purpose for which the consumer price index is to be used.

In situations where consumption is based largely on barter among households, the notion of a consumer price index seems inappropriate.

Insurance

Life insurance and pension fund contributions are not appropriately included in a consumer price index, but there seems to be general agreement that household expenditure on insurance which provides some reimbursement of expenditure on medical or emergency services or on the repair or replacement of damaged or stolen goods should ideally be included. There appear to be two alternative internally consistent methods of doing this:

(1) The weight should be payments less claims paid (expenditure on cars, furniture, etc., paid for by insurance claims being dealt with in the same way as all other expenditure on these things); the price indicator should relate only to the service provided by insurance companies of collecting premiums and paying claims.

(2) The weight should be gross premium payments (the weights in the rest of the index for expenditure on cars, furniture, etc., excluding the part paid for by insurance claims); the price indicator should also relate to gross premium payments.

Method (1) measures the cost of the administrative functions and risk-pooling provided by insurance companies. A rise in repair and replacement costs or a rise in risks will only raise this component of the index if it raises the companies' costs or profits. Method (2), on the other hand, looks at the issue purely from the consumers' point of view, measuring the cost to them of a certain level of security against the consequences of fire, accident and theft. Thus, a rise in either repair and replacement costs or in risks will raise the cost to consumers of obtaining the level of security which they had in the reference period, just as a rise in the difficulties of providing beef will raise the cost to them of obtaining the amount of beef they bought in the reference period. Adjusting changes in premium payments to eliminate any part reflecting changes in risks, so that they reflect only changes in the cost of the service rendered by insurance companies together with changes in the cost of the repairs and items insured, might be thought desirable. This would amount to measuring "quality adjusted" changes in gross premiums.

The choice will probably have to depend upon the relative feasibility of these alternatives. This will depend upon national institutions, so no generalisations can be offered. The main issues are as follows:

— Is it easier (1) to establish weights which do not distinguish expenditure financed by insurance claims from other expenditure and to deduct claims paid from premiums to obtain a weight for net premiums, than it is (2) to establish weights reflecting gross premium payments and to exclude from expenditures on cars, furniture, and so on, those which are financed by claim payments? In (2), claims paid to reimburse the consumer will have to be deducted from his or her expenditures which the claims helped to finance. In (1) it is the other way round; claims paid on the consumer's behalf directly to the suppliers of repairs, replacements, medical treatment, and so on, will have to be added to his or her own expenditure. In (1), in order to obtain net premium payments from the gross payments recorded in a household survey, the share of gross premium payments in the reference period which were received back as claim payments will probably have to be ascertained from insurance companies.

— How can an index of the cost of the administrative and risk-pooling service provided by insurance companies, as required by (1), be calculated?

— How can an index of the cost of the insurance cover provided by insurance companies, as required by (2), be provided? This requires the measurement of premiums for a number of clearly specified types of insurance. But this is not all, since the question arises whether, in order to ensure "constant quality", the gross premiums should be corrected both for changes in risks and for changes in the prices and repair costs of the goods insured. More simply, the correction might be limited to the changes in the prices and repair costs of the goods insured, thus accepting any increase in premiums stemming from increased risks as a price increase. In this case the premiums on a sample of insurances for specified objects would each be deflated by an appropriate price sub-index. More simply still, there might be no correction at all, in which case the quality being held "constant" would be the security of the consumer, rather than the volume of the repairs, replacement and treatment paid for by claims.

Even an indicator of this latter type can be complicated. The article "Le problème de la mesure de l'évolution des primes d'assurance de dommages et de son introduction dans l'indice des prix à la consommation français" [The measurement of liability insurance premium trends and their inclusion in the French consumer price index], by M. A. Marret, reprinted in Appendix 2 (with a summary in English), explains how such an indicator can be calculated.

Other financial services

Administrative charges for credit-card accounts, various bank services and portfolio management, together with fees paid to accountants and tax advisers, are all equivalent to prices paid for services. In principle, therefore, they should be included in a consumer price index if some of the consumers in the reference group make use of such services, whether or not interest charges on mortgages and other forms of credit are included. It is a question of fact whether they are large enough to be worth including. Even when they are non-negligible, specific units of such services have to be definable for price collection to be possible. The annual charge for a credit card and the fee for a standard tax declaration are two possible examples.

Expenditure abroad

The resolution of the Fourteenth International Conference of Labour Statisticians specifies that the extent to which expenditure abroad is included in the index should be made clear. The issue of principle arises, as already noted, with respect to expenditure on holidays abroad and cross-border shopping. For some purposes, the whole of the cost of holidays is relevant, while for the analysis of inflation, for example, it is only their domestic component (e.g. travel on a national airline) which is of interest. The same applies to items which some households buy on cross-border shopping expeditions. As with all these issues, there are practical considerations as well. The only feasible way of measuring the cost of overseas holidays may be to collect the prices of package holidays, and these often involve the problem of seasonal unavailability. Cross-border price collection may be impracticable.

Jewellery

In certain countries some purchases of jewellery may be more in the nature of an investment than of consumption expenditure, in which case it would be well to exclude them from the index. Thus purchases above a certain cut-off value might be excluded.

Plutocratic or democratic weighting?

Consumer price indices normally use weights which reflect the composition of the estimated aggregate expenditures of the reference population. This means that households with above-average expenditures have an above-average influence on the weights. Such weighting has been named "plutocratic". An alternative, named "democratic", would give equal importance to all households by averaging expenditure proportions over the whole reference population instead of summing expenditure amounts. The index would then measure the evolution of prices as they influence the average household rather than as they influence average consumption expenditure. It would be a simple average of separate indices for each household, i.e. the basket of goods and services whose price movements it measured could not be described simply in terms of consumption during the weight reference period. Rather, it would be what one household would have consumed had the share of its expenditure on each item equalled the mean share over all households.

A democratic index would thus give less weight to items which are not bought by the majority of households, even though the amount spent on these items by a minority of households is large.

If the index is primarily used for current cost accounting, as a general measure of inflation, or for national accounting deflation or retail sales deflation, then plutocratic weighting is clearly appropriate. On the other hand, for some indexation purposes, democratic weighting may be judged more appropriate. However, the choice between the two can be avoided if it can be shown that, in practice, they would give almost the same result.

Some countries exclude a few top and bottom percentiles of the income distribution from the household expenditure data used to provide weights. One reason may be the practical one that it is not clear what types of household are included in these income brackets or that the data relating to their expenditures are unreliable. The exclusion is also sometimes explained on the grounds that the spending patterns of these households (especially of the very rich ones) can differ very considerably from those of the rest of the population, and that this could have an effect on the weights. Depending on the cut-off points, this may mean that the omission of such households largely removes any difference between a plutocratically and a democratically weighted index. This implicitly admits the case for democratic weighting, raising the question as to whether an explicit choice of democratic weighting would not be more appropriate for the main purposes served by the index. The computation of separate indices for different population groups, distinguished (among other things) by their expenditure levels, will also reduce the significance of the problem.

It should be noted that even where, as is in fact usual, the index is intended to be plutocratic, a democratic element may inconsistently creep in. This would occur if population data were used as an expenditure surrogate to weight different regions in the calculation of an overall index when expenditures per head varied systematically between regions. Consistency requires that if, for example, northerners are poorer than southerners, the weight given to northern expenditures should be *less* than the northern share of the population. Thus regional population shares each multiplied by regional average income may provide reasonable weights.

Consumption: Acquisition, use, or payment?

An explanation of the difference between them

Consumption expenditure can be conceived and measured in three ways which it is important to distinguish. The recommendation defines them as follows:

— *Acquisition* indicates that the total value of all goods and services delivered during a given period, irrespective of whether they were wholly paid for or not during the period, should be taken into account.

— *Use* indicates that the total value of all goods and services actually consumed during a given period should be taken into account.

— *Payment* indicates that the total payments made for goods and services during a given period, without regard to whether they were delivered or not, should be taken into account.

For practical purposes these cannot be distinguished in the case of non-durable items bought for cash and they do not need to be distinguished for many durable items bought for cash. But the distinction is important with purchases financed by some form of credit, notably in the case of major durable goods, which are acquired at a certain point in time, used over a considerable number of years and paid for, at least partly, some time after they were acquired, possibly in a series of instalments. Housing similarly provides a flow of services after it has been acquired. Thus reference-period consumption may be taken as including the acquisition of dwellings during the reference period or as the reference-period use of the stock of owner-occupied housing. Mortgage credit, on the other hand, means that the timing of acquisitions of dwellings differs from the timing of payments for them. Thus reference-period consumption can also be taken as including the owner-occupied housing for which payment was being made during the reference period.

Note that differences between the three concepts of consumption are not merely a matter of timing. If payment follows acquisition, interest may be charged in addition to the equivalent of the cash price. When use extends over several years, the value of this use will reflect the price level of those years, not the price at the date of acquisition.

Owner-occupied housing

The nature of the problem

There are many possible ways of dealing with owner-occupied housing in a consumer price index and practices vary widely between countries. Hence, it was not possible for the Fourteenth International Conference of Labour Statisticians to recommend one particular solution. The three main reasons why the solution that is best in one country may not suit others apply here. First, the relative importance of different uses of the index varies, and these different uses require the index to answer different kinds of question. Thus, there is the issue of specifying the question to be answered by the index. Second, there are differences in the data requirements of the different solutions and the relative costs of meeting these different requirements varies between countries according to institutional circumstances. Third, a point that applies only to the approach involving the imputation of rents, the existence of rent control on rented dwellings or a great difference in the types of dwelling that are owner-occupied from those that are rented may create difficulties.

The solutions as answers to questions

It is convenient to start by examining the first issue, listing the possible solutions and then specifying the question to which each of them provides an answer.

The three main groups of solutions are as follows:

— the value of market acquisitions of dwellings for owner-occupation;

— the cost of using owner-occupied dwellings; and

— the payments made by owner-occupiers.

The first solution relates to the value of a market flow of goods to the reference population and is thus particularly relevant for the analysis of current price changes. The second solution, which is concerned with actual consumption, poses the question in a way which interests an economic theorist and necessitates imputations. The third relates to how much money households need to pay out (i.e. to cash expenditure) in respect of their dwellings, and is therefore relevant to the evaluation of money incomes.

The questions to which each of these three types of solution offers an answer are as follows:

— *Net acquisitions*. What is the change through time in the cost of reference-period net acquisition of owner-occupied dwellings by consumers?

— *Use*. What is the change through time in the user cost of reference-period consumption of the services of owner-occupied dwellings?

— *Payment*. What is the change through time in the cash outlays corresponding to the reference-period cash outlays in respect of owner-occupied dwellings?

The reason why net, rather than gross, acquisitions are suggested in the first solution is that sales as well as purchases of existing dwellings are important, at least in developed countries. An obvious possibility (which applies equally to transactions in other second-hand items) is to treat these sales and purchases symmetrically, so that sales constitute negative expenditure. Given price data for transactions in both new and existing dwellings, positive weights would then be used for purchases of new and existing dwellings and negative weights would be used for sales of existing dwellings.

In practice, the price data for existing dwellings will rarely distinguish between purchase and selling prices, with the result that a single set of prices will have to be weighted by the algebraic sum of these two weights.

This sum will be zero if net sales of existing dwellings by the reference population to, or from, the rest of the economy are zero, so that households only sell and buy them from each other. If this is the case, the consumer price index should include only new dwellings. The rationale for thus ignoring sales and purchases of existing dwellings is that if the reference population is simply selling to itself, the prices that it pays itself cannot affect the cost of its reference-period consumption. (The amount it pays to lawyers and estate agents for facilitating the transactions should be included in the index along with other services that consumers pay for.)

The sum may not be zero when the reference population does not encompass the bulk of the country's population, or when there are considerable sales of dwellings to tenants by landlords (whose business transactions are outside the scope of a consumer price index).

(a) *More detailed questions*

Figure 2 elaborates in greater detail the major possibilities that have been proposed or are used under each of the three solutions. The choice made will determine both the weight for owner-occupied dwellings in the overall consumer price index and the way in which the sub-index for owner-occupied dwellings is calculated. Formulating the three questions previously listed in more detail now yields the following set of more specific, alternative questions.

(A) *Net acquisitions*. What is the change through time in the total purchase value of a sample of new owner-occupied dwellings similar to the new owner-occupied dwellings acquired by consumers in the reference period?

(B1) *User cost (1)*. What is the change through time in the mortgage interest and conventional depreciation at replacement cost in respect of a sample of owner-occupied dwellings similar to consumers' owner-occupied dwellings in the reference period?

(B2) *User cost (2)*. What is the change through time in the opportunity cost of the invested capital value, plus depreciation, less accruing capital gains, in respect of a sample of owner-occupied dwellings similar to consumers' owner-occupied dwellings in the reference period?

(B3) *User cost (3)*. What is the change through time in the estimated rental value of a sample of owner-occupied dwellings similar to consumers' owner-occupied dwellings in the reference period?

Figure 2. Treatment of owner-occupied dwellings

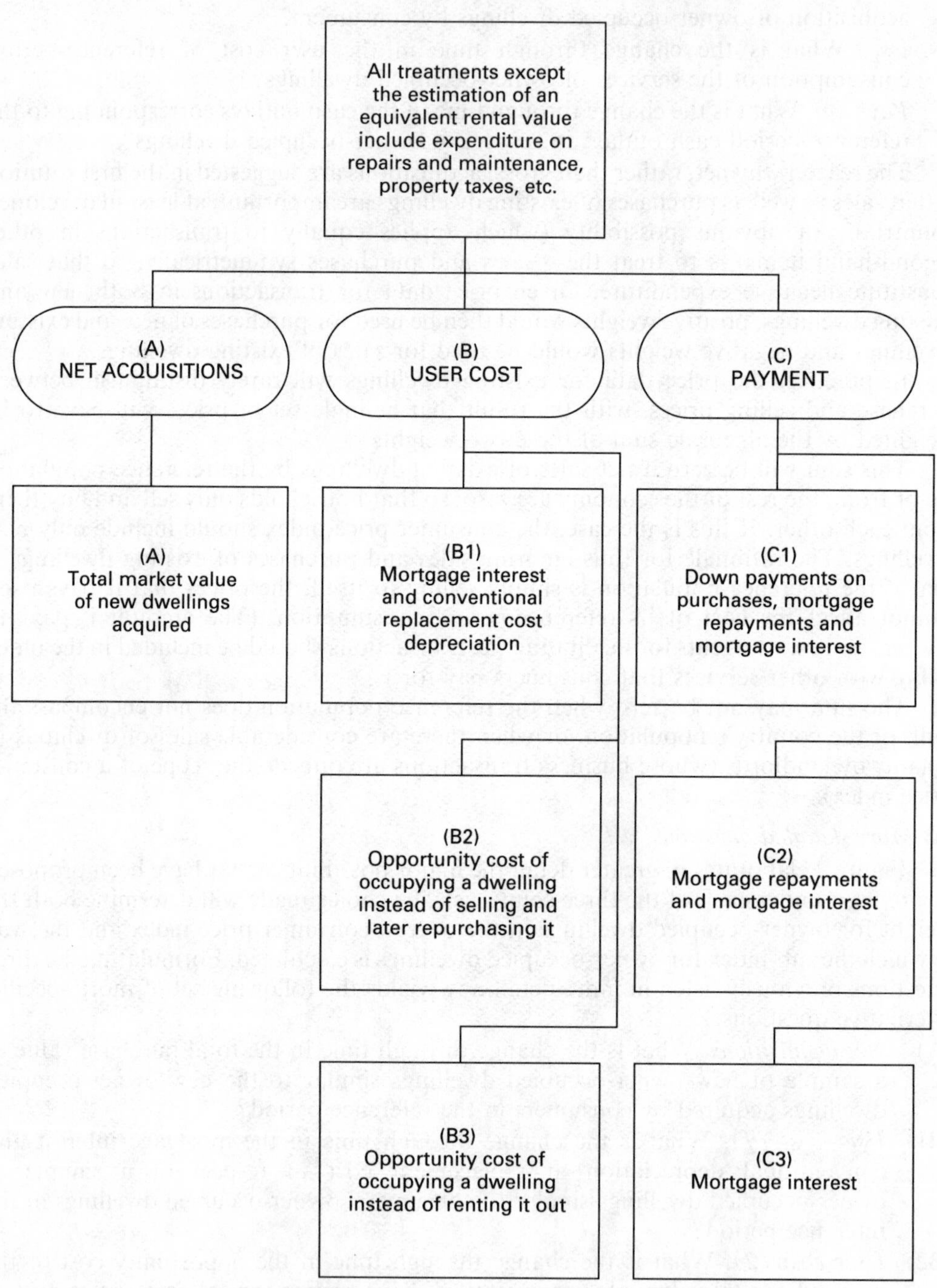

(C1) *Payment (1)*. What is the change through time in the cash outlays on down payments on purchases, mortgage interest and repayments in respect of a sample of owner-occupied dwellings similar to consumers' owner-occupied dwellings in the reference period?

(C2) *Payment (2)*. What is the change through time in the cash outlays on mortgage interest and repayments in respect of a sample of owner-occupied dwellings similar to consumers' owner-occupied dwellings in the reference period?

(C3) *Payment (3)*. What is the change through time in the cash outlays on mortgage interest, excluding repayment elements, in respect of a sample of owner-occupied dwellings similar to consumers' owner-occupied dwellings in the reference period?

All these questions refer to a sample which is similar to reference-period acquisitions or to dwellings owned by their occupiers in the reference period. On the user cost or payment basis, this should, at least in principle, be a sample of dwellings which are currently as old as those owned in the reference period were then, since one of the characteristics relevant to "similarity" is age. Thus the sample should not consist of an unchanging set of dwellings unless the age of dwellings is irrelevant to their quality.

The answer to question (A) treats owner-occupied dwellings in the same way as most consumer price indices treat acquisitions of cars, furniture and other durable goods whose purchases are often partly financed by credit.

The first answer under the user cost approach, (B1), answers a question which an accountant might ask.

(B2) and (B3) perhaps require a little more explanation, since they both reflect the approach of many economists to the concept of user cost and its relevance to a consumer price index. The basic idea is that the cost of using anything is the value of the opportunity sacrificed by using it, and that this cost forms part of the owner-occupier's consumption. There are, however, two such alternative opportunities and hence two measures, (B2) and (B3). One would be to let the dwelling to a tenant. The value of this opportunity is the rent that the owner could obtain; it is what he as tenant notionally pays to himself as occupier. The other would be to sell the dwelling and buy it, or a similar dwelling, later on at the end of the period for which the cost is being calculated. To explain this second alternative, some algebra will help.

Consider a period of a year. Assume that the owner could sell the dwelling for P at the beginning of the year. If the relevant one-year index of dwelling prices is I and if, at constant prices, the addition of one year to the age of the dwelling depreciates it by a fraction d, its value at the end of the year will be $IP(1-d)$. Assume further that the value of the mortgage outstanding at the beginning of the year equals a fraction f of P. Then, if the mortgage interest rate during the year, expressed as a fraction, is r, the owner's debt at the end of the year will amount to $fP(1+r)$. Thus the owner starts the year with a net asset value of $(1-f)P$ and ends it with a net asset value of $IP(1-d) - fP(1+r)$. The difference, $(1-f)P - [IP(1-d) - fP(1+r)]$, is the loss (which will be negative if I is large!) during the year.

By selling the dwelling for P at the beginning of the year, and paying off the mortgage, the owner could invest the rest of the sale proceeds, $(1-f)P$. If the yield obtainable from this investment, expressed as a fraction, was y, the owner could end the year with a capital sum of $(1-f)P(1+y)$, a gain of $(1-f)Py$.

The cost of ownership during the year is the sum of the loss from ownership and the gain sacrificed by not selling:

$$(1-f)P - [IP(1-d) - fP(1+r)] + (1-f)Py$$

which can be rearranged as:

$$dIP + fPr + (1-f)Py - (IP - P)$$

and which can be negative if dwelling prices are rising sufficiently fast. Its components are:

dIP depreciation

fPr mortgage interest

$(1-f)Py$ earnings forgone on owner's equity

less

$IP - P$ gain in owner's equity

(This expression for user cost is simplified by omitting selling and buying costs and by ignoring any tax relief on mortgage interest.)

The selection of y poses a problem, since it requires the statistician to decide how owner-occupiers would invest the money they could get from selling their dwellings, if they were to sell them.

It will be noted that user cost could be *negative* if dwelling prices rose fast, i.e. if I was high. A negative cost simply means that it would be better to keep the dwelling, even unused, than to sell it and then buy it back a year later.

Trial calculations applying this approach have produced a widely fluctuating index. It is therefore tempting to reject it. But an approach should not be rejected because one does not like the answer, provided that it is a valid answer. The approach undoubtedly yields a valid answer, so the real issue is whether the *question* to which it responds is a good one in the context of a consumer price index! In any event, most advocates of the relevance of user cost have tended to favour (B1) or (B3), at least in principle. In some countries, however, (B3), which requires the estimation of equivalent rents for a sample of owner-occupied dwellings, is ruled out on practical grounds because the vast majority of owner-occupied dwellings are too different from rented ones to make imputation possible.

For the mortgage interest component in (B1), (C1), (C2) and (C3) it is necessary to estimate what would be the current interest payments on a sample of dwellings with the same age-distribution of mortgages outstanding as the owner-occupied dwellings of the reference period. The methodology for this estimation is discussed below.

The questions (B1), (C1), (C2) and (C3), since they partly or wholly relate to the present payment consequences of past dwelling acquisitions, obtain current answers which will partly reflect the evolution of past dwelling prices (and of past mortgage rates, if interest rates on outstanding mortgages are not altered when current mortgage rates change).

It has been suggested that the real, rather than the nominal, interest rate on mortgages should be measured, so that, for example, if the mortgage interest rate is 12 per cent and prices are rising at 9 per cent, the real cost which should be measured in the consumer price index is only 3 per cent. However, if such a reduction in the real value of a debt is allowed for, should not any appreciation in the real value of an asset be similarly treated? The idea seems to lead towards (B1) rather than to modify the specification of the other possible questions.

While user cost (B2) and user cost (B3) will differ when they are independently measured, it is possible to define the return forgone on owners' capital, in such a way as to make them equal. This has been pointed out by Robert Gillingham and provides a justification for the use of the rental equivalence method in the United States. Instead of the return being *measured* in terms of the yield obtainable, for example, by investing in shares or bonds it is *assumed* to reflect the rental value and capital appreciation obtainable by investment in housing. The return on an owner's equity is thus *defined* as the return which would equate *rental value plus the growth in the owner's equity* with *mortgage interest and the return on the owner's equity*, so that user cost (B2) and user cost (B3) are defined to coincide.

This result is an appealing one for those who believe that a question about user cost is the most useful, since it allows theoretical justification in terms of (B2) and practical estimation in terms of (B3). If mortgage rates or dwelling price movements change, the opportunity cost of the owner's equity will change, but user cost will not, so long as rents in rental markets are unaltered. It thus escapes the peculiar results which can otherwise be obtained with user cost (B2), stemming from the volatility of dwelling prices, and it conveniently avoids the problem of deciding what alternative investments would have been chosen by homeowners had they not put their money into home ownership. Its applicability is, of course, limited to economies where rent control is unimportant and the same types of dwelling are both owner-occupied and rented.

The difference between (C1), (C2) and (C3), is simply that (C2) excludes the down payments on dwelling purchases in the current period, while (C3) also excludes the repayment of loans, on the grounds that such down payments and such repayment does not form part of consumption. The argument that payment for an asset should be excluded from a consumer price index can also be urged against the appropriateness of (A). On the other hand, it might be asserted that the purpose of a consumer price index is to measure changes in prices paid by consumers for all the goods and services that they buy. Which of these two contradictory positions is to be taken should depend upon a consideration of the purposes to be served by the index, a question to which we now turn.

(b) *Different questions for different uses of the index*

Which of the questions formulated above is the most useful to have answered must obviously depend upon the uses of the index.

For much macro-economic analysis, especially in countries where other price indices are lacking, the consumer price index is used as a general indicator of inflation, measuring changes in the price level of current output. The same is true, however, even in countries which, whilst having other less frequent price indices, publish a monthly consumer price index. In this context, given that prices and interest rates may move independently, it is probably best to have an index which does not reflect any interest rates; they can easily be measured separately.

Presumably the inflation to be measured is a matter of the prices currently being charged. Hence, no retrospective element relating to prices in previous months and no imputed prices should be included. Since changes in past prices and changes in past and/or current interest rates can affect the cash outlays of owner-occupiers, the payment approach appears to be inappropriate for economic analysis. The same applies to the user-cost approach to the extent that it involves imputations or, in so far as movements in interest rates affect it, even in the absence of price changes. An index limited to the repairs and maintenance of owner-occupied dwellings or one also incorporating the prices of new dwellings might therefore be preferred if the analysis of inflation were the primary purpose of the index.

For the evaluation of money incomes and, even more, for indexation, the questions which have to be answered are perhaps those corresponding to the payment approach. On the one hand, households may need to pay out more money in one period than in another, even though no currently acquired goods or services have changed in price, either because the original cost of the dwellings owned in the later period exceeds that of those owned in the earlier period, or because interest rates have risen. This applies to both payment solutions, the second of which excludes the capital element. On the other hand, households do not need to pay out more money simply because some imputed component of user cost has risen. A rise in the imputed rent that a family is deemed, as tenant, to pay to itself, as landlord, has no effect on its cash outlays, so the appropriateness of the user-cost approach seems doubtful in this context.

In a national accounting context, user cost (B3) is applied, but this need not dictate the treatment of owner-occupied dwellings in the consumer price index. The main case for the relevance of the questions answered by the user-cost solution stems from those economists who believe that a consumer price index should be placed within a rigorous "cost-of-living" framework which has meaning within modern economic theory. Such an index would measure the change over time in the cost for a given consumer of achieving a given level of satisfaction and must therefore incorporate a flow of services approach to owner-occupation costs. In practice, some approximation to this general theoretical formulation is necessary.

Data requirements for the different solutions

The problem of specifying the question to be answered by the index was the first issue named above in introducing the discussion of owner-occupied housing. The second issue relates to considerations of the cost and reliability of data. All seven of the possibilities distinguished require the use either of some kind of dwelling price index or of a rent index. If one or other of these is much more expensive or difficult to compile reliably than the other, it may be sensible to ignore the solution which requires it. The same applies to other data requirements. On these practical grounds, particular national circumstances may mean that certain solutions have to be dismissed. Hence, the next step is to examine the data needed for each solution. Data on repair and maintenance costs and on property taxes are needed in all cases, except for (B3), rental equivalence, if these costs are borne entirely by landlords and thus included in rents. The other data requirements are as follows:

Weight		Price index	Other data
A	Market value of new dwelling acquisitions	Quality-adjusted new dwelling prices or building costs	
B1	Interest and estimated replacement cost depreciation	Quality-adjusted prices for all dwellings or building costs	Reference period age distribution of outstanding mortgage amounts, mortgage terms, depreciation rates
B2	Estimated user cost	Quality-adjusted prices for all dwellings	Opportunity cost of capital, expected future dwelling prices, depreciation rates
B3	Estimated rental value	Rents of comparable dwellings	
C1	Interest and mortgage repayments, plus down payments	Quality-adjusted prices for all dwellings	Reference period age distribution of outstanding mortgage amounts, mortgage terms
C2	Interest and mortgage repayments	Quality-adjusted prices for all dwellings	Reference period age distribution of outstanding mortgage amounts, mortgage terms
C3	Interest	Quality-adjusted prices for all dwellings	Reference period age distribution of outstanding mortgage amounts, mortgage rates

(B3) requires an imputed reference period rental value of owner-occupied dwellings to provide a weight while (B1) requires a reference period capital value (for the calculation of depreciation). Rental values may be converted into capital values, or vice versa, by applying a standard ratio. In either case, a number of methods is possible. They are discussed in the chapter on price collection.

The expense of obtaining these data and their reliability will obviously vary from one country to another, depending on institutional factors. One example is that in some countries no data are automatically collected from mortgage lenders or elsewhere concerning the prices and characteristics of the dwellings in respect of which they have granted loans. A second example is that in some countries owner-occupied dwellings are massively predominant and/or are very different in type from rented dwellings. In the first case, it will be difficult or expensive to calculate quality-adjusted price indices for different types of dwellings. In the second case, the estimation of equivalent rental values is the problem.

Other difficulties may arise with respect to:

— the opportunity cost of capital for owner-occupiers. This is an elusive concept and, in any case, will vary from one owner-occupier to another because of income-related differences in marginal tax rates;

— the construction of quality-adjusted price indices for new dwellings, which can be very difficult, even when there are plentiful data on sale prices by type of dwelling. Locational differences alone can cause enormous differences in value between physically similar dwellings.

Mortgage interest

Since interest payments on mortgages enter into several of the solutions, a more detailed discussion of the problem of measuring them is called for.

To simplify the discussion, suppose that the price reference and weight reference periods coincide and that just one elementary aggregate index for mortgage interest is to be computed, rather than several distinguished by region or type of owner-occupied dwelling.

The simplest procedure would compare updated interest payments for the reference period with their reference period total value. The update would multiply the latter by an index of dwelling prices and multiply again by the ratio of the average current rate of interest on mortgages to the reference period interest rate. But this raises problems both of principle and of practice. They include the following:

— the problem of fixed-interest mortgages, where changes in the current rate do not affect the rate paid on existing mortgages;

— the fact that the amount of debt, and hence of interest payments, in any period does not reflect the level of dwelling prices of that particular period, but the prices at which the dwellings were bought, i.e. prices over a long series of previous periods;

— in a household income and expenditure survey, respondents may not be able to break down their mortgage payments into separate repayment and interest components, so that reference period interest payments may not be directly measurable;

— some of the money raised on mortgage by the reference population may have been used for other purposes than buying the dwelling, including business investment. So it may be desirable, though perhaps not possible, to exclude that part of mortgage interest from the reference total.

More complex computations may therefore be necessary and/or desirable. Unfortunately, there are big differences between countries, both in the way mortgages are arranged, and in the availability of data on property transactions and on mortgage finance, with the consequence that no general exposition of such complex computations can be provided. However, by way of illustration, it may be useful to provide one example for one specific set of circumstances.

Accordingly, let it be supposed that all mortgages used to help finance the purchase of dwellings for occupation are variable-interest mortgages and that there is no shortage of data (or unwillingness to make estimates!). Reference period (period t) interest payments in respect of dwellings bought by their present owner-occupiers n periods previously, in period $t - n$, can then be computed as the product of the following terms, each of which relates to dwellings acquired in period $t - n$ by the reference population:

average price of dwellings bought;
number of dwellings bought;
proportion of purchases mortgage financed;
average mortgage as fraction of purchase price;
proportion of dwellings still occupied by original purchaser;
proportion of surviving mortgages not repaid;
average interest rate on mortgages in period t.

Summing over all n, from $n = 0$ to whatever was the longest mortgage period granted among the surviving mortgages, yields total reference period mortgage interest.

Updating to the current period involves calculating what interest would be paid now on a similar "basket" of dwellings. Similarity can be taken to mean unchanged values for all but the first and the last of the above seven variables between reweightings of the index. Thus, the calculation for each period succeeding n will bring forward, by one period, the average price used for each cohort of dwellings and will apply the current rate of interest.

A final complication deserves mention for countries where mortgage interest payments are deductible in the calculation of income tax. If the principle is applied that subsidies and rebates which are universally available should be treated as effective reductions in the prices whose movements are measured by the index, then in such countries, the above calculation should be performed using the product of eight terms. The eighth, additional, term is the fraction of income retained after deduction of income tax at the standard rate (assuming that this rate applies at least to a majority of owner-occupiers). The logical consequence would be that, say, a rise in the standard rate of income tax would lower the consumer price index!

Consumer durables bought on credit

Purchases bought on credit, mainly consumer durables, raise the same problems as owner-occupied dwellings.

In terms of what is practicable, however, user cost (2) and user cost (3) can be dismissed from consideration. Furthermore, any separation of interest payments from repayments of principal is generally unfeasible in the case of consumer credit.

What, if any, are the main reasons of principle for treating consumer durables differently from housing? Four have been suggested:

(1) They are treated differently in the national accounts. But while the compilers of the consumer price index will presumably be required to supply data to the compilers of the national accounts, the two do not have to adopt the same conventions unless the dominant purpose of the consumer price index is to supplement the national accounts.

(2) Because of their lesser durability and, in most cases, decline in second-hand value, the acquisition of consumer durables is less of an investment than is the acquisition of dwellings and the payment for them is scarcely saving. This argument is relevant only if neither the acquisition of dwellings nor payments in respect of them are included in the consumer price index.

(3) A mortgage arrangement is the only practical way in which most households can become owners of a dwelling and is a long-term commitment, unlike hire purchase and credit card arrangements, so the cost of servicing mortgage arrangements is a legitimate proxy for owner-occupiers' costs. This implies that a payment basis is appropriate for dwellings but not for consumer durables, because consumer credit is more optional and less permanent. However, the acquisition of ice-cream is even more optional and even less permanent.

(4) If owner-occupied dwellings are, for whatever reason, treated on a payment basis, the inconsistency of treating consumer durables on an acquisition basis may be justified when a major use of group indices for consumer durables is to deflate retail sales.

In addition to these arguments of principle, there is the more practical argument that the effort of dealing with consumer credit as well as with (the much larger) mortgage credit is not justified; a consideration related to cost.

If these arguments are not accepted, the case for treating consumer durables and owner-occupied dwellings, as far as practicable, in the same way is a strong one.

Advance payment and delayed payment

Air travel and package holidays are often booked, and at least partly paid for, in advance. Hence, the issue arises of whether they should be priced at the time when they are taken (the time of both acquisition and of use), or at the time they are paid for. In practice, this second alternative implies recording price changes at the time they come into force, which, in the case of package holidays, means at the time new catalogues are issued.

A similar problem arises when consumers order a motor-car at a fixed price, making at least partial payment long in advance of the delivery date.

Finally, there is the point that public utility services, such as electricity, phones, etc., involve the opposite case of payment after use. The practical alternatives of dealing with their prices are discussed in the chapter on price collection; here it suffices to note that there is a choice, in principle, between recording a price increase when the future payment that will have to be made for current consumption rises, or recording it when the current payment for past consumption rises.

The treatment of indirect taxes and subsidies

Indirect taxes

The principle is that the index should relate to what consumers have to pay for the items within its scope. Thus both taxes embodied in a price, and sales taxes that are added to a price, should be included. Such taxes are paid to the seller. More broadly, taxes which are paid directly to the State, rather than to the seller, but which are inescapable costs to consumers of particular items of consumption, should also be included, both in weighting and in price collection. Property taxes on dwellings, television and radio licence fees, driving licence and car licence fees are all examples.

Subsidised prices

There seems little doubt that the prices measured should reflect government subsidies which lower prices, when the subsidies are such as to affect the prices paid by *all* buyers of a particular item. In such cases, expenditure data obtained from a household survey and used for weighting will also be lowered by the subsidy.

It is less obvious what should be done with selective subsidies which lower prices only to those consumers who fulfil certain conditions. Examples are provided by subsidised milk for families with small children and rent reductions for public housing tenants with low incomes.

In such cases careful consideration of the purposes to be served by the index may indicate what, in principle, is preferable. An increase in such subsidies raises the real incomes of the subsidised group, but may not be regarded as reducing inflation. However, there is also the practical point that if the subsidies are paid by reimbursing consumers, the effective price paid cannot be ascertained from the sellers. Hence, it may be best to follow the procedure which, *(a)* is simpler to explain and, *(b)* easier to implement. A full account of a group's economic situation requires that both their income and the prices they pay should be taken into account, and it seems a good idea to treat subsidies which partly depend on factors other than the mere act of purchase (e.g. on some aspect of family circumstances) as transfers, that is to say as additions to income rather than as subtractions from prices. This preserves the desirable symmetry of treatment between the weights used and the prices measured, in which expenditures and prices are either both measured gross or both measured net.

A more complex case arises when certain types of personal expenditure are wholly or partly allowed as deductions in the computation of income tax. In some countries, for example, there is a concession of this kind for certain medical expenses. These deductions result in a reduction of the effective cost to taxpaying consumers, so, at least for some purposes served by the index, should ideally enter into its calculation. But since considerable time may elapse between the expenditure and the payment of less income tax, and since the amount of tax reduction obtained by each taxpayer may depend upon his or her whole tax situation, it would be a bold statistician who would choose to attempt to allow for these tax concessions in compiling the index.

The above remarks about subsidies apply to government subsidies, where the government pays money to sellers or buyers in respect of purchases by members of a selectively subsidised group, or where the government is the seller and charges a lower price to such people. They also apply to assistance with purchases given by employers to their employees.

Net price indices

For some purposes, a consumer price index which does not include indirect taxes or subsidies may be required. Such indices are discussed in the article "Adjusting the CPI for indirect taxes", by H. W. J. Donkers et al., reprinted in Appendix 3.

Should the index relate to a point in time or a period?

This choice is evidently more important with a quarterly index than with a monthly one, though, as in the rest of this manual, the exposition runs in terms of a monthly index. If used for deflating income, expenditure or sales, the index should obviously relate to the period of time to which the money flow in question relates. For economic analysis, where the index will be used in conjunction with other economic statistics, most of which relate to a period rather than to a point in time, it seems appropriate that the consumer price index should do the same.

As with the other choices discussed in this chapter, considerations of principle have to be weighed up against various practical considerations. In the present instance, the first is that without rapid inflation there will be little difference between, for example, the change in the index from Monday 1 January 1990 to Tuesday 1 January 1991 and from the average for January 1990 to the average for January 1991. But this will not be the case if inflation is rapid and its rate changes.

The next consideration should be that, given the same number of observations, the sampling error may be different. In practice, all price observations cannot be made within a single day, let alone at one point in time, so the real issue is whether they are spread over a few days to provide an approximation to a point-in-time estimate or over the whole month to provide a whole-month estimate. However, which of their sampling errors will be the greater cannot be established *a priori*. In either case, items priced once a month should be priced at the same time in each month, so that the interval between observations is the same for all such items.

The costs of collection may be different, too. Limitation to a few days requires many collectors for a few days each month, with the possible advantage that they may be taken from other government work without disrupting it. The index can then be computed once the price collection is complete, so can be published quickly. It has the disadvantage that the price collectors will develop less expertise than if they spent more time on price collection.

A final point is that, with the point-in-time approach, major price setters, notably the government, can influence the index according to whether their price changes take effect on a day just after or before the day for which their price information is obtained. Since prices are often collected centrally from such price setters, it should be possible to obtain information from them about both the amount and timing of such price changes at the end of each month, so that in applying the period-of-time approach, an average price for the whole month can be calculated.

The choice and weighting of elementary aggregates

3

The nature of elementary aggregates

The next two chapters divide the construction of an index into two parts. Using the name "elementary aggregate" for the strata, the index is a weighted average of price indices for all the elementary aggregates. These jointly cover all the expenditure within the scope of the index. This chapter deals with their choice and weighting, i.e. with stratification. The next chapter deals with the sampling within each stratum and a later chapter examines the calculation of the elementary aggregate price indices using the sample price data.

The notion of an elementary aggregate should be clear from figure 3. It is the basic building block of the consumer price index, being an aggregate of purchases over a defined set of items (a composite item) in or from a defined region at a defined set of outlet types, e.g. long-grained rice of brand A from large stores in the north-west region. It is thus defined as a cross-classification of type of item, type of outlet and region. If, however, regional and outlet type weights are not available, then an elementary aggregate is simply defined in terms of the items of goods or services it includes. It is then the same as a composite item. An index is calculated for each elementary aggregate and this often has to be done without the use of explicit expenditure weights for its components. (If separate weights are available for separate parts of an elementary aggregate, then perhaps it should not be a single elementary aggregate, but should be further split into two or more smaller ones.) The indices for elementary aggregates are not necessarily sufficiently reliable to be individually published, but the compilation of elementary aggregate indices is an essential step in using price observations so as to maximise the reliability of the much more aggregative group indices and the all-items index.

The individual price observations each relate to a selected variety of the representative item in question, except where the specification of the representative item is so precise that it indicates an absolutely unique item, i.e. an item consisting of a unique variety. The issue of the appropriate tightness of these specifications is discussed later, in the chapter on price collection.

The weight for each elementary aggregate should represent expenditure on the whole elementary aggregate and not just on the sample of particular items at particular outlets chosen to represent it. Thus, if bread in the northern region constitutes an elementary aggregate, the weight reflects total expenditure on bread in the northern region, not just the sales of those bread outlets in the north from which prices are collected.

Figure 3. Elementary aggregates and other concepts illustrated

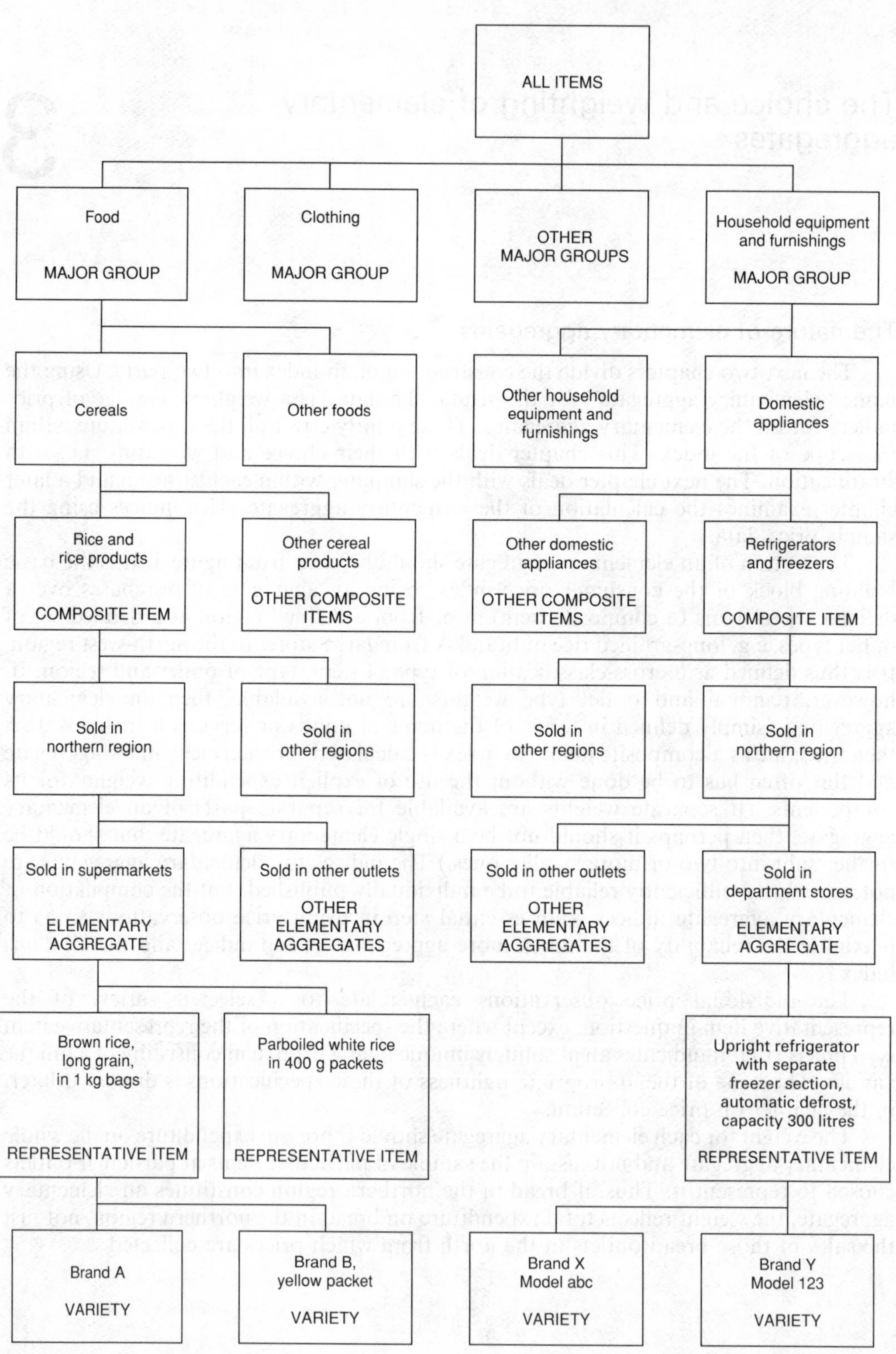

Principles of selection

The selection of elementary aggregates has to weigh up a number of considerations, listed in the following set of headings. No generally valid recipe for combining them is possible, though the first is clearly mandatory. When constructing a new index it is perhaps best to start with the available weighting data and then to consider whether to combine some groups into larger elementary aggregates and, even though rough weight estimates must be used, to split others into smaller elementary aggregates, in order to seek to minimise error. The classification *desiderata* spelt out below must also be taken into account.

Clarity

Elementary aggregates should be so chosen and described that any item within the scope of the index, and hence any price quotation, can be unambiguously assigned to only *one* of them.

Minimise error

This topic is discussed in the article "Reduction of errors in a consumer price index", by D. J. Sellwood, reprinted in Appendix 4. His analysis, to which the reader should refer, suggests that:

— Elementary aggregates, particularly those with large weights, should as far as possible be made up of related items which are likely to be subject to similar price movements. This is in order to reduce the possible effects of both sampling and non-sampling errors in the estimates of the elementary aggregate indices. (Similarity of price movements may occur within a region, for imported items, for items whose labour or raw material requirements are similar, for items sold by a particular type of outlet, for items whose prices are similarly influenced by taxes and subsidies or for seasonally influenced items.)
— A corollary is that items whose prices might be expected to move in a markedly differently way should not be grouped together in the same elementary aggregate.
— Whether or not regional or outlet-type group sub-indices are required, regional or outlet weights should be used to define separate elementary aggregates if possible, even though only rough estimates of these weights are available.
— A large number of elementary aggregates, with roughly equal weights, is to be preferred to a small number with very different weights. Equal weights would rule out any correlation between elementary aggregate indices and their weights, and positive correlation increases the effects of errors.

The scope for applying this last suggestion may be limited, though it should be borne in mind both in dividing expenditure into composite items and in stratifying by region. If regional sub-indices are not published, and if regions are made up of aggregations of administrative areas, some degree of similarity of size can be sought.

Classifications

Types of expenditure

The classification used should be such that it permits aggregation into *(a)* the eight major groups of the System of National Accounts, and also, *(b)* into the most detailed ones used for publication of group indices (whose choice is discussed later). It is also desirable that, as far as possible, it should be capable of mapping into the classifications used for household expenditure surveys and used for other statistics where deflators are needed, for example data on retail sales.

Some consistency with the classification of elementary aggregates used in the International Comparison Project may also be desirable.

No elementary aggregate should cut across these classifications by including items from more than one of the groups distinguished in any of them. The choice of group indices is discussed in another chapter. The national accounts compilers may need group price indices for each of the groups in their consumption expenditure classification. (These may be different and more detailed than the group indices which are published.)

The classification should, as far as possible, include in each group some items which are continuously available on the market. Thus, an elementary aggregate consisting exclusively of fashion goods will create problems. Another point worth considering is that the classification may usefully include groups of items which, though currently unimportant, are expected to grow in significance. Thus, if sales of frozen foods, though small, are expected to expand rapidly, their specific inclusion as a group which can be separated out in the future is a good idea.

Outlet types

Beyond the application of the general principles stated above with respect to the availability of weights and the parallelism of price movements, a practical reason for separating out a particular outlet type, such as a major chain of food shops, is that the prices charged may be obtained centrally.

Regions

A "region", it will be recalled, may not be a geographically contiguous area; it may consist, for example, of towns of a certain size. It will usually be defined in administrative terms. A particular case of this is to be found in federal countries where indirect taxes, and hence some price movements, may differ between the member provinces. But this last possibility apart, the use of administrative boundaries does not necessarily mean the use of large administrative units; the regrouping of smaller administrative units may produce "regions" which are more likely to have similar price movements within their boundaries or which contain households with similar purchase patterns. For example, even a simple distinction between rural and urban areas may reflect quite large differences in the weighting of housing and food expenditure of households. In some countries climatic differences may cause widespread regional variations in the composition of food expenditures or in the importance of fuel.

Sales within a region versus purchases by its residents

This distinction is important because some of the steps in sampling depend upon whether the sample selection is related to regional sales or to purchases by the residents of a region.

Most household expenditure surveys give purchases by a sample of the residents of the sampled zones; they rarely break them down by outlet type and outlet location. On the other hand, prices collected from a sample of outlets in a zone relate to their sales to both residents and non-residents and any information obtained in the outlets about their relative sales of different items will rarely distinguish the two. The imaginary and much simplified arithmetic example in figure 4 serves to explain the complications which result.

Let us assume that there are only eight elementary aggregates formed by the cross classification of two regions, urban and rural, two composite items, clothes and food; and two outlet types, shops and markets. The left-hand column of the diagram shows the breakdown of expenditures. Town dwellers account for 41 per cent of the total. But urban purchases have a larger share of the total, namely 55 per cent, because, it is

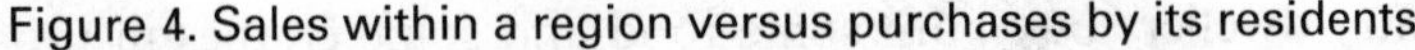

Figure 4. Sales within a region versus purchases by its residents

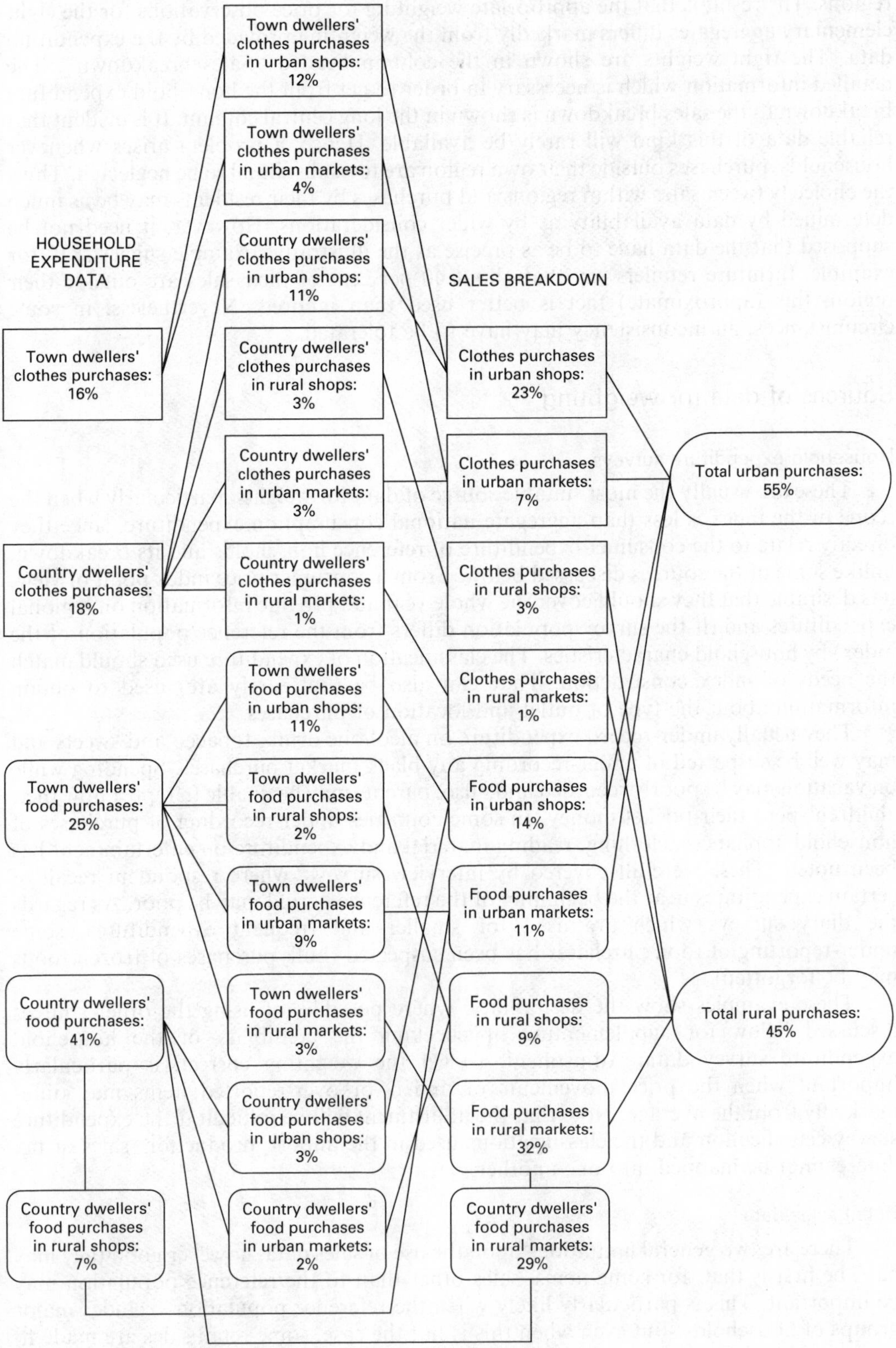

HOUSEHOLD EXPENDITURE DATA

Town dwellers' clothes purchases: 16%

Country dwellers' clothes purchases: 18%

Town dwellers' food purchases: 25%

Country dwellers' food purchases: 41%

Country dwellers' food purchases in rural shops: 7%

Town dwellers' clothes purchases in urban shops: 12%

Town dwellers' clothes purchases in urban markets: 4%

Country dwellers' clothes purchases in urban shops: 11%

Country dwellers' clothes purchases in rural shops: 3%

Country dwellers' clothes purchases in urban markets: 3%

Country dwellers' clothes purchases in rural markets: 1%

Town dwellers' food purchases in urban shops: 11%

Town dwellers' food purchases in rural shops: 2%

Town dwellers' food purchases in urban markets: 9%

Town dwellers' food purchases in rural markets: 3%

Country dwellers' food purchases in urban shops: 3%

Country dwellers' food purchases in urban markets: 2%

SALES BREAKDOWN

Clothes purchases in urban shops: 23%

Clothes purchases in urban markets: 7%

Clothes purchases in rural shops: 3%

Clothes purchases in rural markets: 1%

Food purchases in urban shops: 14%

Food purchases in urban markets: 11%

Food purchases in rural shops: 9%

Food purchases in rural markets: 32%

Country dwellers' food purchases in rural markets: 29%

Total urban purchases: 55%

Total rural purchases: 45%

assumed, country dwellers buy both some food and some clothes in urban shops and markets, whereas town dwellers buy only a little food and no clothes at all in rural regions. The result is that the appropriate weighting for price observations for the eight elementary aggregates differs markedly from the weighting provided by the expenditure data. The right weights are shown in the column headed "Sales breakdown". The detailed information which is necessary in order to get from the household expenditure breakdown to the sales breakdown is shown in the long central column. It is evident that reliable data of this kind will rarely be available. Hence, a problem arises whenever households' purchases outside their own region are too substantial to be neglected. Thus, the choice between sales within regions and purchases by their residents may be as much determined by data availability as by wider considerations. However, it need not be supposed that the data have to be as precise as the illustrative example suggests. If, for example, furniture retailers say that about 40 per cent of their sales are outside their region, this (approximate) fact is better used than ignored. Nevertheless, in some circumstances, an inconsistency may have to be tolerated.

Sources of data for weighting

Household expenditure surveys

These are usually the most suitable source of data for weights, particularly when the scope of the index is less than aggregate national consumption expenditure, since they directly relate to the consumer expenditure of reference households and its breakdown, unlike some of the sources discussed below. From a consumer price index point of view, it is desirable that they should cover the whole year and provide information on regional expenditures and (if the survey population differs from the reference population of the index) by household characteristics. The classification of expenditure used should match the needs of index construction. They can also be (but rarely are) used to obtain information about the type of outlet and location of purchases.

They usually under-record expenditure on alcoholic drink, tobacco and sweets and may well be suspected of under-recording any black market purchases. Spending while on vacation may be poorly recorded and, also, parents may be unable to report how their children spent their pocket money. In some countries under-recording of purchases of household appliances, clothing, reading material and expenditure on entertainment has been noted. These were all covered by interview surveys, where respondent recall of certain expenditures near the beginning of the reference period may be poor. As regards the diary surveys which are used for smaller and frequent expenditures, some under-reporting of food purchases has been suspected (bulk purchases of frozen foods may be forgotten).

These examples show the desirability, where possible, of using the other sources discussed below for supplementing or checking the credibility of the household expenditure survey data. Adjustment, to get the weighting correct, is particularly important when the price movements of under- or over-reported items may differ markedly from the average. Note that the adjustment will be difficult if the expenditure survey classification and the classifications used in the import, production, sales or tax data cannot be mapped into one another.

Retail sales data

There are two general limitations upon the use of sales data, however good they may be. The first is that, for some items, sales other than to the reference population may be important. This is particularly likely when the reference population excludes major groups of households. But even when this is not the case, some retail sales are made to government and business customers, whose purchases are not part of private consumption. The second limitation, as already noted, is that sales data by region are of little use when purchase data by region are required, and when sales to out-of-region purchasers or to purchasers not in the reference population are considerable.

Retail sales data can be of various kinds. In socialist economies the socialised trade system usually includes a regular reporting system which provides a mass of sales data. (In peasant markets price but not sales data are usually collected.) These sales data can be used as major sources for estimating weights, at least when the reference group is sufficiently broad to account for most retail sales. In mixed economies retail sales data are generally scarcer. Some may come from market research firms or retail trade associations. The statistician should take the trouble to find out what is available and see whether it can be used.

There may be retail sales surveys which provide information for broad groups of items, by region and by type of outlet. If not, the statistical office should consider whether such a survey should be instituted, bearing in mind that most retailers keep accounts, though not necessarily in great detail. If data are obtained through such a survey, it may be necessary to estimate the breakdown of each broad group of items into its component items.

In any event, where a very large proportion of sales of a particular group of items, such as food, are made by chainstores, an annual survey of those chainstores may be fairly easy to undertake. This should then be carried out, the data being used for central outlet selection, even though, for other outlets, the selection may have to be decentralised and less well based.

Better still, some countries have enterprise directories which include retail enterprises, which are reasonably accurate and which contain information about turnover or employment (which can be assumed to be roughly proportional to sales within each kind of retailing). The price statistician who is fortunate enough to have such information at his disposal should use it for probability proportional to size sampling for each branch of retailing or for weighting of outlet types.

At a later stage, once zones for price collection have been selected, local surveys of sellers can be undertaken to provide sales data for outlets in those zones.

Production and trade statistics

With items which are primarily consumer items, or where business use can be estimated, total availability can be estimated as production plus imports less exports less change in stocks. Consumption equals total availability less the amounts used as intermediate inputs, which also have to be estimated where relevant. For example, some food items and some cookery equipment will be bought by restaurants and hotels as well as by households. Such an approach can be of use, in particular in small economies, where the supply of many items derives exclusively from imports. However, this is only useful when the import statistics are reliable and smuggling is unimportant.

Tax statistics

These yield data on the consumption, in particular, of alcohol and tobacco, which, if bootlegging and smuggling are minimal, may be more reliable than questionnaire responses concerning expenditure on these items.

Point-of-purchase surveys

These are household sample surveys of the reference populations in towns and villages selected for price collection. They provide expenditure estimates by item group by outlet. The results are useful not only for weighting but primarily for selecting where to collect prices. They are especially helpful when more than one consumer price index is to be produced, related to different reference populations. The only argument against them, and unfortunately it is a powerful one, is their cost. The task of coding responses giving the name, address or description of an outlet for each recorded expenditure is a considerable one, and the response burden is significantly larger than in a customary expenditure survey. When this argument is decisive, and relevant retail sales data are inadequate, the possibility of ascertaining only outlet types as part of a household expenditure survey should be considered. This adds a little to the burden of carrying out such a survey, but not much, since it can be limited to asking a simple question for each of a number of expenditure groupings.

National accounts

National accounts estimates of private final consumption expenditure can be used as the main source of weights for types of expenditure when they are detailed and when the reference population includes all households, though it may be necessary to supplement and correct them by more detailed information obtained from a household expenditure survey.

The use of national accounts estimates, of course, merely transfers some of the work from the price statistician to the national accounts statisticians. The price statistician should, however, check that they are not based exclusively upon the household expenditure survey but combine information derived from other sources as well, such as retail sales, production, tax or trade statistics. Furthermore, allowance must be made for any differences in scope and definitions, such as the inclusion in the national accounts of the expenditure of non-profit-making organisations and foreign tourists, or the ways housing expenditure and medical care are treated. In any case, it will presumably be the price statistician who has to make the estimates, however rough, of the breakdowns by outlet types and by regions.

Population censuses

When regional weights for total expenditure are not available from a household expenditure survey, census data on the geographic distribution of the population, and perhaps on regional differences in household size and composition, may be utilised. But if so, they should be used together with data (or even rough estimates) of regional household expenditure levels, for which incomes may serve as a proxy. It is important to remember that the use of population data alone makes the implicit assumption that expenditures per head or per household are the same in all regions. Any assumption of this sort should, however, be examined very carefully and should be made explicit rather than implicit. In one country, where a population weight of 0.19 had been given to the urban population, taking account of the higher levels of expenditure of urban households raised the weight to 0.58.

Selection and weighting in practice

Data availability

Data availability (and cost considerations) will determine the extent to which the principles of selection, outlined above, can be applied in the stratification of expenditure into the elementary aggregates that compose an index. At the one extreme, a large number of small, homogeneous and (very approximately) equally weighted elementary aggregates may be distinguished and reliably weighted. At the other extreme, elementary aggregates may be defined only in terms of the classification of type of expenditure, without any breakdown either by type of outlet or by region.

A possible intermediate case would arise where regional and outlet-type breakdowns were available, but not disaggregated in terms of each other or by type of expenditure (or not in as much detail). Estimates of the weight of any elementary aggregate in the three-way classification could then be obtained as the product of its regional share of total consumption, its outlet-type share of total consumption and its expenditure-type share of total consumption. But it is extremely unlikely, for example, that the share of radio and television set purchases from department stores will be the same fraction of the consumption of metropolitan households as of that of rural households. Hence, the procedure would entail error. Even a very approximate adjustment for this is better than none at all.

Another intermediate case would arise where no regional breakdown of expenditure was available.

In such cases of inadequate data it would usually be best to make estimates, using whatever relevant data are available. As an example among many possible cases, suppose that population data by region are available, and that a household income and expenditure survey has provided some information about the relation between income or expenditure levels and various demographic variables. A regional distribution of consumption can then be estimated which, though very approximate, will be preferable to the (implicit) assumption that prices should have the same weights in all regions.

Similarly, if it is known that around two-thirds of the grocery trade is in the hands of national chainstores in the western part of the country and only half in other parts, this is information which should be used. The type or types of expenditure in the expenditure classification which consist of grocery items should then each be split into at least four elementary aggregates, however poor the information about the western share of grocery sales in the national total.

It is important to note that data do not always have to be recent in order to be useful in estimating weights. The structural composition, as distinct from the level, of many factors often changes but slowly. Many rural/urban differences, for example, persist over long periods. This reinforces the point that elementary aggregates should not be defined and weights estimated simply by type of expenditure. Region is also important, except perhaps in small island economies, and outlet type also usually deserves to be taken into account.

Omitting unimportant expenditures

A household expenditure survey, which in most cases will be the main source of data for weighting, should include everything, if only to ensure that the information furnished by respondents is complete and consistent. But this does not mean that everything has to be included in the index; on the contrary, the collection of prices and the computation of the index should exclude very minor items of expenditure whose inclusion would have no discernible effect.

In order to illustrate this, let us assume that some households buy pipe cleaners, snuff and shoe polish but that aggregate expenditure on these items is trivially small so that collection of their prices is unnecessary. In terms of these examples, such cases can be dealt with as follows:

— put pipe cleaners into an elementary aggregate called "Miscellaneous" and exclude this elementary aggregate both from the calculation of weights and from the computation of the index (this is equivalent to including this elementary aggregate and assuming that its elementary aggregate index is identical to the weighted mean of all other elementary aggregate indices);

— include snuff when calculating the weight for the elementary aggregate "Tobacco" (which may also include cigarettes) but do not seek to include snuff among the representative items in it, i.e. the items for which prices are collected;

— include shoe polish when calculating the weight for some elementary aggregate such as "Household cleaning materials", but do not seek to include shoe polish among the representative items selected.

The last two of these three examples illustrate the appropriate method to use when the price of the item to be neglected is likely to move in parallel with the important items in one particular elementary aggregate; this could be, for example, because of common ingredients or similar tax treatment. The first example applies the method that is appropriate when no such obvious parallelism can be found.

Frequency of reweighting

Statisticians know better than the public that small changes in weights usually have little effect upon an index. Nevertheless, to find out whether the changes are small, a new set of weights has to be estimated. In any case, it is important that the public have faith in the accuracy of a consumer price index. Hence, updating of the weights at reasonable intervals is desirable. There is a lot to be said in favour of an annually chained index, but where this is not possible, a five to ten year frequency should be aimed at.

Substitution bias

Economic theory asserts that fixed weight indices have an upward bias because consumers will reduce their (relative) purchases of those items whose prices rise (relatively to the rest). By thus substituting some cheaper items for other, newly dearer items, they will be able to buy a set of goods and services which is just as good as the original one but which costs them less than the new cost of the original set. The net cost increase to them of this measures the rise in the "true cost of living". It follows that, other things remaining equal, a chain index will theoretically rise more slowly than a fixed weight index.

The logical correctness of this argument does not necessarily mean that it is important. On the one hand, various econometric investigations of this "substitution" showed it to have minor effects on the value of an index, at least as regards substitution between groups. On the other hand, actual changes in weights seem to result, to a considerable extent, from other factors: alterations in habits and tastes; the introduction and spread of new products; and changes in the relative importance and location of different types of household.

Whether or not price-induced substitution dominates changes in weights, if actual weights are changing, then the weights used in the index should ideally also change.

Maintenance

New items

If a new good or service is so different from existing ones that it does not fit within any of the composite items distinguished by the index, it will not be feasible to include it until the next general reweighting. But the index can respond to changes in the market if minor weight changes are made within unchanged totals for larger groupings when a new product does belong to an existing composite item. If it is a substitute for existing items, a quality adjustment will be in order. However, once it is apparent that this is a new kind of item, that its sales are substantial and that its price no longer reflects novelty value, it should be linked in, so that its introduction does not affect the level of the index.

New outlets

Similar remarks apply to new outlets. New retailers, the opening of new branches of chainstores and the construction of new shopping centres can all bring about a need to change the sample of outlets from which prices are obtained. If the market share of one type of outlet increases it may be worth dividing an elementary aggregate index into more than one, linking the weighted average of the new ones to the old one. But there are also other reasons why it may be necessary to increase the number of outlets from which prices are obtained. The need arises when, in what has been a fairly stable market, price competition becomes more severe so that prices fluctuate rapidly and vary more between outlets.

Maintenance involves more than responding to changes. It also involves checking whether, and where, there is a need to improve the system of weights. If the prices obtained for an elementary aggregate display dissimilar behaviour, a matter which should be periodically checked, then obtaining weights to enable it to be split and/or an increase in the number of price observations obtained should be considered.

Finally, it is important to remember that even when a complete reweighting is not possible, data may be available for partial reweightings. In addition to the cases of new items and outlets just discussed, such new data may permit updating either at a high level of aggregation or at a low level. In both cases they should be utilised.

Sampling within elementary aggregates: Zones, outlets and items 4

Since a consumer price index is an estimate, based upon sample data, we are concerned with the choices of:
- — sample of the zones within each of the regions covered by the index;
- — sample of items in a sample of outlets;
- — sample price collection times within the month.

Practical constraints

Geographic spread

The statistician who knows that price movements in different places are very highly correlated may feel able to produce a good index without a wide geographic spread of price collection. In addition, the importance of making reliable assessments of quality change, in particular for clothing, make it more important to have well-trained price collectors in a limited number of areas than a poorly qualified staff scattered all over the country. But collection from more places than is necessary to provide a good estimate may be unavoidable, partly to make it clear to the users that it is a national index and partly in case price movements in different areas cease to be parallel.

Limiting costs by concentration of price collection

It is evident that for a given number of prices, the greater the number of price collection zones, the higher the costs of supervision and travel. This explains why most countries select fairly compact geographic zones (within each region if there is more than one) as the first stage in sampling.

Sampling within regions

If there are no regional weights, elementary aggregates being defined for the whole of the territory covered by the index, then the sampling will treat that whole as the one and only region. Within each of the one or more regions, if it is a large area, there will have to be a selection of a sample of zones within which prices are collected.

If price movements were known, or suspected, not to be parallel in different zones of a region, and if the relevant estimated regional consumption could be split between them, then these zones should not be in the same region! In that case, stratification should have been carried further to create smaller regions. But, given that no zonal breakdown of consumer expenditure is available, the selection and, indeed, the delimitation of zones, has to be a matter of common sense. Thus, suppose that a region has been defined as all towns other than the capital city. Population data may suggest which are the towns where expenditure is greatest. The possibility of divergent price movements in different areas may suggest that the small number of towns where prices are to be collected should not all be in the same corner of the country.

The weight for each region (for each expenditure type and outlet type) has, somehow, to be spread between the sample of zones within it selected for price collection. This may be done by using a simple mean of all the sample observations. This, of course, amounts to giving them equal weights. If it is known that one zone is much more important than the others, it is better to give it an arbitrarily larger weight.

Sampling of outlets and items purchased by residents

Given *(a)* the weight of an elementary aggregate; *(b)* its specification in terms of type of expenditure, region and outlet type; and *(c)* the selection of sample zones within the region, we now turn to the selection of the precise prices to be collected. This involves specification of the representative items and the selection of their varieties and of outlets. These selections are necessarily linked for the very practical reason of ensuring that items which are selected are available in the chosen outlets, and that they are likely to remain available.

What is an item?

An item is a definable good or service which has a price. There are, however, some cases where the matter is less obvious because the price paid is the sum of a number of components, so that it is necessary to decide whether the item is to be treated as a single whole or whether the components are to be treated separately. Examples of such cases are *à la carte* restaurant meals, cars (where the buyer pays a basic price plus the cost of various options), household appliances with an optional service contract and the rental of a car, which may include extra payment for insurance.

Where the buyer has no choice, so that all buyers pay for the same set of components, there is no problem, only the total matters. But where a choice does exist for buyers, the statistician also has a choice: between treating the components as separate items and selecting a representative combination of components as constituting a single item.

Consider a simple case where all purchasers buy component A but only a fraction of them buy the optional component B, and where the prices of A and of B do not change in the same proportion. Then the item can be defined as: A plus a fraction of B; or two items can be distinguished, A and (with a smaller weight) B. But if the fraction is not known, the only practical possibility is to define the item arbitrarily either as A alone or as A + B together, whichever is believed to be most common.

Three cases where the fraction is likely to be known are discussed separately in the next chapter. They are multi-part tariffs for public utility services; mail-order purchases; and rental payment for dwellings where there are separate charges for heating.

The different methods

Ideally, the selection of outlets and items would rest upon a complete "census" of all the relevant zonal expenditure by type of expenditure and by outlet. Since this is impossible, in practice, there are various ways to obtain the sample. A point-of-purchase household sample survey can provide an estimate of all the relevant zonal expenditure by type of expenditure and by outlet. Alternatively, sampling from a list of outlets can be used, preferably using probability proportional to size if some measure of the sales of each outlet (or a proxy variable, such as employment) is available. Failing this, and failing a simpler version of a point-of-purchase survey, such as a household expenditure survey which merely ascertains the type of outlet for each recorded expenditure, but not the name and location of each particular outlet, the selection of outlets must rest upon local knowledge as to which outlets are important and/or typical. This latter method, which is the crudest, does however have non-sampling advantages in scheduling the work of the price collectors.

It is evident that the selection method applied in practice will depend upon the availability of ready-made information, the size and complexity of the economy of the country and upon the resources available to the statistician for designing and conducting the calculation of the index. Five methods out of a multitude of possibilities are described below. The first of them, which is largely inspired by the probabilistic method used by the United States Bureau of Labor Statistics, is the most demanding. It is here termed the "reference method", since other less complex and less expensive methods can be described as simplifications of it. The four simpler methods described all presuppose the availability of certain statistical data. Where this is lacking, as is the case in some less developed countries, sensible guesstimates based on local knowledge will have to be used.

The following discussion of this reference method and the four particular variants described below all suppose that the aim is to obtain prices for purchases by residents of a zone. Figure 5 shows how the discussion is arranged. A later section takes up the different case of obtaining prices for sales within a zone.

The reference method

This is a two-stage sampling procedure: selection of a sample of outlets followed by selection of a sample of items.

Selecting outlets

The selection is based upon a point-of-purchase survey of a sample of households resident in the zone. Information is obtained, for each item of expenditure, about how much has been spent in each outlet where purchases have been made, together with the names and addresses of all these outlets. This provides a list of outlets, some of which may be outside the zone, with the total sales by each of them of each item (or group of items) to the sample households.

The sample of outlets is then drawn from this list proportionally to these total sales. The estimator of the index for each item for the households of the sample zone is then the simple mean of the price relatives, or the relative of mean prices, calculated for the outlets in the sample. An outlet drawn more than once in the sample will be counted more than once in calculating this. Alternatively, substrata could be formed and weights attached to the outlets then selected.

Figure 5. Sampling of outlets and items purchased

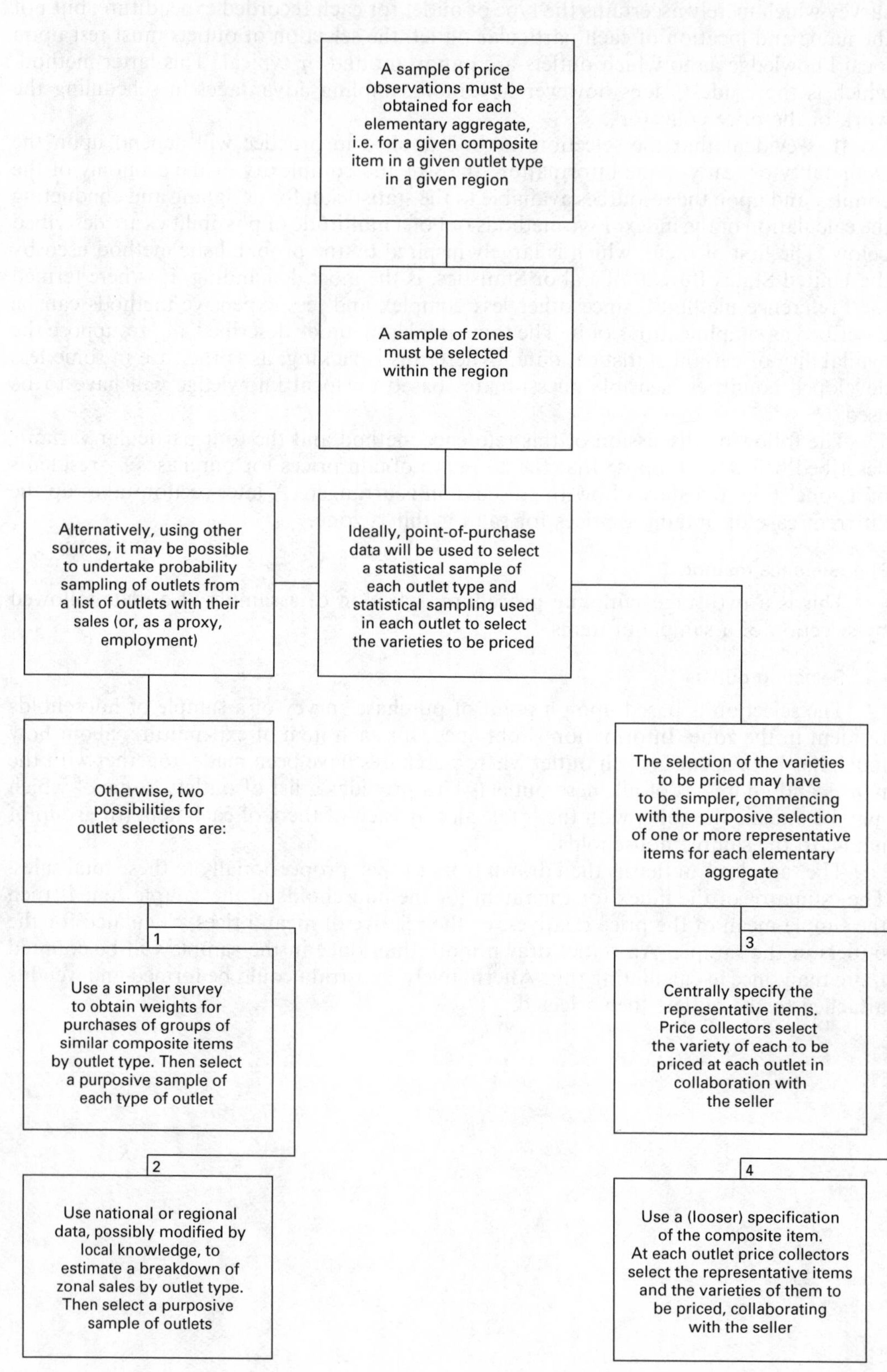

A sample of price observations must be obtained for each elementary aggregate, i.e. for a given composite item in a given outlet type in a given region
A sample of zones must be selected within the region
Alternatively, using other sources, it may be possible to undertake probability sampling of outlets from a list of outlets with their sales (or, as a proxy, employment)
Ideally, point-of-purchase data will be used to select a statistical sample of each outlet type and statistical sampling used in each outlet to select the varieties to be priced
Otherwise, two possibilities for outlet selections are:
The selection of the varieties to be priced may have to be simpler, commencing with the purposive selection of one or more representative items for each elementary aggregate
1
Use a simpler survey to obtain weights for purchases of groups of similar composite items by outlet type. Then select a purposive sample of each type of outlet
3
Centrally specify the representative items. Price collectors select the variety of each to be priced at each outlet in collaboration with the seller
2
Use national or regional data, possibly modified by local knowledge, to estimate a breakdown of zonal sales by outlet type. Then select a purposive sample of outlets
4
Use a (looser) specification of the composite item. At each outlet price collectors select the representative items and the varieties of them to be priced, collaborating with the seller

Selection of items at each outlet

At each selected outlet items within each expenditure category of the survey must be selected for pricing. If the outlet has been selected more than once in the sampling, then a corresponding number of items must be selected.

The selection results from a random process which again involves sampling in successive stages. It is based on the fact that one can move from the description of a composite item to the precise identification of a particular variety via a hierarchy of descriptive levels. Thus, to get from a composite item called "refrigerator" to "refrigerator with freezer of brand M, model R" one might envisage the following series of hierarchical levels and choices:

Ordinary refrigerator, Refrigerator with freezer, Freezer;
capacity of the refrigerator: < 50 l, 51-150 l, 151-250 l, > 250 l;
capacity of the freezer: < 20 l, 21-40 l, 41-70 l, > 70 l;
cabinet: enamel, plastic;
brand: A, B, C, . . . M, . . .;
model No.: N, O, P, . . . R . . .

The nature of each level depends on the choice at the preceding level. For example, if, at the first level, the choice was "Ordinary refrigerator", then the third level above would be irrelevant and there would be a different list of brands and models. Similarly, if the first-level choice was "Freezer", then the second-level above would not apply and the freezer capacity brackets would be different, maybe
< 50 l, 51-100 l, 101-200 l, 201-300 l, > 300 l, etc.

Selection of a variety at an outlet thus takes place in successive stages:

— At the first hierarchical level the respondent person at the outlet is asked for the distribution of turnover between the different types. Thus, still in terms of the same example, he or she might answer that ordinary refrigerators account for 50 per cent, refrigerators with freezer for 30 per cent and freezers for 20 per cent. The price collector then follows a procedure for selecting, with a probability proportionate to sales value, one of these three types as a function of their relative importance.

— At the second level the collector obtains estimates of the shares in turnover of the different refrigerator capacity size groups within the sales of refrigerators with freezers. The response might be, for example, 10 per cent for < 50 l, 20 per cent for 51-100 l, 50 per cent for 151-250 l, and 20 per cent for > 250 l. Again, the price collector follows a procedure for selecting, at random, one of these size brackets as a function of their relative importance.

The process continues in this way until a unique variety has been selected by this method of progressive decomposition. It is worth pointing out that the collector may have to modify the list of alternatives at each hierarchical level in order to adapt the interrogation to apply to the range of items that are available in the outlet in question.

Note that since the sampling at each outlet is done in terms of its turnover, i.e. of all its sales whatever the place of residence of the purchaser, there is a slight departure from the purism of the place of residence approach. However, it will only rarely happen that the composition of purchases within a composite item will differ much between residents of the sampled zone and all the other customers of a given outlet, though one can think of exceptions such as when farmers come to town to buy farm clothes and cars.

Problems with the method

Despite the merits of principle of the method, its implementation in practice is not easy for the following reasons:

— It is costly since it requires a special household survey in the selected zones to obtain the point-of-purchase data. It may be possible to integrate this with an expenditure survey, but at the cost of making it more extensive and complex. In the United States the separate point-of-purchase survey obtains the names and addresses of business establishments where households make their purchases for each of about 140 categories of items, and the interviews take about 1½ hours. In either case, the sample size has to be adequate within each selected zone.

- It is more costly than the centralised collection of certain prices which, as discussed in the next chapter, may be reliably carried out in certain circumstances.
- It is also expensive because a point-of-purchase survey yields data on purchases by the households of a zone, not purchases within the zone, so that price collection will have to extend to outlets outside the zone where the households of the zone make purchases. Even if expenditure away from home, on holiday, is treated differently from other out-of-zone expenditure, such outlets may be widely dispersed. Shopping trips outside the zone and shopping done during visits to other places may be important; even if they are not, the cost of obtaining a few price observations in locations scattered outside the zone can be very considerable.
- It requires a detailed, exhaustive and sometimes technically complicated hierarchy of classification of all the varieties of all the items included in the composite item. What is more, the classification needs to be continuously kept up to date.
- The price collectors have to be given rigorous training in the application of the statistical sampling procedures as well as in quality evaluation, since substitutions may well be more frequent with this method of item selection than with purposive sampling. This means that it is desirable for them to be specialists in price collection rather than ordinary local officials who devote a day or two of each month to price collection.
- It requires the close collaboration of people in the outlets and this may be difficult to secure. The necessary interviews with sales personnel may take several hours.

The four particular variants presented below are various practical approximations to the reference method which, wholly or partly, avoid the problems just listed. They are not mutually exclusive, since various combinations are possible, but they suffice to exemplify the whole range of possibilities. The first two simplify outlet selection and the second two simplify item selection. Their feasibility is linked to the availability of existing information. As they are all simpler than the reference type of procedure, they unavoidably fall short as regards the precision of the results, though it is not possible to say by how much. It may be possible to compensate for this by increasing the number of prices collected, though this naturally entails higher costs.

The use of simpler methods than the reference method is forced upon most statistical offices by cost considerations and staff limitations. Such methods are more acceptable the more the particular situation corresponds to any of the following sets of circumstances:

- Movements of the prices of the individual items are fairly similar within relatively homogeneous groups, apart from temporary price movements such as those for vegetables resulting from changes in the weather, or those due to bursts of price competition between shops. The homogeneity that is relevant here relates either to the physical characteristics of the items (e.g. bread) or to their having a common origin (e.g. wooden furniture). Greater homogeneity diminishes the length of time over which the validity of the generalisation needs to be checked.
- Price movements within the items included in a composite item are conditioned in some way by a limited subset of these items. This subset is not necessarily the major part of the composite item. An example might be the price of milk (when prices are not regulated) within a composite item consisting of milk and milk products, such

as cream, butter and cheese. In such cases, price observations can be limited to prices of the subset.

— Even when their level is not uniform, price movements within a local area vary only slightly according to outlet for a given item (apart from bursts of price competition between shops, special offers and the like).

— Price movements for similar items in different regions tend to be parallel because transport and communications facilities are such that the amount of traffic between them is extensive.

1. Outlet selection using zone-level statistics

This involves a household survey in each zone, in the same way as the reference procedure, but of a simpler kind. Instead of obtaining a detailed list of purchases by type by outlet, purchases are simply divided between types of outlet and between those within the residence zone and those outside it. Thus, instead of ascertaining purchases of dairy products by individual outlet, an estimate will be obtained of such purchases in all local supermarkets together, in local street markets, etc. The households surveyed may be asked to record purchases by individual outlet but, at the stage of coding the data, the only details to be recorded will be the type of outlet and whether it is local or not. Cost is saved because this kind of survey, which makes acceptable a smaller sample size than in the reference procedure, is less detailed.

The selection of outlets for price collection can be done under the assumption that, for each composite item, prices move in the same way in all the outlets of a given type within the zone. (If the assumption can be extended to outlets outside the zone, price collection there can be avoided.) The selection is done separately for each outlet type distinguished. The lack of information about the turnover of individual outlets necessitates the implicit assumption that they all have the same value of sales of the composite item, so that the sample outlets can be selected with equal probabilities. A simple average of the observations will then provide the price estimate for the outlet type and these can be combined into a weighted average for all the outlet types selling the composite item. Alternatively, if the number of outlets sampled for each outlet type is proportional to the estimated value of purchases of the composite item from that outlet type, then a simple average for all the outlets of all types can be used.

The assumption about parallel price movements for each outlet type justifies delegation of the selection of outlets for price collection to the supervisors of the price collectors, with a quota of outlets of each type. If this is done, the sample chosen must be examined centrally in order to check the quality of the sample. Delegation of the selection to the price collectors themselves would incur the risk that their choice would be influenced by such irrelevant considerations as their individual ease of access to the outlets. (It might also be influenced by the friendliness of the reception accorded to them there, but while this may be irrelevant for sampling, it can be an advantage for obtaining the data.)

Prices will have to be collected from outside the zone if the assumption that these prices move in the same way as prices within the zone cannot be supported, and if these purchases are large enough to matter. In many cases, however, the places where purchases are made outside the zone will be largely common to different zones. The most obvious example is when people go on shopping expeditions to a large town, maybe the capital city. Price observations made in a few such central places can then be used in the computations for several zones.

2. Outlet selection using more aggregative statistics

This variant applies when the breakdown of expenditures is unknown at the zonal level but is known only for the whole region, for a group of regions or even only for the whole of the territory to which the index relates. One then has to assume that whatever is thus known is also valid for the zones where outlets are to be selected. On this assumption, the method described above for the first variant can then be applied.

Obtaining the necessary data on the distribution of expenditure between outlet types at a regional or national level is certainly less difficult and expensive than obtaining it for every selected zone in every region. Data from trade sources or from a distribution census can be used, though at the price of ignoring any difference between the pattern of purchases by the residents of a region and the pattern of sales by outlets in a region. Alternatively, survey data on purchases by outlet type can be obtained at a regional level with a much smaller sample than if estimates at zonal level are sought.

Using national level data may obviously lead to error. Thus, if it is known that open air markets account for about 25 per cent of the sales of fresh fruit in the country as a whole, it may none the less be obvious that the figure is much higher in a particular region even though no regional statistics are available. This is an example of a case where it is better to make rough estimates for weighting purposes, than to achieve a spurious accuracy by using only inadequate statistically quantified information. Consultation between the central office and people who know the various regions should make it possible to arrive at estimated regional breakdowns of the purchases of each composite item, by outlet type within the region, and by outlet type outside it. If, for example, when a rural and an urban region are distinguished, it is known that many rural dwellers make some of their major purchases in the towns, then prices obtained in sample towns should be used in calculations for the sampled rural zones as well as in the calculations for the towns selected to represent the urban region.

When a large share of retail trade is in the hands of chainstores, for example co-operatives, data may be available from the headquarters of the chainstore which can be used for drawing a sample of its outlets. How this is done must depend upon the nature of the data. The point is that the data should be used, even though recourse has to be made to more primitive procedures for selecting samples of all other outlets. Furthermore, and this leads us to the next section, the data may make possible the use of a statistical procedure for selecting the representative items priced in the outlets of the chainstore, leaving the selection for other outlets to *a priori* procedures.

3. *A priori* selection of representative items

The nature of this variant

Both of the two variants just described could perfectly well be combined with the reference case procedure for sampling within a composite item at each selected outlet in order to choose the precise items to be priced. But, as noted above, this procedure involves problems which often necessitate some simpler way of selecting varieties. The possible simplification here is analogous to that just discussed for the selection of outlets.

Each composite item could be split into subgroups, a reasoned choice of representative items made within each and the results combined. In the case of more homogeneous composite items, one or more representative items can be directly selected.

When considering alternatives such as this, which are less demanding of data, it must be borne in mind that the ability of statisticians to make sensible choices may match their ability at sampling. It should not be forgotten that statisticians who deal with consumer prices have advantages that are denied to those who deal with, for example, foreign trade prices. One advantage is that the purchase of consumer goods and services is part of their own everyday experience. They can thus better appreciate the characteristics of the items they price, and understand the advice of experts such as wholesalers and store buyers, than if they dealt, for example, with complex capital goods. Another is that they have regular personal contact with respondents in the outlets, so can ask questions and observe the conditions under which sales are made. It is simple common sense to guess that items made from the same raw materials, or items imported from the same country, are likely to display parallel price changes. At least for items frequently bought, statisticians can use their qualitative knowledge as consumers and easily obtainable advice to make, and gradually refine, reasoned selections within a composite item of subgroups of items for which parallel price movements seem likely. They can then select and centrally specify representative items for each of the subgroups, in order to proceed to the subsequent stage where the price collectors select varieties for price observation at each outlet. Thus, a distinction between major kinds of cheese, or a decision to ignore duck eggs in a country where nearly all eggs are hens' eggs, are examples of the application of reliable, though unquantified, information.

Varieties

With purposive sampling, the variety chosen by the price collector in a particular outlet for a particular representative item should obviously be one which is typical of that item, is likely to remain in stock for some time and is of a quality which can be ascertained. This latter requirement stems from the need to be able to find a good substitute should the variety chosen cease to be sold. When a whole range of qualities is available, a variety of middle-range quality should generally be chosen. The price differences from higher- and lower-quality varieties can then be used to make a quality adjustment should the manufacturer of the selected item change it in a way which affects its quality.

Concluding remarks

The rather home-made procedure just described can have major consequences if it is not carefully controlled. The quality of an index depends very much upon the way it is constructed at the most detailed level of observation. The choice of representative items and any weighting of them must therefore be carried out with extreme care and must be continually checked. In particular, care must be taken to avoid the trap of concentrating on items which come to mind readily because they are bought very frequently; it is the amount of expenditure which is relevant.

4. Selection of items in the outlets

As an alternative to the *a priori* selection of centrally specified representative items, those within the definition of a composite item could be selected separately at each outlet. If this is done, the price collector or his or her supervisor has to make the choices which, in the reference method, are approached by passing through a hierarchical series of selections.

Since this method of successive decomposition requires extensive knowledge on the part of the collector, a frequent shortcut is to seek the best selling variety of one or more of the best selling items included in the composite item at the outlet in question. In many cases the best selling variety (or varieties) will make up a major proportion of the outlet's turnover for the composite item. However, care must be taken when this is not the case and when sales are spread over many varieties, with none predominant. In such circumstances it is incumbent upon the price collector to remember that what really matters is not just which variety sells the most, but also which best represents the price movements for the item(s) it is to represent. Furthermore, it may be desirable for the central office to require a certain proportion of prices collected to relate to the second best selling item. Thus, if Brand X is thought to have over half the market, and Brand Y is believed to have about a third, it could be a mistake to allow price collectors to select Brand X in almost 100 per cent of the outlets because it was the best seller in nearly all of them.

Without centrally provided specifications the central checking of price collectors' reports will clearly be limited or, alternatively, require that minute attention be paid to detailed item descriptions which the collectors would be required to provide. Hence, this variant suffers from an important disadvantage, except when the range of items in the outlets is very limited.

Sampling of outlets and items sold within a region

The reference method and the four possible variants described earlier all relate, in principle, to obtaining a sample of prices paid by residents of the region rather than a sample of prices of items sold within the region. It is evident, however, that the simpler are the procedures used to sample within an elementary aggregate, the more the distinction becomes blurred. The same is true if one starts with the aim of sampling according to region of sale. Thus, the distinction may be less important in practice than one would like it to be in principle. A random selection of zones of purchase instead of zones of residence has the advantage that all the outlets to be chosen will be within the zone; this keeps down costs. On the other hand, the data may be more difficult to obtain. In this case they cannot be obtained from a survey among the zone's residents; they should ideally come from a survey of outlets, at least for those types of expenditure where non-resident purchases are thought to be important.

The issue in practice is one of how well the desired data can be approximated and this obviously depends upon the available retailing data. It may be necessary to use purposive sampling based on local knowledge about the major shopping centres and about the amount and direction of travel into these centres. Within each outlet, selection of the best selling variety of the composite item (or for each of one or more items chosen to represent it) at the outlet in question is even more justifiable than within a place-of-residence framework, since in the present case it is sales to all customers which are relevant.

Sampling in time

Whether price collection is spread over a few or many days will depend upon whether the aim is to estimate a point-in-time or a period-of-time index.

Where prices change infrequently or where it can be foreseen whether or not they will soon change, price collection can be undertaken less frequently. More generally, there is a trade-off between cost and accuracy, and if resources are short, one of the following strategies may make sense:

- collect half of the sample of prices for one or more elementary aggregates in one month and the other half in the following month;
- collect a subsample of prices monthly and only collect the remainder of the prices in the sample in alternate months;
- collect prices only when a small sample of retailers report that prices have changed or will change.

In the case of rents, the first strategy is often used, only the sample is split into three, four or six subsamples and the collection of the data rotates between them.

Sampling of rented dwellings

The weight reference period sample

In the case of most items in the index there are often no data for weighting or selecting representative items, let alone varieties; such expenditure data as are available have already been used in selecting and weighting the elementary aggregate which those items are to represent. But it may be a different matter with rented dwellings. A population and housing census may provide an enormous amount of detail that can be used for sampling rented (and owner-occupied) dwellings. Such a census, in effect, does for housing what a complete point-of-purchase census would do for food, clothes and other items.

If the census (or other listing) of dwellings used for drawing the sample does not distinguish rented dwellings from owner-occupied dwellings, then it will be necessary to ascertain which of the dwellings in the sample are rented and to allow for their probable proportion of the total in choosing the sample size.

Note that it may be possible and desirable to supplement the census by data on new dwellings completed since the date of the census, obtained for example from construction permits. If the sample includes owner-occupied dwellings, it may also be desirable to check on them when rent data are collected in order to include any which have subsequently been let to tenants.

Updating the sample

It is fairly common practice to renew the sample of rented dwellings by, for example, replacing a quarter of it every year, thus retaining no dwelling for more than four years. (In some countries renewal is much faster than this.) It is best done in such a way as to ensure that some new dwellings are included in the replacement subsamples.

What are the reasons for replacement and why is there a justification for adding dwellings which did not even exist in the weight reference period?

First, consider the following as some practical reasons for replacement:

- the rent survey may be undertaken as part of a labour force survey where households are rotated out of the sample after a certain number of periods;
- in a separate rent survey, the response burden may justify some maximum number of periods over which people are asked to provide the information;
- there is attrition because some rented dwellings are demolished, converted to other uses, become vacant or become owner-occupied.

Next, consider the point that if care is not taken to replace some of the originally selected dwellings with new dwellings, the average age of the dwellings in the sample will grow through time and the average number of years since their rents were last determined may also do the same. The first fact might possibly be held to mean that the average quality of the dwellings in the sample is falling. But in most countries it is the second fact which is important, because the way the rental housing market works is such that the rents of new tenants exceed the rents paid by existing tenants for comparable accommodation. Since new rented dwellings necessarily contain new tenants, a sample in which new dwellings were increasingly under-represented as time passes would provide an underestimate of rent levels and might well provide a poor estimate of rent changes.

Price collection

5

Specifications

The purpose of specifications

Specifications, which are provided centrally, tell the price collector what items are to be priced. They are thus essential, except where items are entirely selected by collectors within each outlet. The statistician responsible for drafting them will need the help of people who know about the items in question. Such help should be sought from manufacturers, importers, wholesalers, retailers, public analysts and trade associations.

A specification may be so tight that it enables the price collector to identify the item without exercising any discretion at all. In such a case there is no distinction between the representative item and the variety. Such a tight specification will have to be very detailed and quite lengthy for a heterogeneous composite item like women's shoes, but may, despite its completeness, be relatively brief for a homogeneous item like Super petrol or for a volume-selling branded article which is nationally sold.

If the specification is looser, the price collector has to choose the particular variety to be priced. In this case, he or she should supplement the specification by noting sufficient further descriptive details to provide a unique identification of the variety priced. As an aid to this, the specification may be accompanied by a list of the characteristics which are to be described, providing a framework for recording these further details. This then helps the price collector by telling him or her what to look for. Alternatively, the collector may be provided with a particular detailed description which merely serves as an example, to be modified in each particular case.

While the specification serves to tell the price collector what item is to be priced, in all cases where it is not very tight it is important that the collector should supplement it by recording further descriptive details. This serves two further purposes. First, there is an exact record of the variety that was priced so that even if the collector is replaced by another person, the identical variety will be priced next time. Second, the specification, and any additional description, should also note those readily describable characteristics of the item which determine its value for money in the eyes of consumers. In the case of a washing machine, for example, these include capacity, external finish, degree of automation and type of drying. Quality judgements can then be made in the event of replacement of the variety by another. Such information is essential, whether such adjustment is done by the price collector or at the centre. When it is the price collector who makes the judgements, the facts on which they are based should be recorded, both to ensure that he or she does the job thoroughly and so that the centre can check (all or some of) the judgements.

In the case of branded goods, precise identification of a variety is easy. Even so, descriptive details should be collected to make clear whether any attachments or options are included and so that, when a substitution has to be made, quality judgement will be possible.

Specifications should state the nature of the preferred units to be priced: . . . per litre, per 100 grammes, per pair, per 500 ml plastic bottle, per 2½ pound bag, per packet of ten, per visit, per ticket . . . and so on and so forth. The price collection form should require the collector to state whether the price collected refers to this standard unit, and, if not, what other unit was used. It is necessary to be particularly careful where, to give an example, two or three tins sell for less than two or three times one tin. The units preferred should be those that are most common.

Tight versus loose specifications

It is fairly obvious that tighter specifications, by leaving less discretion to the price collectors, require less judgement and training on their part. On the other hand, and equally obviously, tight specifications entail the risk that an outlet does not sell the item exactly as specified or that, even if it does, it may be unrepresentative in that particular outlet. Examples of specifications are given in box 2.

The importance of these opposing considerations depends partly upon the intelligence, training and reliability of the people who collect prices. It also depends very much upon the kind of items involved. Some quality judgements require more specialised knowledge than others. The risk of non-availability of tightly specified items is least for standard foods and for branded items where a few major brands are available nearly everywhere. Thus, quality judgements for cars are best made at the centre, with very tight specifications being provided to the price collectors for one or two models of each major make. Clothes and furniture, on the other hand, often require loose specifications even though quality judgements require some training and experience. This is because there are so many makes, styles and models of these things, that different outlets rarely sell exactly the same goods.

One common practice is for there to be a number of alternative centrally provided tight specifications. In this case, each collector would be free to price in each outlet a variety of the one which was most representative there. This would continue to be priced there for as long as it remained available, being replaced by one of the others if it ceased to be sold there. Upon such substitution, prices from other outlets could be used to impute a price reference period price to the replacement.

Tight specifications are of no use if the price collectors cannot use them. For example, even if the distinction between a home-produced and an imported foodstuff is relevant to price movements, it should form part of the specification only if the collector can easily distinguish the two. Similarly, weight is not useful information for identifying things which are not sold by weight and which do not vary much in weight. The point is that specifications should relate to what customers are prepared to pay for, not to laboratory measurement.

A final factor in the choice between tight and loose centrally provided specifications is that tight specifications allow regional comparisons of prices. Regional comparisons may be needed by government even if they do not take the form of index numbers. Tight specifications also allow the calculation of meaningful average prices. An average can, of course, be calculated and used for index number calculation (as an alternative to using an average of price relatives) but the point here is that statistics of the average prices of particular consumption goods or services may be useful in a direct way. First, they enable the central office to pick outlier prices and query them and also to make check comparisons with any other available price data. In other words, with a meaningful average price it is easier to use supplementary information to help determine whether

Box 2. Examples of specifications

The examples are arranged mainly in increasing order of the tightness of the specifications. The less tight the specification, the more details should be recorded by the price collector. Some of the examples provide a checklist for this purpose, while others leave the characteristics to be noted to the discretion of the price collector.

Potatoes

1. Imported, 1 kg.
2. Old "Whites" (Majestic), 1 lb.
3. Preferably bagged, 1-3 kg. Standard quantity is 2 kg. Washed or poor-quality potatoes are not acceptable. If new and old season potatoes are on sale, the bestseller should be priced.

Beef

1. Beef without bone. 1 kg. Fresh, indicate the cut.
2. Beef, fresh home-killed. First quality. 1 lb. State the price of one of the following: chuck; sirloin (without bone); silverside (without bone), round; back ribs (with bone); fore ribs (with bone); brisket (without bone); rump steak.
3. Boneless stewing beef. Lean boneless chunks or cubes of beef, cut from various portions of the carcass; pieces generally cut into 1-2 inch squares; contain a small amount of fat. 1 kg. Brand A. Exclude beef for "fondue" or other speciality trims.

Milk

1. Milk, fresh. State whether cow's or goat's milk.
2. Pasteurised milk; butter fat content 2.6-3.3 per cent. Fresh. ½ litre bottle, exclude bottle deposit.
3. Fresh milk, pasteurised and homogenised, with vitamin D added. Butter fat content at least 3.25 per cent. 1 litre or ½ litre sold in carton or bottle. Exclude milk sold in containers larger or smaller than specified, all non-homogenised milk, all milk without added vitamins and certified raw milk. Specify grade, make, size and type of container. Exclude bottle deposit if sold in bottles.

Men's shirt

1. Shirt, collar attached, medium priced, price of one shirt. State the make, material and size.
2. Shirt. Plain short-sleeved shirt in cotton/polyester imported from Hong Kong, Singapore or Taiwan, China.
3. Men's shirt. Cotton; long sleeves; neck measure 13-14 inches; white or light blue. One. Select the volume seller and indicate the material and make.
4. Men's shirt. Long sleeves; Country Club; Timberline; twill weave, brushed poly/cotton fabric. Styles: 242C-250 (plain colours) or 242C-260, 242C-284. Size: M, SM or XL. 97-99 cm.
5. Men's shirt. Select the volume seller and indicate the following:
(a) name of style;
(b) manufacturer;
(c) brand name;
(d) country of origin: no indication, France, Federal Republic of Germany, Italy, Netherlands, Belgium, other European countries, others;
(e) nature of the fabric: natural fibre, artificial fibre or synthetic fibre;
(f) quality of the fabric;
(g) name of the fabric;
(h) neck size, sleeve length, pockets, number of buttons;
(i) quality rating: A, B or C.

Women's shoes

1. Women's fashion shoes, 1 pair.
2. Women's casual shoes, 1 pair. Fashion shoe, medium priced.
3. Women's shoes, medium size, either of the following:
(a) "Hawaianas" model, unisex;
(b) "Pampero Moccasin" (e.g. Boyero).
If these are not available, the price collector should select a similar one that is selling well.
4. 1 pair ladies' leather shoes, with glued outsole of synthetic material, one-piece 35-70 mm heel, lined, size 37-40 (4-6½). Only shoes intended for indoors or warm/dry outdoor use may be included, shoes may have simple decoration, such as a buckle or rosette and the synthetic outsole may include some blended rubber.

Box 2. Examples of specifications (*continued*)

5. Women's court shoes.
(a) Jane Debster. High fashion styles. Uppers: black or coloured, calf, patent, suede or leather. Sole: synthetic. Styles: Alibi, Bond, Bridget, Dynasty, Tiffany, etc. Size: 7½ B FF (4-11) S.;
(b) Sandler of Boston. Uppers: synthetic patent, leather or suede. Sole: synthetic. Styles: Apollo, Ballet, Cannes, Charm, etc. Size: 7½ B (4-11) S.;
(c) Bellini. Imported, e.g. China, California styles. Synthetic upper and sole. Styles: SDL 9097 Balsam, SDL 6185 Salina, SDL 9081 Barton, etc. Size: 7 (5-10) S.;
(d) Diana Ferrari. Court shoes. Leather upper, synthetic sole, leather-covered heel. Styles: Aggy, Hot, Loya. Size: 8 (5-10) BM.

Iron

1. Dry automatic iron with temperature dial control.
2. Steam iron with 1 kW rating, with lead. 1 unit. Ratings up to 1,100 watts are acceptable but a non-steam iron is not.
3. Electric iron, simple model, 1 unit:
(a) Atma 1070, light, handle of any colour;
(b) Atma 1075, heavy, handle black;
(c) Wemir International, handle of any colour.
Price any one of the make and model indicated. If these are not available, price the volume-selling brand and indicate the model, colour, etc. (Do not price a steam or spray iron.)
4. General Electric, F34055, self-clean, surge, light weight, plastic handle, 4-metre cord.
5. Make a selection using the following checklist:
Type: steam iron; steam and dry; travel iron; dry iron.
Sole plate: polished aluminium; non-stick (Teflon).
Features: self-cleaning steam vents; spray; water level gauge.
In subsequent periods, the computer-printed price collection form repeats the particulars of the iron selected, for example: steam iron, non-stick (Teflon), spray, with water level gauge, General Electric, F38066.

Television repair

1. Replacement of TV tube. State size and service charges.
2. Cost of repair. Make a selection of the type of repair using the following checklist:
(a) type of repair: replace colour picture tube; replace/rebuild tuner (channel selector) for colour set;
(b) location of repair: in-shop repair; in-home repair;
(c) brand of TV repaired;
(d) labour charge: flat rate; hourly rate; initial charge plus hourly rate; other;
(e) description of picture tube: new; rebuilt; triangular gun; in-line gun; screen size in inches; brand name/number;
(f) description of tuner: new; rebuilt; defective tuner rebuilt/reinstalled; conventional control; remote control; with one-control colour tuning feature; brand name/number;
(g) other parts required: name of part; brand/part number;
(h) is travel or transportation charge included?
(i) is tax on repair included: tax on labour; tax on parts?

Restaurant meal

1. Two- or three-course set meal. State its components.
2. Indicate the components of each meal and price three different meals. Service charges are to be recorded separately.
3. Record the prices of the following dishes:
(a) Milanese steak;
(b) ravioli;
(c) fish and chips;
(d) ¼ litre of wine or soda;
(e) bread;
(f) dessert;
(g) a fixed menu.
Indicate the type of service, type of wine, type of dessert and the components of the menu.

prices are being measured accurately and whether the specification chosen is a representative one. Second, apart from the index number context, publication of average prices may be welcomed by the public and be useful for economic analysis.

It should be noted that the use of loose, rather than tight, specifications does not necessarily lead to a wider range of varieties being priced. If collectors seek the best selling brand or model when selecting a variety under a loose specification, it might turn out that the identical one is chosen everywhere. Thus, tight specifications could be written so as to require some collectors to obtain the price of Pepsi, whereas a loose one might result in them all ascertaining the price of Coca Cola!

There are different problems when the items to be priced are selected by probability sampling within each outlet, as in the United States consumer price index. Here, the price collector needs a classificatory scheme for all the items on sale falling within a particular composite item so that he or she can sample within it, with probability proportional to sales. But once the selection is made, the collector must record the characteristics of the selected items in terms of the classification in sufficient detail to identify them uniquely and to enable a quality judgement to be made should a substitution become necessary.

Revising specifications

Specifications should be regularly reviewed in order to see whether they need to be revised. A need for revision may be indicated by: (i) a large number of missing quotations; (ii) a wide or increasing variation in the distribution of prices obtained, suggesting that the specification may be insufficiently precise; or (iii) a large number of substitutions. New specifications may be needed if the sales of an originally unimportant item have grown large.

Some particular problems

Meat

Fresh meat can vary very much in quality in a way which is fairly obvious to a good cook but which it is difficult to quantify. There can be big variations in the quality of the carcass, the way the carcass is butchered, the cuts, and the amount of bone and fat sold with the meat. In such circumstances, precise specifications are impossible and precise descriptions cannot be provided by the individual price collectors. It is then all the more important that meat prices are obtained regularly, on the same day of the week, for what appears to the collector and to the seller to be the same item.

In some countries, however, quality descriptions may be reasonably well standardised and the way meat is butchered may be uniform. In such cases, collectors can be issued with clear instructions, including pictures of the different cuts, so that there can be little ambiguity.

Services with goods

Prices for durable goods and sometimes for clothing may depend upon whether or not delivery, installation, fitting and similar services are provided without extra charge. Hence, the specifications or detailed descriptions of such goods must be very specific on these matters.

Clothing

Fashion and style can be important determinants of how much people are willing to pay for clothes. Unfortunately they are very difficult to describe objectively and create grave problems for quality comparisons. Since there is less standardisation than with many other kinds of good, tight centrally provided specifications are not feasible. Hence, this is perhaps the field where most training and instruction should be given to price collectors.

This is no excuse for ignoring the characteristics which can be objectively checked such as, whether or not garments are lined, what material they are made of, and so on. Furthermore, it should encourage the search to include representative goods which are not so subject to fashion, for example nightwear and underclothes. These can have specifications of the sort: "Child's T-shirt in pure cotton, short sleeves, lockstitched collar and sleeves, single colour, size 8 years." Note that a fairly large number of representative items will have to be distinguished with specifications of this type if the whole range of products is to be covered. Thus, a particular type of underclothing cannot be represented only by an item made of cotton, since price movements may be different for other textiles.

Items more subject to fashion can only have looser specifications. An example might be: "Ladies' trousers in synthetic fibre (55-70 per cent) and wool (30-45 per cent), belt incorporated, currently fashionable shape and width." The price collectors will then have to find (and describe more precisely) a model which is currently selling well in each particular outlet. Incidentally, it is probably best to avoid terms such as "average quality" in specifications, since quality and price levels may differ considerably between outlets.

When a new fashion in clothes is introduced, garments often start off at high prices which are reduced throughout the remainder of the season; the final end-of-season sale being at a particularly low price.

It could be argued that this downward path of prices within each season reflects a deterioration in quality. Right at the beginning of the season, the purchaser obtains a garment which will be in fashion for six months, while at the end, the garment is out of fashion. But it would be a bold statistician who registered no price decrease.

A problem therefore arises in this connection. If there is an overlap, and prices are linked without quality adjustment, the price differences between last season's fashions and the new ones being implicitly regarded as reflecting quality differences, then the index will only register price decreases and be biased downwards. There will be a similar downward bias if, alternatively, fashion prices are omitted for one month (which implicitly assumes that their prices change in parallel with the prices of all other clothes, whose prices continue to be obtained regularly).

To avoid such bias, new-season fashion items must be selected which are directly comparable with corresponding previous-season fashion items and the whole of the price difference regarded as a price increase; unless there is some quality difference which has nothing to do with the change of fashion. Thus, the price collectors, for example, must, with the aid of the retailers, seek to select a new-season afternoon dress which is of the same quality as the one it replaces and which is as much in fashion now as the other one was when it was newly introduced.

Alternatively, artificial overlap prices may be introduced by imputing previous-fashion prices for the first month of the new fashion equal to the prices collected for the previous-fashion items before they went on sale and had their prices reduced.

The easiest way to surmount the fashion problem is, of course, to specify only representative clothes for which fashion changes are minimal, such as ordinary socks and shirts. But what is easiest is not always best.

Controlled and free market prices

When the prices of certain items are controlled or centrally determined by the government, it is clearly easier to obtain these prices centrally than to collect them from outlets. But this practice is acceptable only if the centrally determined prices are universally observed. Field inquiry is necessary to ascertain whether what is supposed to happen does in fact happen.

The problem is much more difficult when there are parallel markets, that is to say where limited quantities are available at the controlled price (which may be subsidised); but consumers can purchase as much as they can afford in a free market (which may be a black market). Here, it is desirable to record both sets of prices and to average them according to the relative quantities sold through the two channels.

Supplies passing through legal and controlled channels may well be known to the government, particularly if government shops or subsidies are involved. If the volume varies from what it was in the weight reference period, then the weights given to sales in the two channels can be adjusted. In the extreme case of controlled supplies drying up completely, then the free market price should be weighted by the whole of expenditure on the item in the weight reference period.

Statisticians may be reluctant to obtain black market prices. However, their job is to measure, not to appraise, and if black market sales are important enough to constitute a significant part of consumer expenditure, then the statisticians or their families will know how to ascertain black market prices, though information on quantities might be unobtainable. Conversely, if black market sales are restricted to small groups of the population, then there is no need to cover them.

Shortages

The problem of what to do when shortages develop, so that queues form or items become totally unavailable is the source of great difficulty. (There is, of course, a symmetrical problem when the opposite happens, and the availability of an item is so much increased that queues shorten or disappear.)

A theoretical answer is that the price used for calculating the index should be what the price would have to be to limit sales, without queues, to their newly reduced level. But this remains a theoretical answer, because of the impossibility of estimating this notional price, unless a black market develops, in which case this is the price that should be collected.

The easiest practical solution, in the absence of a black market price, is to use the prices actually charged for such limited supplies as are available and to carry forward the prices last observed in other outlets. This was done, for example, when large stocks of domestic apples caused a government to decide to ban the importation of the most important kind of foreign apple, a kind which had its own weight in the index. Domestic apple prices then rose, but the use of the "unchanged" price for the imported apples exerted some restraining influence on the apples component of the group index for fruit. Since different kinds of apple are clearly fairly close substitutes, an alternative would have been to impute a price rise to imported apples equal to the observed price increase for domestic apples.

In more extreme cases, where close substitutes are not available and where no significant black market develops, so that demand is restrained by queuing and informal rationing rather than by price, the easy solution seems to be the right one. Although consumer purchases are then limited by the shortages, prices can be obtained for the small quantities that are available, at least in some shops, and price collectors can ascertain the (centrally fixed) prices that were charged before supplies ran out, or that would be charged were supplies available. The situation then is not that the index is wrong. It is that the index by itself is totally *inadequate* to describe what is happening. Availability has fallen *instead* of prices rising; there are *two* phenomena to be measured, so *two* measures or descriptions are required. Instead of measuring changes in what reference period consumption would cost consumers, the consumer price index must now be described as measuring changes in what reference period consumption would cost consumers *if all items were still available*. When the new shortages appear to be fairly permanent, or when reference period shortages disappear, then reweighting is called for.

Price reductions and supplements

What should be measured is the actual regular transaction price paid by consumers, which may differ from the recommended or list price. If there is a generally available cash discount, the cash price is the one to record, not the price charged on credit sales. Where the unit price of an item differs according to the number in the pack or its weight or size, the price for either the minimum quantity or the most usual quantity should be reported and a note made of what that quantity is. Indeed, there may be a case for pricing separately more than one size or weight for important items.

Sale prices

These should be reported and noted as such so that the fall in price, and subsequent rise, is not regarded as an error. But when the low price is a clearance price for stale, shop-soiled or otherwise imperfect items, or it is for something which is limited in availability, it should be ruled out and a substitute found. As far as possible, this is something which should be foreseen in advance and avoided by making a substitution *before* the clearance sale starts. However, clearance prices should be included if they are a permanent and widespread feature of the market. In some European countries so-called "clearance sales" have been growing in importance and have gradually been held earlier in the year than previously. For example, "clearance" swim-suits, which once could be bought only after the summer holidays, can now be bought at their beginning.

Special care has to be taken with items which are sold in "Sales", but which are not regular stock, having been obtained by the retailer just for the sale. While such items may be sold at low prices, they may well be of lesser quality than the regular stock. An example is provided by the "Special offers" by department stores, twice a year of a whole range of towels, sheets and other domestic linen. These often represent good value for money, thus reducing effective prices, because the price reductions are larger than the values of the quality reductions. If consumer expenditure in such "Sales" is great, the price reductions should be reflected in the index, after adjustment for the quality difference.

Bonus offers

If the bonus consists of an extra amount of the item and the total quantity remains within the range of sizes in the specification, then it is possible to note both the new size and that it is a sale price. But if the bonus consists of providing some other item "free" along with the item bought, then the price must be adjusted downward by the estimated retail value of the "free" item.

Rebates and discounts

If a rebate or discount is given on purchase, then the net price should be reported. But, if purchases have to accumulate to a certain amount before any rebate is gained, it is probably best to ignore the rebate, as with annual dividends on co-op purchases. If discounts are confined to particular groups of customers, then price discrimination is involved.

Price discrimination

If different prices are charged to different customers as standard policy for the outlet, for example, when "trade" customers or employees are charged a low price, then the basis for the difference should be ascertained, the most appropriate price for most consumers chosen and a note made to explain the choice. But if, to take a different example, pensioners are accorded a low price, then (assuming that they form part of the reference population) this price should be recorded separately and explained.

Stamps

Sometimes purchasers are given special stamps which can be accumulated and subsequently exchanged for goods and services. If a discount is available as an alternative to such stamps, then the discounted price should be recorded. Otherwise the stamps should be disregarded.

Trade-ins

In general, the price reduction (below the nominal price which is generally obtainable) by trading in an old item is very difficult to evaluate, since the trade-in value may be negotiable in each case. It is therefore best to report the cash price which the seller will accept. Even in the case of cars, where trading in is common, dealers will often be ready to quote a cash price.

Sales taxes

When an indirect tax is not included in the price of individual items in a shop, but is instead added on when the customer pays for the item, great care must be taken to record the price including tax. To make sure of this, with items whose price is normally quoted pre-tax and in areas where a general sales tax is added to the bill, the price collection forms should require the collector to indicate whether or not the price recorded does include the tax.

Tips for services

Where tipping is customary, or a compulsory "service charge" is included, for example on a restaurant bill, the conventional or compulsory amount should be included in the price. This applies not only to such services as taxis, restaurants and hairdressers, but may also apply even for services which in principle are free, but which, in practice, can rarely be obtained without what amounts to a tip.

Problems of timing

Periodic payments

Problems arise with items which consumers pay for only quarterly or annually, such as annual subscriptions and fees.

If a price, paid annually, alters for all renewals made after a certain date, it will roughly be the case that one-twelfth of consumers pay the new price in each month. Hence, the price change could be split into 12 successive price changes of one-twelfth of the actual amount. Alternatively, and more simply, taking an acquisitions approach, the new price can be fully taken into account as soon as it is introduced. The index then measures current prices paid by buyers, rather than including some historic prices.

In other cases the timing is synchronised, so that all consumers have to pay in the same month and no payment is made in other months. School fees due three times a year or a licence fee payable every January constitute examples. The simplest way of dealing with this is to treat these payments as if they were made in equal instalments over the period covered. It may be sensible, when inflation is rapid, to raise them proportionately to some relevant indicator such as teachers' salaries so as to avoid a large jump next time the fees are recorded.

Fixed timing within each period

The interval between price observations should be uniform for each outlet. Since the length of the month varies, this uniformity has to be defined carefully. Price collection days (and sometimes times) need to be set in advance, preferably days of the week when purchases are concentrated, unless retailers are less prepared to co-operate when they are busy, and avoiding holidays except for items with large sales during holidays, such as petrol and restaurant meals. A fixed interval is impossible because of the varying length of a month and the timing of holidays. One solution is to take sequences of four, four and five weeks, so maintaining a quarterly period; another is to follow a rule such as collecting on the regular market day or on Wednesday through to Friday of the first full week in the month. Regular timing is particularly important when inflation is rapid.

In the case of foodstuffs sold in market-places, the time of day as well as the day of the week is important. In Africa at least, these prices are usually high in the mornings and low in the evenings.

When the collection is spread out over a large part of the month (this has a practical advantage when full-time price collectors are employed) different neighbourhoods can be scheduled for price collection at different times of the month. This not only makes the use of the collector's time more efficient, but also has the advantage of providing a spread of collection dates for many representative items.

Rapid inflation

If the aim is to compute a point-of-time index, price collection has to be spread over a very small number of days each month. The more rapid the inflation, the smaller that number of days should be. But if the aim is to compute an index relating to the average over the month, then the fact that prices are changing rapidly increases the number of observations that should be collected.

In either case, the interval between successive price observations at each outlet must be held constant. For example, prices might be obtained from one particular outlet on the 6th and 18th working days of each month, and on the 2nd and 14th from another outlet.

Practical collection procedures

Field collection

When price collection first starts at a particular outlet, a personal visit is necessary. It may be useful to precede this by sending a letter to explain the nature and purpose of price collection. In any case, the collector must make the acquaintance of someone in the outlet, find the varieties to be priced, record their prices and descriptions and agree arrangements for subsequent price collection.

The steps to be followed for subsequent price collection are set out in figure 6. This flow chart shows the sequence of steps and some of the contingencies which have to be covered in the instructions to price collectors. (It is not intended as a model for conveying those instructions.)

In some cases, this subsequent collection may be done by telephone or by mail, where the postal service is reliable and prompt and where the collector is sure of the collaboration of the outlet and can be certain that the respondent knows the exact identity of the items whose prices are sought. Clearly this will reduce costs, a fact which is liable to tempt statisticians into adopting this method without adequate checking. Care should be taken that it does not provide an excuse for limiting price collection to outlets with telephones or to areas with a good postal service. In any case, it limits collection to outlets willing to collaborate, i.e. willing to bear some of the costs saved by the

Figure 6. Price collection procedure

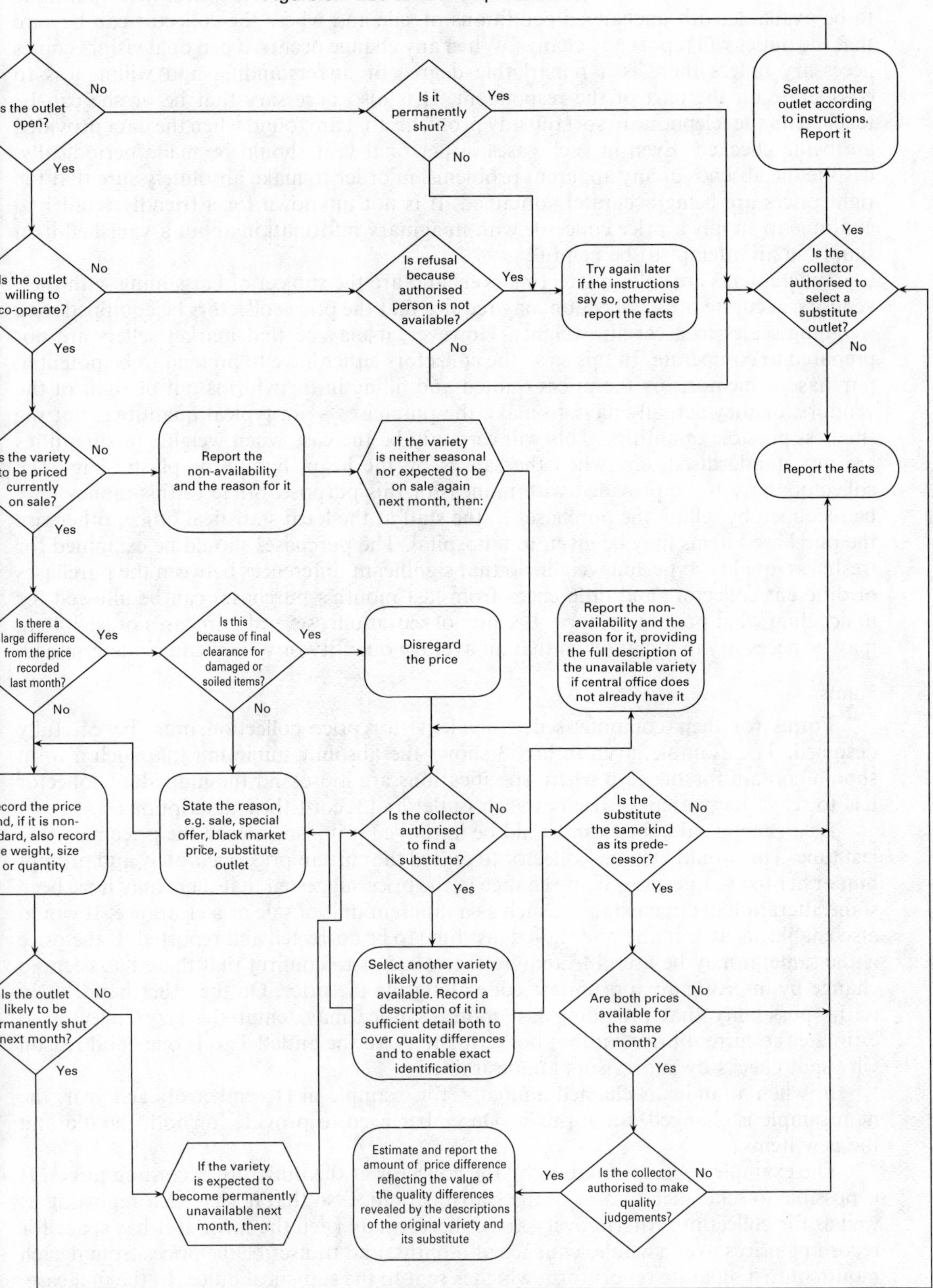

statistical office! Furthermore, it will only work well when the identical items continue to be available with unchanged conditions of sale and where the collector can be sure that the outlet will report any change. When any change occurs, a personal visit becomes necessary unless there is a remarkable degree of understanding and willingness to co-operate on the part of the respondent. It is also necessary that he or she can be reached on the telephone to sort out any problems that are found when the data provided are being checked. Even in such cases, a personal visit should be made periodically, despite the absence of any apparent problems, in order to make absolutely sure that the right prices are being accurately obtained. It is not unknown for a friendly retailer to continue to supply a price collector with imaginary information about a vanished item simply in an attempt to be helpful!

Where items are sold in street markets and are the subject of bargaining with their vendors, accurate price collection may require that the price collectors be equipped with weighing scales to ascertain weights. However, it may be that market sellers are not prepared to co-operate. In this case, the collectors either have to pretend to be potential purchasers, memorising the prices quoted and filling in their forms out of sight of the vendors, or they actually have to make the purchases – in typical quantities, not the smallest possible quantities. This will certainly be the case when weights or quantities are not standardised, e.g. when the sale is by the heap, bundle or plastic bag. The collectors have to be provided with money for this purpose. Some of this money may be recouped by selling the purchases to the staff at the local statistical office; otherwise the purchased items may be given to a hospital. The purchases should be examined for freshness, quality, type and weight, so that significant differences between the purchases of different collectors and differences from last month's purchases can be allowed for in deciding what prices to record. Because of variations, several purchases of each item may be necessary in a market so that an average quantity or weight can be determined.

Forms

Forms (or their computerised equivalent) for price collection must be carefully designed. The example given in box 3 shows the absolute minimum that such a form should contain for the case where specifications are loose and the individual collector has to select the varieties priced at each outlet and record their descriptions.

As a general rule, the form would be improved if it also showed the price recorded last time. This would help the collector to record the current price accurately and prompt him or her to ask questions if any change in the price suggested that there may have been some alteration in circumstances, such as a different unit of sale or a clearance. It would also enable an error in the price noted last time to be corrected and reported. If the price is the same, it may be useful to require the collector to confirm that there has been no change by inserting an appropriate code alongside the price. On the other hand, there is the possibility that providing last month's price may tempt the lazy collector to estimate the current price without bothering to go to the outlet! This is one good reason why spot checks by supervisors are desirable.

If, when an index is chained annually, for example in December of each year, the item sample is changed, the forms in December need to provide for both the old and the new items.

The example is of a form used by the collector at the outlet for recording prices. It is possible to send such a form to the statistical office, so that it serves for reporting as well as for collecting. Alternatively, the collector may keep the form, if it has space for recording prices over a whole sequence of months, and transcribe the prices from it each month onto a separate report form which is sent to the statistical office. In the first case, where the form used for collection is also used for reporting, there are two main possibilities: *(a)* a form with space for recording prices over a whole sequence of months

Box 3. Extract from a simple price collection form

(N.B. The collector fills in the last four columns, leaving "Brand or make" blank when inapplicable. Usually there will be a separate questionnaire for each type of item or for each outlet.)

Month: Date: Collector's name: Outlet name:

#	ITEM	DESCRIPTION	BRAND or MAKE	UNIT	PRICE
12	1 kg potatoes				
23	1 kg fresh beef. State the cut				
49	Fresh milk. State cow's or goat's				
84	Men's shirt, collar attached, medium size. State make, size and material				
91	Women's fashion shoes, 1 pair				
105	2- or 3-course restaurant meal				
108	TV repair. State type				

which is shuttled backwards and forwards monthly between the collector and the office; and *(b)* that new collection and report forms are printed out by the computer each month – they can contain the prices recorded in the previous month alongside the spaces for recording the current month's prices.

Whichever of these possibilities is chosen, it is necessary also to make provision for each of the various possible complications in price reporting. The price report form as described above is therefore not sufficient. It should be extended (or supplemented by a further form) with the aid of a check list or a set of codes to allow reporting of any of the following when relevant:

- outlet unwilling to co-operate;
- outlet shut;
- outlet likely to be permanently shut next month;
- outlet has changed its line of trade;
- item seasonally unavailable;
- item not currently available and unlikely to be in stock again;
- item not currently available but likely to be in stock again;
- item unlikely to remain available next month;
- price includes/excludes tax;
- sale price;
- normal price, following sale price
- change in the unit of quantity;

– the item is a substitute for that priced last month;
– other reason for significant difference in price;
– price reported last month was incorrect.

Knowledge of these facts is important. For example, if an item is unlikely to remain available next month, a substitute can be selected now, so that overlapping prices are obtained. Noting that a price is a sale price enables subsequent price changes to be understood, and prevents a sale price being related to a regular price if any quality comparison becomes necessary. The form must require the collector to report or to request any necessary follow-up action. Thus, if, for example, it is necessary to find a substitute and if the collector is to do this and either propose a quality adjustment or explain that quality is the same, so that the adjustment is zero, part of the form (or a special form) must provide the necessary space. (An example of a separate quality-adjustment report form is provided in box 5; see page 78.) Another space, or a separate form, must also be provided for collectors or their supervisors to report on outlet substitution, so that they can provide, as a minimum, the name, address and type of the new outlet.

All these facts should be recorded on forms, not in a non-standardised way in individual notebooks belonging to each collector; this is because some of the information will be needed at headquarters and some may be useful to those taking over price collection from another person.

Centrally collectable prices

The economy and speed of collecting prices centrally where they are definitely known to be uniform are evident. Although the possibilities vary from country to country, the tariff structures for public utilities, including the post office, are usually readily ascertainable. Newspaper and periodical prices are often set nationally; so are insurance premiums, though care must be taken to avoid central collection when, in fact, agents have discretion to offer rebates or discounts. Even when set centrally, premiums vary according to age, health, crime rate, make of car, etc., so that formulating precise specifications demands care.

However, though controlled prices can be ascertained from the price control authorities equally easily, there is room for very grave error in simply assuming that these prices are uniformly implemented. On the one hand, the controls may be widely evaded; on the other hand, the fact that a controlled price has been fixed does not guarantee that the item is actually available in the shops.

Mail order sales

It is relatively simple to obtain prices from mail order catalogues, though it should be checked whether the items selected are still available, since some items, particularly clothes, may sell out. It cannot be assumed that mail order prices all move in the same way as other prices; the weight given to mail order prices, therefore, should be be limited to the estimated share of mail order sales in the total consumer expenditure to be covered by the index. When the mail order catalogue selection changes, quality judgements will often require more information than can be obtained from the catalogue, necessitating recourse to discussion with the mail order business.

The effective price of mail order goods to consumers depends partly upon freight or postage charges which in turn depend upon the total size or weight of an order. Hence, it is best to use catalogue prices only, setting the index weight for postal prices to include the postal charges paid to the mail order firm by its customers as well as postal charges paid directly by consumers.

Distribution chains

In some countries a large share of retail sales of standardised convenience items such as groceries and various household articles is either in the hands of a few sizeable retail chains or in the hands of retailers who are supplied by a few large wholesalers. In the first case, prices may be fixed at headquarters; in the second case, lists of recommended prices may be provided to the retailers by their wholesalers. The system may cover not only the regular prices but also special offers, since these are frequently centrally planned in connection with press and television or radio publicity. Such arrangements obviously provide the possibility of collecting the price data centrally from the head offices of a few large businesses. This is much cheaper than collecting the same number of prices from separate outlets scattered over the country. Furthermore, the detailed sales data available in the head offices may be used as a sampling frame for probability proportional to size selection of the varieties whose prices are obtained.

Though the advantages are obvious, it will rarely be certain that the prices fixed centrally are always the prices charged, and it will be even less certain, in the case of wholesaler recommended prices, that retailers always follow the recommendations. The reasons common to both cases are: *(a)* that a price change may not come into effect in a shop until stocks labelled with the old prices have been sold out. The time this takes will vary from case to case; *(b)* the managers of shops in a chain may have discretion to meet local price competition, so both they and independent retailers may, from time to time, follow their competitors and depart from the centrally fixed or recommended prices; *(c)* they may also do this in special local or regional promotions and sales campaigns; and *(d)* some of the independent retailers may systematically cut their prices on one or many items.

It follows from this that price lists should not be used until and unless there has been a systematic comparison between the movement of these prices and the movement of those actually charged in a large sample of shops. The sample can be drawn using the detailed sales data available in the head offices as a sampling frame for probability proportional to size selection of the shops. This comparison should not be limited to a two-month period, since it can easily happen that there are some fairly widespread seasonal patterns of divergence. The comparison will show which subset of the varieties sampled from the price lists indicate only small and occasional divergences between centrally fixed and actual price movements.

Once the choice is made to use price lists, it should be regularly reviewed. This means that, every few months, the prices of the selected varieties should be collected from the sample of outlets for comparison with the list prices. Given that they are thus collected, they should be used in the computation of the index. Thus, at the level of prices of individual varieties, the calculations will in effect be rebased on actual observed prices every few months. However, any discovery of a large divergence should immediately trigger off the abandonment of central collection of the list prices and reversion to the regular monthly collection of actual prices at the outlets. The need to organise price collection so as to make this possible, and the need in any case to carry out price collection once every few months for the purpose of checking, mean that the savings from central price collection are limited.

One example of the need for care in the central collection of prices is that of retail petrol (gasoline), where the prices charged by filling stations used to be obtained from the oil companies. When price competition started, it became necessary to organise price collection all over the country from a sample of filling stations. It was found that price wars sometimes led to rapid price fluctuations in particular areas, raising the question of whether prices should not be collected more than once a month.

Problems specific to particular items

Tariff structures for electricity, gas, etc.

Although it is relatively easy to obtain data about tariff structures, there are some problems. When the structure of bus fares or train fares changes, it is necessary to compare the averages of the new and the old ticket prices for a representative set of journeys. In the case of electricity and other public utilities there is the complication that multi-part tariffs may create a difference between the average of consumer bills and the bill of a consumer with average consumption. Consider, for example, a two-part electricity tariff with a fixed charge and a kilowatt-hour charge. If these may change in different proportions, then either they should be treated as two prices, each with its own weight, or the total bill per kilowatt-hour for a consumer with some specified level of consumption will have to be calculated.

Alternatively, as a second example, there may be one kilowatt-hour charge for the first X kilowatt-hours per month, and another, lower, charge for usage in excess of X kilowatt-hours. If the tariff is changed, so that X falls, while neither charge alters, there has in effect been a price reduction and the index should reflect this.

Another problem with respect to utility services arises where consumption is metered and paid for in arrears, so that payment follows use and acquisition, which in this case coincide. If there is a tariff change, it will not be implemented for a customer until after his or her next meter reading.

Under some billing systems, the old and the new tariff rates are averaged, each weighted by the proportion of the interval covered by the bill for which they were in effect. Thus, effective rates due in respect of consumption will rise gradually during a transition period in a way which can be estimated and incorporated in the index. Alternatively, a payment approach can be adopted – all consumption after the date of the rate change being treated as taking place at the new rate.

Under other billing systems, the new tariff rates are charged on the whole of all consumption metered and billed after the date of the tariff change. If this has been announced well in advance, it can be taken to apply to all consumption which will be billed at the new rates. The old and the new tariff rates can then be averaged during the transition period, each weighted by the proportion of consumers who will be billed before and after the date of the tariff change; this means that the index will start to rise before that date. This consumption approach obviously cannot be applied when the length of advance notice of the tariff change is less than the billing interval. Otherwise, a payment approach will simply include the new rates all at once, from the date of the tariff change or, if meters are read, on average, every n months, $n/2$ months afterwards, which is when consumers will on average start to pay more.

Books

Books constitute a particular example of the problem of quality change. The movement through time in the prices of a selection of books published in the price reference period, even if they remain in print, can differ from the movement in the prices of new books. Hence, one possibility would be to obtain the average price per page of, for example, the ten currently best-selling novels, all hardback or all paperback. Alternatively, the publishers' decisions on the print run could be used to select books of expected equal popularity.

Dwelling prices

Some of the ways of dealing with owner-occupied housing require an index of dwelling prices, i.e. of the prices of houses and apartments. This section examines the construction of such an index, either for new dwellings alone or for both new and existing dwellings.

There are four possible sources of data, though not all of them will be available in all countries. When more than one source exists, the choice between them must depend upon such factors as their accessibility, quality, coverage and so on. They are listed as follows:

(1) Data from mortgage lenders relating to the dwelling prices paid by their borrowers (or by a sample of them). The data may come from a statistical sample of such lenders or from a group of them which belong to an organisation or which are subject to some particular governmental regulation. In the latter case, the mortgages provided by members of the group may differ systematically from a random sample, for example by being limited to certain types of borrower or to certain types of dwelling or by being limited within a certain maximum amount. It will then be necessary to consider whether this introduces any bias. Similarly, the exclusion of purchases not financed by mortgages may or may not be a serious defect. Note too that the data may relate to mortgages which are approved or to mortgage completions, between which there may be a considerable difference in timing.

(2) If there is a tax on sales of dwellings or some form of official registration of transfers, the government administrative apparatus may furnish data.

(3) Professional valuers can provide market value estimates for a sample of dwellings.

(4) A sample of builders can be asked to provide for a specified town or region, either *(a)* data about their sales or their concluded contracts, or *(b)* estimates of the prices they would charge for (or the costs of) building dwellings of a type specified in some detail by the constructors of the index.

Method (3) can provide prices for a collection of existing dwellings, while method (4) can only provide prices for new dwellings. If any of the first three methods is used and if existing dwellings are included, it will generally be necessary to rule out the prices or values both of dwellings which are occupied by a tenant and of dwellings which are sold to the existing tenant, since such transactions often take place at special prices.

Methods (1), (2), and, in some cases, (4) *(a)* will provide data about a different collection of dwellings in each successive period, so that calculation of a single mean price in each period would be wrong. There are two possible procedures. The first is to establish a number of categories of dwellings, to calculate a mean price for each category and to combine them using constant weights. (For example, if apartments, terraced houses, semi-detached houses and detached houses were distinguished, together with five regions and three sizes, there would be 60 categories.) The second procedure is to use hedonic regression to estimate the effect of each of a number of such characteristics upon price in each period, so that the price of a dwelling with a standard or average set of characteristics could be computed in each period. This procedure is, in effect, a systematic version of method (3). It is discussed further in a later section of this chapter.

With either procedure, the choice of characteristics must be limited to facts that are available and yet comprise those which contribute most to the variance in prices. Hence, no general recommendation about them can be proposed.

Method (4) *(b)* provides prices in successive periods for dwellings with constant specifications, so these prices can be used in the same way as the prices of most items entering into the calculation of a consumer price index.

The same will be true, in some cases, for method (4) *(a)*, when builders have standard models (usually of houses rather than apartments) which they construct over a period of years. However, the problem of quality change has an extra dimension in the case of dwellings because differences of location between physically similar houses may be responsible for quite large price variations. Correction has to be made for these, as well as for other quality differences. Since such locational differences are reflected in site values, one possibility is to ascertain the value that the site would have without the house upon it, as estimated by the builder, to subtract this from the price of the house and to use the residual "house value" for calculating the house price relatives. While this would circumvent the locational difference problem, it would exclude general changes in site values from the index, which may or may not accord with the purposes to be served by it.

The form used for collecting prices under method (4) *(a)* must identify the builder, the location and the exact model name or number of the dwelling being priced. At its first pricing, each dwelling's features must be carefully described, a representative choice being made where there are optional features. The form should list those features which are generally relevant to price. What these are will, of course, depend upon circumstances; they may include – number of rooms; type of construction and of structure; exterior finish and style; presence or absence of garage, swimming pool and other facilities; type of heating, plus a list of internal facilities which may be included in the price, such as cooking equipment, cupboards, etc. In a country where dwellings are simple, the list will be much shorter.

At each successive pricing, the builder must be asked whether there are any changes in any of these features. If so, a quality adjustment will have to be estimated and justified on the report form by describing and costing the changes. If there is a model change, because a particular model has been discontinued, radically changed, or because it has been superseded by another as more representative, then there will have to be a substitution. It will be an advantage if overlapping prices can be obtained for the old model and its new substitute. It also facilitates checking by the central office if the price collector has to indicate on the form the reasons for any reported price change. Thus, the form might list the following alternative reasons: costs of materials, labour costs, market conditions, physical characteristics and terms of sale.

The terms of sale deserve particular attention. The price should relate to a specified day in the month, not necessarily the day on which the collector interrogates the builder. Legal costs incurred by the buyer should be excluded. If the price is payable to an agent, then it is that price and not the amount received by the builder which is relevant. Cash discounts or additional "free" features granted in order to stimulate sales should be carefully noted; they may not last long.

Rents and imputed rents

Rent surveys

Rents may be obtained from landlords (or their agents) or from tenants. Where there is a large amount of public housing, it will probably be best to collect rent data for this housing from the responsible public authorities, provided that they have good records. The sample of rented dwellings for which rents are obtained from the occupiers should be limited to those with private landlords.

The sample should, of course, be one of dwellings, not of households. In the case where the rents are obtained from tenants, it has happened that a tenant whose report forms showed a change in rent had moved to another dwelling!

A simple rent collection form for use when the data are obtained from tenants is shown in box 4. In almost all cases, the form actually used will have to be longer, but this minimal example can serve as a point of departure for the following discussion.

The first section of the form serves to identify the dwelling and to report whether and why no rent can be obtained. It should list all the possible causes of non-response, and the collector should be instructed how to proceed in each of these cases.

Box 4. Example of a simple rent collection form

Month: Date: Collector's name:

Address:

Month and date of last rent observation:

If the dwelling has become owner-occupied or is empty, or the occupier is absent or refuses to respond, explain the circumstances and leave the rest of the form blank:

Occupier's name:

RENT

Week/month/quarter to which the last rent due relates:

Rent . . . . .

Charge for heating . . . . . .

Extra for garage . . . . . .

If neither of the extra items is charged separately:

(1) Is heating included in the rent?
(2) Is garage included in the rent?

CHANGES IN STRUCTURE OR FACILITIES

Since the last rent observation, has there been any alteration or extension of the dwelling or have any facilities provided by the landlord been added or removed? If so:

(1) Describe the changes:

(2) Was the rent raised or lowered because of these changes?
If so, record the amount. Record only any extra periodic rent or rent reduction allowed because of the change; do not include any lump sum paid by the occupier.

Collector's signature:

The second section seeks to elicit the amount of rent and to clarify what is included. The collector may be required to calculate what the rent would be if certain standard services were included and if other services were excluded. In any case, it is important to ascertain whether there has been any change in what is included and what is not since the last rent observation. Heating charges and a possible garage or parking charge are only two examples of items that may or may not be included, but a complete list should be provided on the form. What it will contain will obviously vary according to national circumstances. Other possibilities include the use of gardens, air conditioning, the services of a concierge and water and sewerage charges.

The question about rent may be extended to include the rent due in the previous week, month or quarter if the rent data for each dwelling in the sample are collected only infrequently, as happens, for example, when the sample is divided into six sub-samples, each of which is interviewed only twice a year. Such a retrospective question may elicit a reasonably reliable response when respondents have a rent receipt book or other written evidence about their rent. The computation of the rent index can then use both these within-round rent comparisons and between-round comparisons. Information about the future dates at which the landlord has an option to introduce rent changes can also be useful.

Questions may also be needed to ascertain and eliminate irrelevant kinds of rent change, such as a rent reduction granted because the owner is a relative of the tenant, because the tenant agrees to perform services for the landlord, or because of the introduction of a rent subsidy.

The third section of the form aims to check for changes in the quality of the residential service provided to the tenant, which are not reflected in explicit charges. The example provided merely poses a general question, but a check list of possible items may be preferred. In at least one country, seasonal changes in car parking arrangements are common. It is probably sensible to neglect minor changes in quality such as periodic redecoration which can be regarded more as quality maintainance than as improvement.

Estimating imputed rents

There are several possible procedures for including imputed rents of owner-occupied dwellings in the index. All of them naturally require a weight reference period estimate of imputed rents for the owner-occupiers in the target population. This estimate may be constructed in at least three ways –

(1) Ask a sample of owner-occupiers to estimate rental values for their dwellings. This might be done as part of the expenditure survey used for estimating weights. It must be made clear that they are being asked to estimate the rents that could be obtained, not the rents that they would find acceptable.

(2) Use rental value estimates made by real-estate professionals.

(3) Impute rents statistically, using data on the rental sample and on its characteristics and on those of an owner-occupied sample. (The main difficulty with this is the importance of non-quantifiable "neighbourhood characteristics" on the desirability of dwellings.)

There are then the following possibilities of constructing an imputed rent sub-index (or maybe a separate sub-index for each of a number of regions):

(a) assume it to move identically with the sub-index for rented dwellings. This, of course, simply amounts to increasing the weight of rents by the amount of the weight for imputed rents;

(b) use a rent index calculated for a sub-sample of rented dwellings which resemble the owner-occupied dwellings more closely than does the full sample of rented dwellings (such dwellings may be deliberately over-represented in that sample);

(c) use periodic rental value estimates for a sample of dwellings made by real-estate professionals;

(d) ask a panel of owner-occupiers to estimate rental values periodically for their dwellings;

(e) impute rents statistically, possibly employing hedonic regression, using data on the current rental sample and on its characteristics and on those of an owner-occupied sample.

With some of these methods, the rent survey will have to provide more data than are required just for the rented dwellings part of the index. Sufficient descriptive data must be obtained in order to establish comparability or the differences in characteristics between rented and owner-occupied dwellings. The relevant facts are many, though some of them need to be obtained only once, when a dwelling first enters the sample. To give an example from one developing country, the rent-determining factors include:

— *Location:* Is the area well drained? Are there any bad smells due to drainage or nearby trade activities? What is the distance to the nearest public transport? What is the distance to the nearest market for fresh food?

— *Construction:* How many floors in the building? How many dwellings in the building? How old is it? On what floor is the dwelling? What are the walls made of? What is the type of roof? Are there windows? Are there any shutters?

— *Facilities:* Is there running water (inside or outside)? Is electricity available? Is there a bathroom (shared or separate)? What are the sanitary facilities?

— *Size:* What is the number of rooms or surface area? Are there any balconies?

— *Rental arrangement:* Is the rent shared between two or more families? Are the premises used for business as well as for residence? Is the rent subsidised or arranged between relatives or linked to the employment of the tenant?

If the rents paid for rented dwellings normally include an amount for such appliances as cookers or washing machines provided by the landlord, then care must be taken to avoid double counting when these rents are used to impute rents for owner-occupied dwellings. Either the rents must be adjusted downward to exclude their appliance component, or the weight given to appliance purchases in the index must be adjusted downward to exclude owner-occupiers' purchases.

A factor that may make the rental equivalence method inappropriate is the existence of widespread rent control. Even when the rental equivalence method is preferred in principle, it may, nevertheless, be ruled out for the practical reason that most owner-occupied dwellings are very different from most rented dwellings. For example, most owner-occupied dwellings may be detached houses while most rented dwellings may be flats or terraced houses.

Consumer credit

The acquisitions basis

The acquisitions approach can be applied in the following way, best explained by an arithmetical example. Let it be assumed that the facts are as follows:

	Reference period	Current period
Cash price	5 000	6 000
Credit price	1 000 cash + 36 monthly payments of 140	1 500 cash + 24 monthly payments of 230

The cash price relative is clearly 6,000/5,000 = 1.20, but what is the credit price relative? For the reference period, it is possible to calculate an "internal rate of return", i.e. the (monthly) discount rate which equates the present value of 1,000 plus 36 monthly payments of 140 with 5,000; it is 1.31 per cent. The corresponding figure for the current period is 1.70 per cent, so that in this example the credit price can be said to have risen both because the price of the object has risen and because the price of the credit has risen. The problem is how to combine these two increases into one credit price relative which can be used in calculating the index. A possible answer is to use the reference period discount rate of 1.31 per cent to compare the two credit prices. At this discount rate, the present worth of 1,500 plus 24 monthly payments of 230 is 6,210. This gives a credit price relative of 6,210/5,000 = 1.24.

A simpler approach could also be adopted, one which is particularly appropriate in the case of credit cards where the amount of credit or interest cannot be broken down according to the type of items paid for. Under this approach, all acquisitions would be treated as if cash had been paid and interest would be treated as a separate elementary aggregate with a separate weight reflecting the share of interest in reference period expenditure. This would be regarded as being paid for the service of allowing the consumer to be in debt. The debt would be regarded in terms of its current purchasing power rather than in terms of the acquisitions it had helped to finance. Thus, the elementary aggregate index for debt interest would be the product of a group index of the prices of items bought on credit and the ratio of the relevant current interest rate to the rate in the price reference period; repayment would not enter the picture at all.

The payment basis

The payment approach relates to reference period initial cash payments on reference period credit acquisitions plus reference period expenditure on interest and repayment of outstanding credit obtained previously in respect of objects owned and used by households.

Reference period expenditure, in this approach, relates to all payments made with reference to the collection of consumer-durable goods owned by households. Thus, it includes payments on durables obtained wholly or partly on credit in the reference period, plus payments on the durables acquired during the preceding period for which some credit is still outstanding, plus payments on the durables acquired in the period before that for which credit is still outstanding . . . and so on, back for the number of years comprising the normal span of credit purchases of the durables. The problem lies in how to compare current period payments relating to such a set of durables with reference period payments relating to it. It is immediately apparent that constancy of the base cannot be interpreted as physical identity, since, as time passes, some of the credit outstanding will be paid off. Thus, if the base included a one-year old car "F.1200", what has to be calculated for the current month is not the current-month payment in respect of that car (which will now be more than one year old) but the current-month payment in respect of a more recent car "F.1200" (which is one year old in the current month).

What is necessary, therefore, is

(a) to ascertain, estimate (or guess!) the whole collection of goods corresponding to reference period payments;

(b) to "transform" it into a comparable collection of goods which would have existed in the current month, if the time schedule of goods acquisitions involving credit in the n months ending in the current month had been the same as that during the n months ending in the reference period;

(c) to calculate the current month payments on down payments, interest and repayments that would have resulted. This requires knowledge not only of credit prices (in the sense of the simple table given earlier) over the past *n* months, but also, in the case of credit with variable interest rates, of interest rate changes.

More crudely, total reference period payment of interest and repayments might be separated from reference period cash purchases and down payments. An ordinary price sub-index would be calculated for the latter. The index for the interest and repayments component would simplify by assuming the average outstanding credit contract to relate to a purchase *x* months ago, thus comparing prices and interest rates *x* months before the current period, *t*, with prices and interest rates *x* months before the price reference period, 0. The sub-index would thus be a lagged version of the ordinary price sub-index, $I_{t-x/0-x}$, multiplied by $(1 + sr_{t-x/0-x})$, where *s* is the estimated share of interest in weight reference period interest plus repayments, and *r* is the prevailing rate of interest on credit purchases.

As already suggested, consistency of treatment between durable goods and dwellings may be abandoned for the purely practical reason that data may be more easily available for the one than for the other. The payment method, in other words, may be feasible for dwellings but not for consumer durables. If this is the case but consistency is regarded as an overwhelming virtue, then the acquisitions basis will have to be used for both. However, consistency is not the only *desideratum*, particularly when consumer credit payments are very small compared with dwelling mortgage payments.

A fuller examination of this subject is made in the article "The treatment of finance-related commodities in a consumers' price index", by T. J. Woodhouse and K. M. Hanson, reprinted in Appendix 5.

Cars: Secondhand prices

If the index requires data on secondhand car prices, a simple way of collecting them may be to use newspaper advertisements, provided that these are sufficiently numerous for a number of popular models and that the advertisements state the year as well as the model and the price. Care must be taken to avoid duplication when several newspapers are used.

If the number of advertised prices is small but car prices are known to change relatively slowly, a certain smoothing of the data by averaging the current month's prices with those recorded in the preceding one or two months may be advisable. Even so, three problems may afflict the use of advertised prices –

(a) dealers may mainly advertise "specials" which are not representative of the majority of the cars they have in stock;

(b) the advertised asking prices may not be the same as the prices actually paid;

(c) the details furnished in the advertisements may not suffice to ensure precise identification of each car's characteristics.

The collection of prices by interviewing dealers would seem to overcome these problems, but experience with such direct inquiry is not always satisfactory. In one country, for example, an experimental collection produced results that could not be used, for the following reasons:

— even in large cities it proved difficult to obtain sufficient usable price quotations to establish reliable price series;
— there were wide variations between dealers in prices charged for the same model in the same pricing period;
— there was even a lack of consistency between dealers in the direction of price movements for particular models of car.

Another possible problem is that cars sold by dealers may be more expensive than those sold privately because of value added: repairs, guarantees, etc.

Then there is the general problem of quality change due to ageing. In 1991, a 1988 model is three years old, so its price can be compared with that of a three-year-old car of the same make and model in the price reference period. It will jump to a four-year-old car after 12 months, but there seems no practical way of avoiding this discontinuity. While rough weights may be available for combining price relatives for different makes of car, they will not usually be available for the preliminary step of combining price relatives for the different years of age of each model. Hence, the number of quotations for each year of age should be considered for use as weights.

If the difficulties of obtaining reliable data on secondhand car prices are too great, there are two ways out. One is to omit secondhand car prices from the index. The other is to use new car prices, i.e. to give these a weight representing both purchases of new cars and the net purchases of secondhand cars.

Both for new and secondhand cars there is the problem of dealing with model changes or the replacement of an old model by a new one, where substitutions and perhaps quality evaluations are necessary. This problem, which is by no means confined to cars, now requires examination at much greater length.

Quality and outlet changes: A major problem

A problem arises with the disappearance of a particular variety from a selected outlet or the closure of an outlet, since this prevents the desired matching of the current and previous prices. If the disappearance is expected to be short lived, for example because the item is temporarily out of stock or the outlet is temporarily shut for repairs, the item can be temporarily omitted. But if this is not the case, the question is whether or not to replace it with a substitute and, if so, how to deal with any difference in value for money between them. In many countries this issue arises particularly acutely every spring and autumn when the selection of clothes in the shops is largely changed.

A decline in the relative importance of an item or outlet also raises the question of replacement, though not with the same urgency. Indeed, it is far too easy for the statistical office to wait until the collector reports that the variety is no longer available or that an outlet has permanently closed. An important part of the work of the supervisors and of the central office should be to select substitutes or to ensure that the collectors select them in good time. This means that the office must accept that part of its task is to follow what is going on in retail outlets, to be aware of new shopping trends and the availability of new products. Within each elementary aggregate, the selected varieties and outlets should be updated whenever necessary to reflect changes in consumption patterns. Hence, the statisticians need to read trade journals, talk to retailers or wholesalers and know about the appearance of new shops or the decline of old shops or markets.

Substitution may be necessitated by the supersession of one variety for another at a particular outlet, by a change of outlets, or by a centrally decided change in the specification of the representative item for which the individual collectors have to select a variety at each outlet. When a substitution is made, the necessary quality judgements may have to be decentralised and entrusted to the price collectors in the field, or they may be made centrally when specifications are tight. For example, the clothing and furniture in the shops may be different in different parts of the country, while electronic goods, photographic equipment, domestic appliances and cars are best dealt with centrally, both because national brands are more common and because more specialist knowledge is required for making the quality judgements. More generally, suppose that a representative item X supersedes Y with the same functions but that X has better specifications or more features. These specifications may well not be precise enough for a quality ratio between X and Y to be assessed centrally. In such cases a separate quality comparison at each outlet is required between the variety chosen there to represent the new representative specification and the variety hitherto used to represent the superseded representative specification.

This discussion all relates to quality or outlet changes *within* elementary aggregates. There are, however, some more important changes which cannot be dealt with within an index but which require a new set of weights, with the revised index chained onto the old one. Thus, the introduction of self-service outlets and of colour television presumably provided new combinations of prices and qualities which, in general, meant that consumers were better off. It might be wished that such improvements in the (vaguely defined) standard of living could be reflected in the (precisely defined) consumer price index as a fall, relative to consumers' disposable incomes. However, the necessary quality judgements lie far outside the statistician's competence; even the less demanding quality judgements which he or she cannot avoid making, and which are now discussed, are difficult.

Quality judgements

Quality judgements take two forms. On the one hand, there is the search for a variety which is of the same quality as the one to be replaced, so that its price can be used instead of the old one. On the other hand, there is the evaluation of any difference in quality between the new and the old variety. In both cases, differences which are relevant to quality as seen by consumers have to be distinguished from irrelevant differences. In the first case, a variety has to be sought for which the relevant differences are minimal. In the second case, the new variety is chosen on other grounds and the problem is to put a monetary value on any differences which are not minimal.

Quality judgements can be avoided when there is an overlap in the availability of the old and new varieties so that prices for both can be obtained at the same time. Then it will be possible, in the first case, to pick a new variety selling at the same price as the old variety and, in the second case, to take the price difference as a measure of quality difference. The extent to which this is appropriate is discussed below in the section on "Linking" in the next chapter. The following discussion concentrates on cases where it is not appropriate or where, because there is no overlap, it is not possible.

When price collectors are obliged to make quality judgements it is, as already stated, a good idea for them to be provided with a check list of the characteristics of the representative items which are relevant for judging the similarities or differences in quality between varieties. Such a list may usefully form part of the specification. This will both help them to perform the task and enable them to report (in the first case) why they regard two varieties as being of comparable quality or (in the second case) what differences exist and justify their evaluation of the quality difference.

An example of a possible simple form for reporting the evaluation of a quality difference is provided in box 5. It does not include a check list because such a form will have to be used for many very different items, but check lists should be made available either as parts of the specifications on the price report forms or as part of the manual provided to price collectors.

The danger of delegating quality judgements to collectors is that their judgements may reflect their personal tastes and preferences, being in consequence highly subjective, so possibly causing cumulative errors. An extreme case would arise if each of a sequence of quality changes ultimately led back to the original quality, yet the sequence of quality judgements as a whole judged the end result to be an improvement. This could happen with clothing, where the distinction between fashion change and quality change is difficult to determine and the fashions of yesteryear tend to reappear after a time. On

Box 5. A quality adjustment report

Date:	Collector's name:	Outlet:

Former variety	**New variety**
Manufacturer or make	Manufacturer or make
Brand and/or style	Brand and/or style
Size, weight or unit	Size, weight or unit
Last price recorded	Current price
Date of last price	
Was this a sale price?	Is this a sale price?
If so, give sale rebate	If so, give sale rebate

Calculation of quality adjustment

Difference in regular prices ________

Less quality increase (plus decrease) ________

Equals pure price change ________

Less increase in sale rebate ________

Equals current price change ________

Describe the new variety:

Describe the quality difference, justifying your evaluation of the quality change:

Collector's signature: Reviewer's initials:

the other hand, it can be argued that subjective judgements by the index compilers are the only possible way in which account can be taken of the subjective judgements of consumers.

Statisticians quite rightly wish to avoid making subjective judgements, the users of the index demanding that it be objective. So the compilers of consumer price indices seek to minimise the degree of subjectivity by the use of various devices: estimating quality differences as proportional to differences in production costs, using tests and relying upon the judgement of "commodity specialists". Hedonic regression has also been proposed. These devices are now each discussed in turn so that it can be seen when each of them might be useful.

What follows relates much more to goods than to services. It has to be admitted that quality changes in services are difficult to identify, let alone to evaluate. Thus, the quality of such (medical care) representative items as a visit to the doctor or a day in the surgical ward of a hospital has perforce to be assumed not to change.

Objective measures

Differences in production costs

Where a quality change reflects an increased use of resources to improve a product, the producers can be asked how much the extra features cost. If this extra cost is grossed up to allow for producer and retail markups (and any indirect tax), to obtain its retail equivalent, the resulting amount can be deducted from the price to obtain a price which is quality-adjusted to be comparable with the price of the previous version of the product. This procedure may be unnecessary if the extra features were previously available as options, since then it may be reasonable to deduct the price hitherto charged for those options instead. Furthermore, it can be applied only with this particular type of quality change. It cannot be applied in the case of quality changes that require no additional inputs but which reflect technological improvement and it is inadequate when a product is improved both because more inputs are used and also because of some design improvement.

Where the extra cost is identifiable, it could be applied to quality changes of durable goods which affect their durability or running costs. However, the justification for the approach is less obvious in such cases than when the extra cost relates to a specific extra feature such as remote control for a television set or larger bumpers on a car.

Quantifiable item characteristics

Examples of quantifiable characteristics are the weight of the contents of a package; the alcohol content of alcoholic drinks; the fat content of butter; the percentage of rayon in a fabric; and the tested fuel consumption of cars. If such quality characteristics can not only be objectively ascertained but can also be valued, then the tests go part of the way towards reducing the need for subjective judgement. Thus, economy in fuel consumption can be estimated in money terms over the average lifetime of a car and discounted to obtain a present value which is treated as the value of the improvement. The reduction in quality from lowering the alcohol content of whisky from 42 per cent to 40 per cent can be valued by examining the relationship between alcoholic strength and price for other drinks. In one country, the value of a rise in the fat content of milk was judged to be zero because in the case of other milk products, the non-fat varieties, once they had been introduced, rapidly took 80 per cent of sales.

Specialist judgements

Specialist judgements of appropriate quality adjustments are objective only in the sense that they are delegated by the statistician to someone else and may deserve more respect than any judgements the statistician might make! But the specialists to whom they are delegated may be very expert indeed in the properties of different materials, the merits of different methods of manufacture, the costs and advantages of different features, and so on and so forth. They may, in short, know what consumers ought to know but rarely do know.

Price ratios elsewhere

In small economies and in economies with quantitative import restrictions there may be changes, from time to time, in the varieties of imported goods which are available in the shops, necessitating a substitution. In this limited set of cases, price ratios between the new and old varieties in neighbouring and similar countries may be used, provided that both varieties are freely available there at the same time.

Another possible case where other price ratios may be used occurs with some kinds of regular seasonal changes. For example, if new-season potatoes come onto the market when old-season potatoes are still available, the average ratio of their prices in the same month over the past few years may be used to make their prices comparable. Similarly with clothes; spring and autumn fashion clothes often differ not only in fashion but also in weight (clothes for the winter being heavier). For this reason, other factors apart, they are likely to cost more. Hence, the average price differential between them over recent years might be used as a quality correction factor.

Hedonic techniques

These are attractive in principle for dealing with quality change, but are rarely used in practice, with the possible exceptions of housing and (though not in consumer price indices) computers. They involve the use of multiple regression to relate the prices of an array of similar items, such as different models of cars, to a number of their characteristics, such as horsepower, provision or not of power steering and amount of passenger space. The estimated coefficients provide implicit prices for each of the bundle of characteristics which make up an item. These can then be used to calculate what would be the price of an item with a standard set of characteristics, reflecting the average characteristics of the reference period consumption of the item, and this imputed price used in the index computation. Alternatively, the coefficients can be used for making explicit quality adjustments, for imputing a current period price to a variety which has ceased to be available, or for imputing a previous period price for a new variety. In the first case, where a quality adjustment is made, the new variety can be substituted for the old one. In the other two cases, an overlap is created so that linking is feasible.

A hedonic regression usually takes the form:

$$P = a + b_1 X_1 + b_2 X_2 + b_3 X_3 + \ldots + u$$

where P is the price (or its natural logarithm), a is a constant term, the X are the various characteristics and u is the error term. The X may either be continuously variable, for example the number of rooms in a house or the size of a television screen, or they may be dummy variables which are zero or one. For example, a dummy variable for a video camera may take the value of one if there is an electronic rangefinder and zero if there is not, and similarly for the presence or absence of a garage with a house.

A necessary, though far from sufficient, condition for a good estimate is that the characteristics entering into the regression are not only quantifiable but are also both meaningful to consumers and directly relevant to the cost of production. A difficulty obviously arises because it is rarely possible to include all the relevant characteristics in the regression, either because they are not all available (for instance, with regard to the state of repair and the quality of the neighbourhood of houses) or because inclusion of them all would leave no degrees of freedom. When a new variety incorporates an important new characteristic so that a new formulation with an additional X is necessary, there is no way at all of imputing a previous period price to the new variety.

As with much econometric work, different data and different estimation methods or functional forms yield varying results to an extent which fascinates the researcher but alarms the official statistician. Collinearity is a problem which affects many hedonic regressions. For example, personal computers with faster CPUs may have larger hard disks. In such cases, the coefficients for the correlated characteristics may not be reliable and one of them may have to be omitted from the regression, the remaining one partly proxying the omitted one. Experimentation with functional forms frequently shows a semi-logarithmic or double logarithmic form to provide a better fit than a purely linear one. A semi-logarithmic form has been chosen for housing and for some consumer durables in a number of cases.

In the field of consumer price indices, the most promising use of the technique relates to the prices of existing dwellings. On the one hand, it is necessary because the dwellings sold in any period will hardly ever be the same dwellings sold in the preceding or reference period, so the need for it is particularly great. On the other hand, a reassuringly large number of price observations may be obtainable with descriptions and measurements of the relevant characteristics. For example, a British study uses about 12,000 house price observations per month, with the following variables:

— House type: detached, semi-detached, terraced, bungalow, flat.
— Number of: habitable rooms, bathrooms, separate toilets, garages, garage spaces.
— Presence of a garden, of a plot of 1 acre or more.
— Central heating: full, partial, none.
— Freehold.
— Location (12 regions).
— Age of property in years.

A practical example of adjusting quality change for vehicles is given in the article "Pricing of new vehicles in the Australian consumer price index", by L. C. Clements et al., reprinted in Appendix 6.

Imposed quality changes

The main example of this particularly difficult problem arises when government imposes technical requirements for new cars for environmental reasons and car prices are increased to meet the extra costs, for example, as in the case of catalysers for cars. Is this a price rise or a quality improvement? We can assume that it reflects a political judgement that the benefits outweigh the costs. Yet individual consumers might prefer cheaper cars without catalysers. It is far from obvious what should be done in such circumstances, and different countries have, in fact, come to different conclusions.

The argument that it is a price rise is simply that it has been forced upon consumers; that even if the new devices had previously been available as options, consumers have now lost the option of not buying them. In other words, it is just like any other tax except that the revenue obtained is spent on producing the cars that bear the tax rather than on something else.

The counter argument is that consumers are now getting more car for more money, rather than the same car for more money (which *would* constitute a price increase). They now buy a catalyser with each car. It might further be argued that, as a result of suffering less pollution, they are getting a better product; they each benefit from the improvement to all the other new cars rather than from the improvement to their own new car alone. In some countries it might be added that the regulations, having been decided democratically, do reflect a belief on the part of the majority of consumers that the change is an improvement.

Once again, the problem can be clarified, if not solved, by looking at it in terms of the uses of the index. Is it for measuring inflation? If so, is a rise in car prices because they now have catalytic convertors inflationary? Is the index designed for wage indexation? If so, should wages rise when cars become more expensive in order to reduce pollution? Is the index to be used for deflating the value of car sales? If so, are more complex cars equivalent to an increase in numbers? These questions should be posed by the statistician, but answering them is not just a statistical matter. This is a good reason for having an advisory committee on the consumer price index.

Outlet substitutions

The last few pages have related to substitutions between varieties. However, substitution may be between outlets, thereby raising a rather different problem of comparability. Thus, take the case where an old-fashioned shop closes down and the only replacement outlet that can be found in the area is a supermarket offering lower prices and a totally different kind of service.

It is difficult to see how the price collectors can be asked to put a value upon the difference. It is more practicable to leave out the price of the item for one month and introduce the supermarket price only when two successive prices have been obtained. But it would have been preferable if the substitution had been made earlier when the supermarket was beginning to acquire a substantial market share, rather than when the old shop had succumbed to the competition and finally closed down. If this had been done, overlapping price observations could have been obtained and the new price linked in, on the implicit assumption that the price difference then represented the service quality difference.

What has just been said relates to substitutions of individual outlets within an elementary aggregate. A general change in the distribution of consumer purchases between different types of outlet should be reflected in a change in the weights of elementary aggregates which are differentiated by type of outlet. If new types of outlet develop sufficiently to take an important fraction of consumer expenditure, then new elementary aggregates should be introduced at the next reweighting. Even if the distribution of purchases moves from a high- to a low-price type of outlet, so that the average price paid by consumers over all types of outlet is reduced, the index should not record a decrease. The consumer obtains different types of service from different types of outlet, even if the items bought are physically identical. The index measures changes in the cost of reference period consumption and this is defined in terms of type of outlet as well as type of expenditure and region. A major change in any of these dimensions justifies reweighting.

Training, employment and organisation of price collectors

Recruitment

There are two possibilities. One is to employ price collectors, many or all of them as part-time employees, to do the work. The other is to use central or local government officials for a few days each month, thus temporarily releasing them from whatever is their main task. The choice will depend upon national circumstances, but should be made so that the same reliable and conscientious people do the work every month, and so that a backup is available should any of the collectors be unavailable.

Training

At its simplest, training will include:

- obtaining a background understanding of the nature and uses of the index;
- accompanying an experienced interviewer; and
- attending a course or reading a manual.

It is a good idea for the statisticians from headquarters to be personally responsible for supervising price collection in the area where the headquarters are situated, so that they have first-hand experience of the problems involved. Equally, it is a good idea to arrange for regular visits to headquarters by groups of collectors and their supervisors; it is good for morale. If they are not able to feel that they belong to a team, that their work is appreciated, that their problems are understood and that the accuracy and conscientiousness of their contribution is crucial to the quality of the index, then they will not do a good job. In addition, the statisticians at headquarters need to keep in touch with conditions in the field and, maybe, can use the opportunity to provide more information about new representative goods or aspects of quality change than can be easily communicated through written office memoranda.

Documentation and manuals

A manual may serve for initial training. Even if it is not used for this purpose, it should enable the collectors to remind themselves of all the relevant rules and procedures. It should be well organised and well indexed so that answers to problems can quickly be found.

The author must know the work intimately, and the draft should be checked by all concerned. It must be updated regularly; the pile of pieces of paper containing amendments should never grow large, but should be replaced by a new consolidated version. One way of achieving this is to have a loose-leaf manual, so that individual pages can be replaced whenever necessary.

Data transmission

A tightly organised system is necessary to ensure that the collectors send in all the information they are supposed to provide. This system must be explained in the manual and in the training. It is useful to provide a check list which must be filled in by the collector or by the local office (if any) to which he or she is attached, and sent with the forms, enabling the central office to verify what has been received. Its nature will obviously depend upon the details of the way in which collection is organised, but, for example, it should tell the collector who to contact in case of difficulties and might ask for the following:

- the collector's name and the name or code of the local office, if there is one;
- the number of price collection forms enclosed;
- whether there is a quality adjustment report for each item substitution made by the collector;
- whether there is a change of outlet report for each outlet substitution made by the collector;

and, similarly, whether other specified requirements have been met.

The same form can also be used by the central office; to record the initial checking and editing of the forms received; whether any queries are sent back to the collector or the local office; and the entry of the data onto worksheets or into the computer.

Computation

6

The whole periodic routine of producing a consumer price index needs to be carefully planned. Circumstances vary to such an extent that this manual can offer no generally useful timetable or critical path analysis of all the steps involved. The diagram in box 6 is, therefore, included simply as a reminder of the kind of schedule of activities that should result from a detailed examination of the logistics of the whole periodic operation of computing the index.

Central checking and data entry

Four kinds of regular checking are necessary:

(1) To ensure that the price collectors' reports are sent in when they are due. If not, it is necessary to find out the reason and take appropriate action to obtain them.

(2) To confirm that the reports contain what they are supposed to contain, i.e. that fields which must be filled in have not been left blank, that numeric fields contain numbers and non-numeric fields do not.

(3) There is the more analytical task of reviewing and editing each return. Substitutions may have to be made centrally or those made by the collectors may have to be approved. Unusual (or simply large) price changes should be queried. Items priced in multiple units or varying weights may have to be converted to price per standard unit. Missing prices must be dealt with according to their cause.

(4) Errors in keying the numbers into the computer or transcribing them onto worksheets must be found and corrected, or avoided.

Note that the way the data are organised in worksheets or in the computer may differ from the way they are organised on reception, since they will arrive at the central office organised by collector, outlet and item. Their origin should, however, be recorded so that reference back can be made should processing disclose any problems with the data. Furthermore, even if codes provided to the collectors to list items and to describe or qualify the prices are used unchanged in the processing, other codes will have to be used for information which comes in from the collectors in non-coded form.

How all the checking is organised will vary from country to country. In some cases, local or regional supervisors will do some of it; in other cases, it will all be done centrally. Some of these tasks can be done by computer, others manually. Therefore, no general suggestion can be made about the sequence of the work or about its division into different parts. But note that since some of the checking may require reference back to the price collectors (or to their supervisors or to respondents when direct-mail

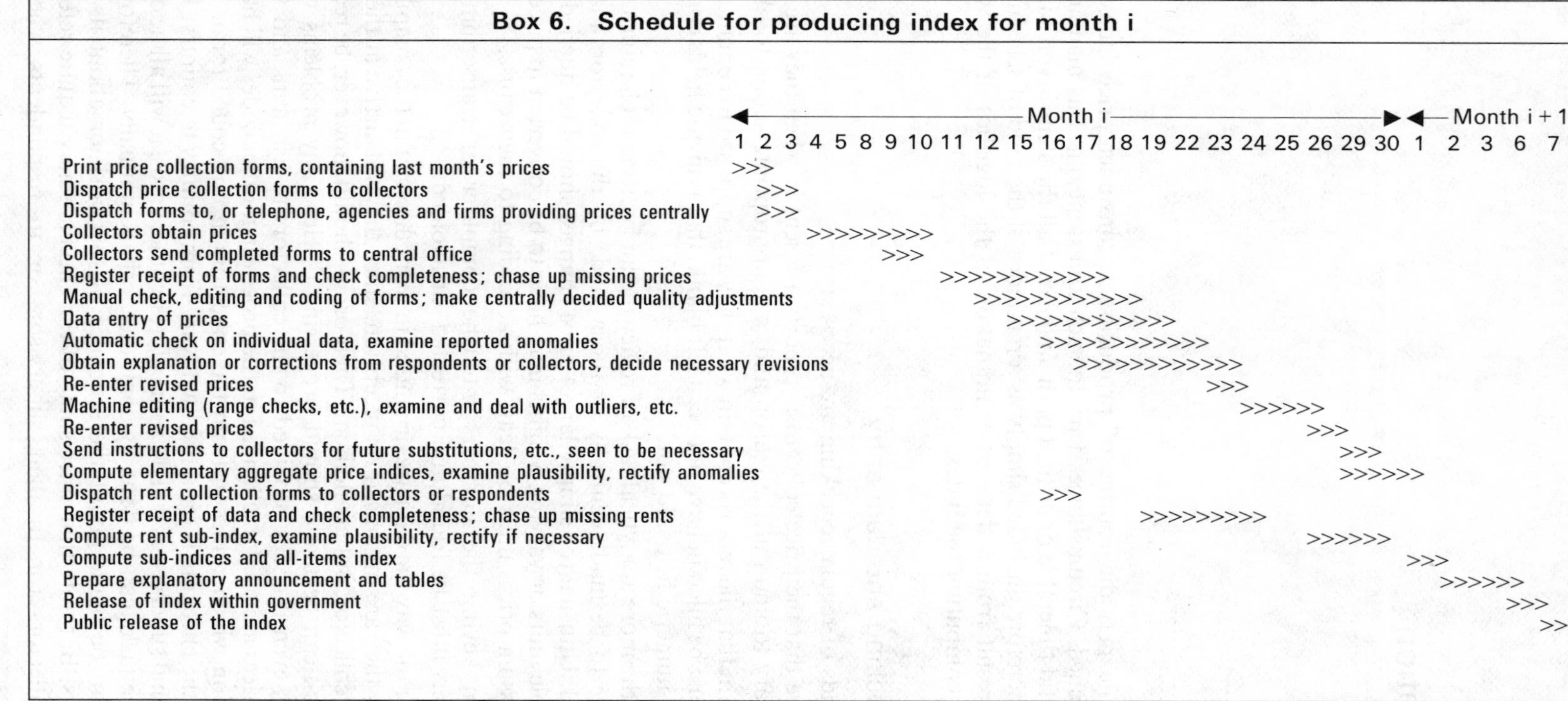
Box 6. Schedule for producing index for month i
Month i
Month i + 1
1 2 3 4 5 8 9 10 11 12 15 16 17 18 19 22 23 24 25 26 29 30 1 2 3 6 7
Print price collection forms, containing last month's prices
Dispatch price collection forms to collectors
Dispatch forms to, or telephone, agencies and firms providing prices centrally
Collectors obtain prices
Collectors send completed forms to central office
Register receipt of forms and check completeness; chase up missing prices
Manual check, editing and coding of forms; make centrally decided quality adjustments
Data entry of prices
Automatic check on individual data, examine reported anomalies
Obtain explanation or corrections from respondents or collectors, decide necessary revisions
Re-enter revised prices
Machine editing (range checks, etc.), examine and deal with outliers, etc.
Re-enter revised prices
Send instructions to collectors for future substitutions, etc., seen to be necessary
Compute elementary aggregate price indices, examine plausibility, rectify anomalies
Dispatch rent collection forms to collectors or respondents
Register receipt of data and check completeness; chase up missing rents
Compute rent sub-index, examine plausibility, rectify if necessary
Compute sub-indices and all-items index
Prepare explanatory announcement and tables
Release of index within government
Public release of the index

questionnaires are used), the timetable for producing the index must allow time for this communication to take place. Sometimes, indeed, it may be possible and desirable to get in touch with respondents at the outlets when there is a suspicion that the price collectors may have been tempted to make life easy for themselves. To save time, the doubtful data may, none the less, be transcribed or keyed in, but with a code which will enable them to be easily retrieved and corrected, if necessary.

In addition to the one-at-a-time checking of the price forms sent in by collectors, there is a further kind of checking for which a computer is more or less indispensable, which involves comparisons between outlets and comparisons over time.

Reports should routinely be generated for most representative items, to help the analyst pick out particular reported prices whose level or change stands out as different from that reported for similar varieties in other outlets or regions, or simply where the change lies outside certain specified limits. Thus, a computer printout can list all prices which either fall well outside the range of prices obtained last time for that representative item, or whose percentage change from last time for the same item in the same outlet fall outside a specified range. (The limits used will vary from item to item and can be amended in the light of experience.) The analyst can then work through the printout, first ascertaining whether there has been a keying-in error, and then examining whether any explanation furnished by the collector adequately explains the divergent price behaviour or whether a query should be sent back to the responsible supervisor or collector. The timetable should allow for this, and anomalous observations should be discarded only if an acceptable explanation or correction cannot be obtained in time.

Other reports should be regularly produced which would enable broader problems to be detected. For example:

— one collector's reports might show many more "outlet closed" remarks than those of other collectors, indicating either laziness on the part of that collector, or a change in retail trade patterns in a particular area;
— variety substitutions for a particular representative item might become more numerous than hitherto, suggesting a possible need for revision of the specification or the choice of another representative item;
— where tight specifications list a number of brands and models of which one is to be chosen, together with "Other; please specify", a large number of prices for this last category will suggest that the specified brands and models are no longer appropriate;
— the dispersion of price changes for a particular representative item might be much larger than it used to be, raising the question of whether it has been appropriately specified.

The routine computer-generated reports should enable those in charge of the index to detect the existence of all such problems.

Computing elementary aggregate indices

Weighting representative items

There is a wide range of possibilities, varying from case to case, as to whether it may be both possible and sensible in effect to divide the weight of an elementary aggregate between the groups of items composing it, each represented by one representative item. Similarly, the weight might be divided between the zones within each region for which prices are obtained. Hence this discussion cannot cover all cases.

Most often there will not be enough information for weights to be attached to the various individual representative items selected to represent a composite item, or to the zones, so they will have to be given equal weights. Occasionally, however, some approximate weighting may be possible using information about sales of sub-categories for each of which, one or more of these representative items has been selected. For example, if one cow's milk cheese and one goat's milk cheese have been specified as representative items within the one composite item of "Cheese", and if cow's milk cheese sales are known to be approximately twice those of goat's milk cheeses, the one representative item could be given a double weight in calculating elementary aggregate indices for cheese. Such weighting may use later information than for the weight reference period. Of course the weight used for the elementary aggregate which they jointly represent must always equal its estimated share in the weight reference period consumption of the reference population.

Any such approximate weighting of the representative items within an elementary aggregate might not be feasible and, furthermore, might create too much complexity if it were attempted separately for each zone. It is perhaps better to use regional or even national information about the market shares of different sub-categories to weight their representative items uniformly within all elementary aggregates where these centrally determined weights are not obviously inappropriate.

Relative of means versus mean of relatives

The discussion of the computation of elementary aggregate indices in this and the following sections simplifies by assuming that no weights are available within an elementary aggregate. The extensions to cover cases where they are used are obvious, but the arithmetic examples are easier to follow in the simple case of unweighted averages.

Box 7 shows, by means of a numerical example, four ways of computing an elementary aggregate index, each of which may be applied either using arithmetic means or using geometric means. It makes three points clear for the simple case where there are neither any missing observations nor any substitutions:

(1) Since the prices in month 5 are exactly the same as in month 0, the index for month 5 should be 100. But this does not happen in one of the eight calculations. The chained arithmetic mean of month-to-month price relatives, however, comes out at 106.15 in month 5. Indeed, this product of the sequence of month-to-month arithmetic means of price relatives starting in the price reference period and ending in the current month will necessarily exceed the directly calculated current to reference period index arithmetic mean if movements of relative prices within the sequence of months are wholly or partly reversed before the end of it. Hence, it is not to be recommended.

(2) The four methods using geometric means yield identical results.

(3) The cumulation of month-to-month relatives of mean price yields the same result as relating the current mean price to the reference period mean price. In other words, the relatives of both arithmetic and geometric mean prices are transitive: the index from month 1 to month 3 equals the product of the indices from 1 to 2 and from 2 to 3, provided that the identical set of items is priced on all three occasions.

The most common methods hitherto used in practice are:

A – the current to price reference period relative of arithmetic mean price.

R – the arithmetic mean of current to price reference period price relatives.

Let *0* be the price reference month and *t* be the current month. Let there be *n* prices. Then,

$$A = \frac{\frac{1}{n}\sum_n P_t}{\frac{1}{n}\sum_n P_o} \qquad R = \frac{1}{n}\sum_n \frac{P_t}{P_o}$$

Box 7. Different methods of calculating an elementary aggregate index in the absence of weights

Simple case with no missing observations or substitutions

Month	**0**	**1**	**2**	**3**	**4**	**5**
Prices						
Variety A	5.00	6.00	5.00	5.00	4.50	5.00
Variety B	4.00	5.00	6.00	7.00	7.00	4.00
Variety C	8.00	7.00	9.00	9.00	8.00	8.00
Variety D	6.00	6.50	7.00	7.50	8.00	6.00
Arithmetic mean	5.75	6.13	6.75	7.13	6.88	5.75
Geometric mean	5.57	6.08	6.59	6.97	6.70	5.57
Period-to-period relatives of mean prices						
Arithmetic mean	100.00	106.52	110.20	105.56	96.49	83.64
chained	100.00	106.52	117.39	123.91	119.57	100.00
Geometric mean	100.00	109.20	108.48	105.74	96.11	83.07
chained	100.00	109.20	118.45	125.25	120.38	100.00
Current to reference period relatives of mean prices						
Arithmetic mean (Method **A**)	100.00	106.52	117.39	123.91	119.57	100.00
Geometric mean	100.00	109.20	118.45	125.25	120.38	100.00
Period-to-period price relatives						
Variety A	100.00	120.00	83.33	100.00	90.00	111.11
Variety B	100.00	125.00	120.00	116.67	100.00	57.14
Variety C	100.00	87.50	128.57	100.00	88.89	100.00
Variety D	100.00	108.33	107.69	107.14	106.67	75.00
Arithmetic mean	100.00	110.21	109.90	105.95	96.39	85.81
chained	100.00	110.21	121.12	128.33	123.69	106.15
Geometric mean	100.00	109.20	108.48	105.74	96.11	83.07
chained	100.00	109.20	118.45	125.25	120.38	100.00
Current to reference period price relatives						
Variety A	100.00	120.00	100.00	100.00	90.00	100.00
Variety B	100.00	125.00	150.00	175.00	175.00	100.00
Variety C	100.00	87.50	112.50	112.50	100.00	100.00
Variety D	100.00	108.33	116.67	125.00	133.33	100.00
Arithmetic mean (Method **R**)	100.00	110.21	119.79	128.13	124.58	100.00
Geometric mean	100.00	109.20	118.45	125.25	120.38	100.00

Let r be an individual $t/0$ price relative so that $P_t = P_0 \times r$. This gives the alternative formulation:

$$A = \frac{\frac{1}{n}\sum_n P_o \cdot r}{\frac{1}{n}\sum_n P_o} \qquad R = \frac{\sum_n r}{n}$$

The difference between the two is, thus, that in *R* all the *r*s are equally weighted, whereas in *A* they are price-weighted; the costlier goods in period *0* have bigger weights. If all goods had identical prices in period *0*, then there would be no difference. If all the *r*s were the same the result would again be $A = R$. But *A* and *R* will be different when neither of these conditions is fulfilled, i.e. when period *0* prices are not all the same and when some prices change proportionately more than others from period *0* to period *t*.

In the light of this difference there is a choice to be made. There are advantages that arise from having average sample prices for elementary aggregates. In the case of reasonably homogeneous composite items, average prices provide price-level data which are useful for other purposes, including international price comparisons. Their publication also allows the public to appreciate the reliability of the index. They can often be compared with price data from other sources, thus facilitating a check. But even if average prices are used in these ways, it is nevertheless possible, with the use of a computer at negligible extra cost, to calculate means of price relatives as well for use in the actual index computation. Conversely, even if mean prices are used to calculate the index, price relatives can easily be computed in order to facilitate the picking out of possibly erroneous price observations. The following points are thus limited to index computation:

(1) *A* attaches equal probability to each physical unit, i.e. to each price, while *R* attaches equal probability to each monetary unit of expenditure. So if the structure of the sample precisely reflected the structure of the universe with respect to quantities, *A* would be appropriate, whereas if it reflected it with respect to expenditures, *R* would be appropriate. But in most cases, with purposive sampling, it will not be possible to say whether either of these conditions is even approximately fulfilled.

(2) The relationship between *A* and *R* and the unknown weighted index which could be calculated if the weights were known can be shown to depend, first, upon the correlations between the *r*s and the weights and between the *r*s and period *0* prices, and, second, upon the dispersions of weights and period *0* prices. The demonstration relates to the universe and some of the propositions about these correlations which may be suggested may be implausible in relation to the sample. But perhaps the following argument does apply to the sample.

(3) Where the sampled goods or services representing an elementary aggregate are fairly homogeneous, there is normally a tendency in the short term for high prices to come down (or rise less than other prices) and vice versa, i.e. a negative correlation between r and P_0. This is because prices which diverge a lot from the mean often move back towards it. Hence, there is a tendency for lower *r*s to have bigger weights, raising *R* relative to *A*.

(4) Matched samples have to be updated from time to time, as varieties or outlets disappear or change in importance. This entails linking the elementary aggregate index estimated from the new sample with that estimated from the old sample. The use of the non-transitive arithmetic mean of price relatives can then introduce an upward bias, a topic discussed in the article by Bohdan Szulc in Appendix 7.

(5) The use of arithmetic mean prices for calculating a price relative does not necessarily imply that all such mean prices are useful or interesting in themselves. Comparing averages of the prices of hairbrushes and combs at two points in time, for example, is one legitimate way of calculating an index even though each of the two averages by itself makes no sense.

Finally, there is the question whether geometric means rather than arithmetic means should be used. Box 8 provides a numerical example of their use. They have one great advantage:

The geometric mean of the price relatives = *The relative of the geometric mean prices*

In view of this superiority, it is not surprising that many statisticians regard the use of geometric means as the best solution.

Why, then, are they so seldom used? One reason is that they make the calculations difficult, but this argument loses its validity once computers are used for calculating the index. A second reason is that it may be feared that their use is too difficult to explain to users of the index. But most indices have features which are difficult to explain, and

Box 8. Sample worksheet for geometric mean calculation of an elementary aggregate index

Item code	Ref. price	Jan.	Price rel.	Jan.	Feb.	Price rel.	Feb.	Mar.	Price rel.	Mar.	Apr.	Price rel.	Apr.	May	Price rel.
H/214	2.89	2.89	1.000	2.89	2.98	1.031	2.98	2.98	1.000	2.98	2.98	1.000	—	—	0.965
H/321	2.89	2.89	1.000	2.89	2.89	1.000	2.89	2.89	1.000	2.89	—		3.00	2.89	1.000
H/304	3.00	3.10	1.033	3.10	3.10	1.000	3.10	3.15	1.016	—	—		—	—	1.000
H/293	3.20	3.20	1.000	3.20	3.15	0.984	3.15	3.20	1.016	3.20	3.30	1.031	3.30	3.30	
H/169	3.25	3.25	1.000	3.25	3.30	1.015	3.30	3.30	1.000	3.30	3.40	1.030	3.40	3.40	1.057
G/005					3.20		3.20	3.20	1.000	3.20	3.35	1.047	3.35	(4.80)	
H/229										3.25	3.50	1.077	3.50	3.70	
Product of relatives			1.033			1.031			1.032			1.198			1.020
N = no. of relatives			5			5			6			5			4
Geometric mean relative			1.007			1.006			1.005			1.037			1.005
Cumulated value×100			100.66%			101.27%			101.80%			105.55%			106.06%

G/005 first recorded in February.
H/321 temporarily unavailable in April; price imputed for May-April comparison as March price times April-March mean relative of 1.037.
H/214 outlet closed down after April.
H/229 substituted for H/304 in April; no overlap. Quality judged to be 0.10 superior so March price of 3.25 imputed for H/229.
G/005 price implausibly high in May, so omitted from calculation.

in any case, the degree of complexity that is acceptable is growing, through time, in most countries. Statisticians should have the courage of their convictions.

It should be noted that the issue of the use of geometric means is relevant only to the computation of elementary aggregate indices and not to their combination into group indices and the all-items index. The elementary aggregate indices are computed using only a sample of prices to provide an estimate of the price evolution for the whole of the expenditure included in that elementary aggregate. Once they have been computed, no more sampling is involved. Elementary aggregate expenditures are additive, so the weighted arithmetic mean of a number of elementary aggregate indices gives the evolution of the cost of the reference period basket defined as the sum of those elementary aggregates. A weighted geometric mean of the elementary aggregate indices would not have a similarly clear meaning.

The subject of this section is further examined in the article "Price indices below the basic aggregation level", by Bohdan Szulc, reprinted in Appendix 7, where the term "micro-index" corresponds to "elementary aggregate index" and "basic aggregate" to "elementary aggregate".

Missing observations

When an individual observation is unavoidably missing, the calculations should omit the corresponding price from the data set with which current prices are compared, so that like is compared with like. In other words, the two sets of prices must be "matched". However, matching can also be achieved by using an imputed price, calculated in one of the following three ways:

(a) by carrying forward the previous observation, thus assuming no price change, the simplest procedure, which is clearly acceptable only when there is not much inflation;

(b) by assuming that the price would have moved in the same proportion as those prices within the elementary aggregate which were recorded;

(c) a missing price may also be imputed by using an observation from another, similar outlet which is not included in the regular price collection.

The third method is illustrated in box 9.

The first method is clearly inappropriate when prices are rising fast. All three methods are likely to impart a downward bias to a rent index, since it is commonly the case that rents increase most upon a change of tenancy, and such a change may involve a temporary vacancy and, hence, a missing observation.

When a whole set of prices is missing because they are collected less frequently than the majority of prices, similar possibilities are open. Obviously, no sub-index for the subgroup including them should be published for these months.

Linking when quality or outlet has changed

When a variety disappears more than temporarily from an outlet, or when a changed specification of a representative item requires new varieties to be selected, a substitute variety has to be found, unless a continuing reduction in the number of price observations on which the index is based is accepted. Similarly, when an outlet closes down, a substitute for the variety which was priced in it has to be found in order to avoid a reduction in the number of price observations.

Box 9. Price imputation for temporarily missing observations

Month	0	1	2	3	4	5
Prices						
Variety A	5.00	6.00	5.00	5.50		5.00
Variety B	4.00	5.00	6.00	7.00	7.00	4.00
Variety C	8.00	7.00	9.00	9.00	8.00	8.00
Variety D	5.48	6.50		7.50	8.00	5.48
Price relatives						
Variety A	100.00	120.00	100.00	110.00		100.00
Variety B	100.00	125.00	150.00	175.00	175.00	100.00
Variety C	100.00	87.50	112.50	112.50	100.00	100.00
Variety D	100.00	118.61		136.86	145.99	100.00
Index of arithmetic mean prices						
A, B, C mean price		6.00	6.67			
B, C, D mean price				7.83	7.67	
Impute price of D in Month 2 as 6.67/6.00×6.50 = 7.23						
Impute price of A in Month 4 as 7.67/7.83×5.50 = 5.39						
A, B, C, D mean price	5.62	6.13	6.81	7.25	7.10	5.62
Index	100.00	108.99	121.11	129.00	126.28	100.00
Index of arithmetic mean of relatives						
A, B, C mean relative			120.83			
B, C, D mean relative					140.33	
Impute 120.83 to D in Month 2 and 140.33 to A in Month 4						
Index	100.00	112.78	120.83	133.59	140.33	100.00
Index of geometric mean prices = Geometric mean of relatives						
A, B, C mean price		5.94	6.46			
B, C, D mean price				7.79	7.65	
Impute price of D in Month 2 as 6.46/5.94×6.50 = 7.07						
Impute price of A in Month 4 as 7.65/7.79×5.50 = 5.40						
A, B, C, D mean price	5.44	6.08	6.61	7.14	7.01	5.44
Index	100.00	111.70	121.47	131.21	128.89	100.00

In the absence of inflation, the D price of 6.50 and the A price of 5.50 could, alternatively, be carried forward to Months 2 and 4.

The practical possibilities are set out in figure 7 and are illustrated by the numerical examples in boxes 10-12.

Case (1a) uses mean price relatives or the relative of means for all, or possibly only some, of the continuing goods or services to impute a price reference-period price for the new variety, so that the current and price reference-period samples remain matched. (The imputation calculation should apply the same method as used in the calculation of the elementary aggregate index.) In case (1b) the number of price observations used in computing the index is reduced for one month, so that chaining is necessary.

In Case (2), where overlapping price observations are available, it is possible to link the price of the substitute directly to the price of the old variety which it replaces. This avoids making an explicit quality judgement. In some cases, the average price ratio over a number of observations in recent years gives a better indication. One example might be the recurrent seasonal replacement of the previous year's potatoes by new potatoes.

But the fact that a price ratio can thus be used does not necessarily indicate that it should be. The proposition that the price relationship expresses the market's judgement of the quality relationship certainly holds if several units of both were bought during the overlap period by many consumers, since this means that, at the margin, many consumers were indifferent between them. But matters are different for indivisible items like cars and clothes. In such cases, some consumers buy one unit of variety X and others buy one unit of variety Y. So, provided that X and Y are competing goods and that they are in the same price bracket, we can infer that the first group of consumers consider that X's quality in relation to its price makes it a better buy than Y, whereas the second group makes the opposite judgement. We can claim that, on average, consumers judge the price ratio to reflect the quality ratio only if purchases of X and Y are of roughly similar total quantities. If, however, sales of X much outweigh those of Y, it must be the case that on average they judge X to have a higher quality in relation to price than Y. In particular, if X is newer than Y and its sales have grown at the expense of Y and if, in consequence, X is to be substituted for Y in the calculation of the elementary aggregate index, an upward quality adjustment will be required. The index compilers will have to judge its size; market behaviour does not judge it for them but merely demonstrates the necessity of a quality adjustment.

In certain cases, a particular kind of average price ratio may be used whether or not there is an overlap. These cases arise where there are clearly distinguished and widely recognised price bands for an item. An example is provided in some countries by shoes, where there are three or four clusters of prices for a given type of shoe and these are recognised by the great majority of shoe retailers. In this case, a substitute shoe chosen from the same price band as a discontinued model can be treated as being of the same quality, while if the substitute is selected from another price band, the average or typical price difference between the two bands can be taken as a measure of the value of the quality difference. The procedure is all the more acceptable when the substitute shoe comes from the same manufacturer as the variety it supersedes.

When a new variety gradually takes over a share of the market from another, it will be possible to obtain overlapping price observations for a series of months. There is then a choice to be made about when, if it is appropriate, any linking is done. The new variety may start off at a high price and then become cheaper as its market share rises. Thus, the price ratio of the new to the old may fall through time, so that the choice of month for linking will affect the index. With an annually chained index, if revised specifications accompany the new weights that are introduced annually, the problem can be escaped (though not solved!) by waiting until the beginning of the next reweighting and respecification to introduce the new item. Otherwise, the linking should take place for the month when, in the light of whatever information is available, it is estimated or guessed that the new variety and others like it have started to sell more than the old variety.

Figure 7. Substitution in CPI computation

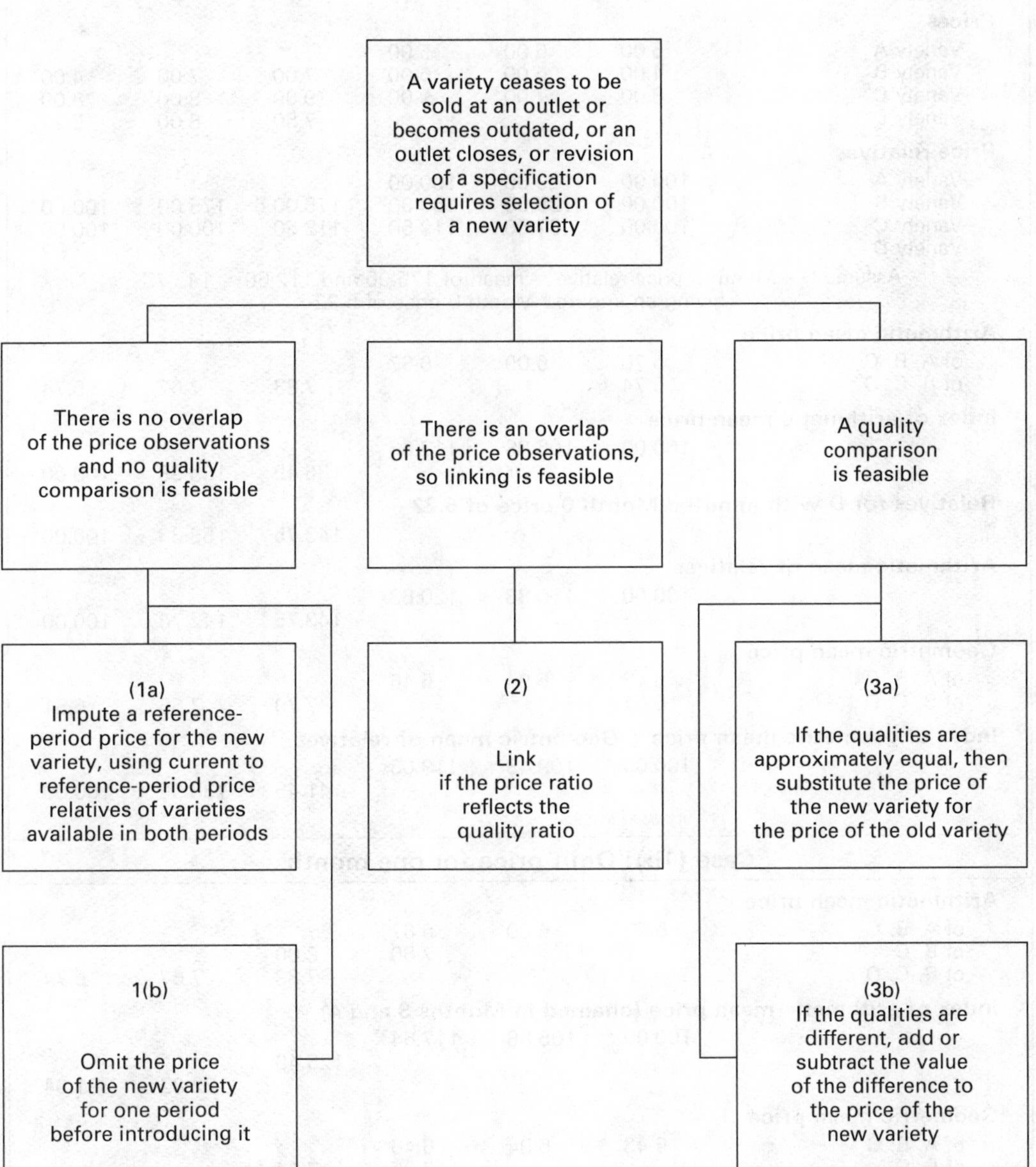

Box 10. Case (1a): Impute a reference-period price

Month	0	1	2	3	4	5
Prices						
Variety A	5.00	6.00	5.00			
Variety B	4.00	5.00	6.00	7.00	7.00	4.00
Variety C	8.00	7.00	9.00	9.00	8.00	8.00
Variety D				7.50	8.00	5.22
Price relatives						
Variety A	100.00	120.00	100.00			
Variety B	100.00	125.00	150.00	175.00	175.00	100.00
Variety C	100.00	87.50	112.50	112.50	100.00	100.00
Variety D				?	?	?

Assume D's Month 3 price relative = mean of 175.00 and 112.50 = 143.75, giving an imputed Month 0 price of 5.22

Month	0	1	2	3	4	5
Arithmetic mean price						
of A, B, C	5.70	6.00	6.67			
of B, C, D	5.74			7.83	7.67	5.74
Index of arithmetic mean price	100.00	105.88	117.65	136.49	133.58	100.00
Relatives for D with imputed Month 0 price of 5.22				143.75	153.33	100.00
Arithmetic mean of relatives	100.00	110.83	120.83	143.75	142.78	100.00
Geometric mean price						
of A, B, C	5.43	5.94	6.46			
of B, C, D	5.51			7.79	7.65	5.51
Index of geometric mean price = Geometric mean of relatives	100.00	109.48	119.06	141.45	138.96	100.00

Case (1b): Omit price for one month

Month	0	1	2	3	4	5
Arithmetic mean price						
of A, B, C	5.67	6.00	6.67			
of B, C			7.50	8.00		
of B, C, D				7.83	7.67	5.74
Index of arithmetic mean price (chained in Months 3 and 4)	100.00	105.88	117.64	125.49	122.82	91.94
Geometric mean price						
of A, B, C	5.43	5.94	6.46			
of B, C			7.35	7.94		
of B, C, D				7.79	7.65	5.51
Index of geometric mean price (chained in Months 3 and 4)	100.00	109.49	119.06	128.59	126.33	90.91

Box 11. Case (2): Link price of D to price of A

Month	0	1	2	3	4	5
Prices						
Variety A	5.00	6.00	5.00			
Variety B	4.00	5.00	6.00	7.00	7.00	4.00
Variety C	8.00	7.00	9.00	9.00	8.00	8.00
Variety D			5.48	7.50	8.00	5.48
Price relatives						
Variety A	100.00	120.00	100.00			
Variety B	100.00	125.00	150.00	175.00	175.00	100.00
Variety C	100.00	87.50	112.50	112.50	100.00	100.00
Variety D			?	?	?	?
In Month 2, D is worth 5.48 and A is worth 5.00, so a unit of A is equivalent to 0.91 of D						
Arithmetic mean price						
of A, B, C	5.67	6.00	6.67			
of B, C and 0.91 of D				7.62	7.43	5.67
Index of arithmetic mean price	100.00	105.88	117.65			
				134.40	131.20	100.00
Relatives for D: divide 0.91 into 5.00 to impute a Month 0 price of D of 5.48						
				136.86	145.99	100.00
Arithmetic mean of relatives	100.00	110.83	120.83			
				141.49	140.36	100.00
Geometric mean price						
of A, B, C	5.43	5.94	6.46			
of B, C and 0.91 of D			7.55	7.41	5.42	
Index of geometric mean price = Geometric mean of relatives	100.00	109.49	119.06			
				139.18	136.74	100.00

Box 12. Case (3a): Quality adjustment

Case (3a) is dealt with similarly to Case (2) except that, instead of correcting the prices of D by an observed price ratio between A and D when they overlap, the price of D from Month 3 onwards when it first appears is multiplied by the estimated ratio of the quality of A to its quality

Month	0	1	2	3	4	5
Prices						
Variety A	5.00	6.00	5.00			
Variety B	4.00	5.00	6.00	7.00	7.00	4.00
Variety C	8.00	7.00	9.00	9.00	8.00	8.00
Variety D				7.50	8.00	7.50
Price relatives						
Variety A	100.00	120.00	100.00			
Variety B	100.00	125.00	150.00	175.00	175.00	100.00
Variety C	100.00	87.50	112.50	112.50	100.00	100.00
Variety D				?	?	?
Arithmetic mean price, judging D 50 per cent better than A	5.67	6.00	6.67	7.00	6.78	5.67
Index of arithmetic mean price	100.00	105.88	117.65	123.53	119.61	100.00
Relatives for D, judging it 50 per cent better than A				100.00	106.67	100.00
Mean of relatives	100.00	110.83	120.83	129.17	127.22	100.00
Geometric mean price, judging D 50 per cent better than A	5.43	5.94	6.46	6.80	6.68	5.43
Index of geometric mean price	100.00	109.49	119.06	125.33	123.13	100.00

Case (3b): Quality adjustment – An alternative

Instead of adjusting the price of D every month, a reference price for period 0 is imputed

Month	0	1	2	3	4	5
Prices						
Variety A	5.00	6.00	5.00			
Variety B	4.00	5.00	6.00	7.00	7.00	4.00
Variety C	8.00	7.00	9.00	9.00	8.00	8.00
Variety D	7.50			7.50	8.00	7.50
The period 0 price for D is imputed when D is introduced, judging D to be 50 per cent better than A						
Price relatives						
Variety A	100.00	120.00	100.00			
Variety B	100.00	125.00	150.00	175.00	175.00	100.00
Variety C	100.00	87.50	112.50	112.50	100.00	100.00
Variety D				100.00	106.67	100.00
Arithmetic mean price						
A, B, C	5.67	6.00	6.67			
B, C, D	6.50			7.83	7.67	6.50
Index of arithmetic mean price	100.00	105.88	117.65	120.51	117.95	100.00
Mean of relatives	100.00	110.83	120.83	129.17	127.22	100.00
Geometric mean price						
A, B, C	5.43	5.94	6.46			
B, C, D	6.21			7.79	7.65	6.21
Index of geometric mean price	100.00	109.49	119.06	125.33	123.13	100.00

This argument concerning a rising market share of X at the expense of Y should not be applied when it is clear that Y is going out of fashion and X is currently fashionable. This often happens with clothes, and it may perhaps be said in this case that Y is losing quality, even though it is physically unchanged, and that X has the quality that Y formerly had, namely that of being in fashion. In the case of consumer durables, on the other hand, the supersession of one model by another one is often the occasion for combining price changes with minor quality changes which are more than purely cosmetic.

In cases (3a) and (3b), a quality adjustment is made. The method shown in the table for case (3a) has the disadvantage that the price of the new variety, D, has to be adjusted every month, which complicates computation. An alternative would be to impute a reference period price for D of 7.50 and use this in the computations for period 3 onward. This is illustrated in box 12. It can be seen that this changes the index of arithmetic mean price in months 3 and 4, but does not change the mean of relatives or the geometric index.

The existence of sufficient comparability to make a quality judgement feasible, as in these two cases, depends upon the new and the old varieties having similar functions. This will certainly be so when they are different varieties of the same representative item. But if, at the opposite extreme, X and Y are different types of representative item within an elementary aggregate (e.g. within electronic goods, where X is a tape-recorder and Y is a radio), there should be no question of quality comparison. Tape-recorders may indeed be substituted for radios as the representative item if their share of the electronic goods market rises, or for other reasons such as difficulty in obtaining suitable radio prices. But this cannot be said to indicate any change in the average quality of electronic goods, so linking is in order.

For cars and other durable goods where quality is nationally uniform and where quality judgement requires technical expertise, quality adjustments made at headquarters (for reasons given above) are preferred to linking, even though overlaps would make linking possible. Thus, new- and old-model cars may both be sold over a period of a couple of months. In such cases, the prices of both should perhaps be obtained for as long as possible, together with an estimate of their relative sales. Then (separately for each outlet) a weighted average of the price of the old model and the quality adjusted price of the new model can be calculated and used in the computation of the index.

A particular case of substitution arises when, for example, a price is usually collected for a 1 kilo packet of detergent but this is not available and the price for a 3 kilo drum is collected instead. In such a case, the latter price cannot be simply divided by three and used instead of the price of a 1 kilo packet. A correction should be made to allow for any difference between the price per kilo in the two packagings.

Newly priced items

When charges are introduced for an item which has hitherto been provided free, as, for example: if bank customers are required to pay for cheque-books which were previously free; if parents have to start paying for school textbooks or; if people have to pay for dental examinations which were previously available without charge; the effective price rises from zero to the amount of the charge. (If the charge is levied by the State and depends upon income, it should perhaps be regarded as a tax rather than as a price.) But even a uniform charge which constitutes a price obviously cannot be automatically included in the computation of the existing index, both because it is an infinitely large percentage price increase and because the item has had a zero weight. A new elementary aggregate or an increase in the scope of an existing elementary aggregate is therefore called for. There are then two possibilities for revising the elementary aggregates and introducing a new set of weights. One is to wait until the necessary information on new expenditure patterns can be obtained and used to revise the index, introducing a new weight reference period. The other, which might be adopted first, and only as a temporary measure pending such a revision, would be to estimate probable expenditure on the new expenditure component, X, and use it to calculate a new set of weights, so that a reweighted index could be spliced onto the old one, starting in $t + 1$, the month after the introduction of the new expenditure item in month t.

To simplify the following discussion, let it be assumed that the weight and price reference periods are the same. The new weights would be calculated by inflating reference period expenditure on each elementary aggregate by its respective elementary aggregate index for month t. Each such revalued elementary aggregate expenditure, together with X, would then be divided into their overall sum including X, to provide new weights for all of them, including the new expenditure item. The index for $t + 1$ . . . would then be calculated as the index for t (calculated with the old weights) multiplied by the index for $t + 1$ . . . (calculated with the new weights and with t as price reference period).

Neither of these procedures will cause the index to rise because of the introduction of the charge. Yet the cost to consumers of their reference period total consumption has risen. Whether, in principle, this ought to be reflected in a rise in the index depends upon the purposes it serves. For measuring inflation and macro-economic analysis, it can be argued that a change from tax finance towards user payment is an institutional change, not a rise in the price level. For indexation, it is a policy question, not a statistical question, whether indexed wages or other indexed payments should be increased because of such a change. Thus, the issue provides another good example of the desirability of some advisory mechanism whereby the statistician can find out what the users want.

If users do want the index to show an increase, and if probable consumer expenditure on the new charge can be estimated as X, then the following procedure could be adopted. (It amounts to comparing the current and reference period cost of a basket which includes the item that was initially free.)

(a) multiply the reference period value of each elementary aggregate by its elementary aggregate index for $t - 1$ and sum, obtaining the $t - 1$ value of the basket;

(b) multiply the reference period value of each elementary aggregate by its elementary aggregate index for t, and sum together with X, obtaining the t value of the basket;

(c) multiply the index for $t - 1$ by the ratio of *(b)* to *(a)* to obtain the index for t;

(d) thenceforth, use the amended index, as in the temporary method described above, where the new expenditure has a weight equal to the share of X in *(b)*.

When an existing charge included in the index is abolished, much of the argument applies in reverse, though the relevant weight is known and there is no choice but to omit the item after the change since there is no longer a price to be collected.

Infrequent observations

Rents, and sometimes certain prices, are collected with less than monthly frequency in a number of countries. This raises the problem of calculating elementary aggregate indices for the intervening months.

The simplest device is to carry forward the most recently calculated index until the next month when observations are obtained. This is most legitimate when the rents or prices in question are changed only at certain customary days of the year, provided that the observations are obtained shortly after these dates. Otherwise, the device may be acceptable, in practice, if the rent or price changes are small.

Alternatively, the most recently calculated index may be extrapolated forward by moving it proportionately to an index calculated for all items which are priced monthly, or an appropriate group index. This may be acceptable if analysis shows that their movements are, in fact, parallel. As with simply carrying forward the most recently calculated index, this device will not introduce any cumulative errors beyond the next month when observations are obtained and used in calculating the index.

Yet another device is to introduce rent changes with a time-lag, by spreading the quarterly change from $t - 3$ to t in equal proportions over the three intervals from $t - 1$ to $t + 2$.

When rents are collected only every n months, it is, however, common to divide the sample into n subsamples, obtaining rent observations from one subsample each month. In this case, each subsample can be given $1/n$ of the total weight for rents, and the rent index calculated using the latest available rents for each subsample.

If the quarterly observations include not only the current month's rents, but also the previous month's rents, the rent index for month t can be calculated both by applying the subsample movement for matched dwellings from $t - 1$ to t to the rent index for $t - 1$, and by applying the subsample movement for matched dwellings from $t - 3$ to the rent index for $t - 3$. A weighted average of the two can be taken.

Rent indices

Rent indices have some special features. An example of one way of dealing with them, that applied in France, will therefore be useful, even though it is not necessarily the best method in other circumstances. A hedonic index, for example, might be worth considering.

The elementary aggregates (as they are here called) of rented dwellings are defined in terms of region, number of rooms and sanitary facilities. For each elementary aggregate, an index compares the current weighted mean rent per square metre, for the dwellings in the sample, with that for the previous quarter. (Conversions are made to allow for the fact that some rents are quarterly, others monthly or weekly, etc.) These indices are then combined, using the previous quarter's total rent for each elementary aggregate as weights.

Data for the previous quarter are adjusted for non-response by multiplying the weight for each dwelling for which a rent was obtained (the reciprocal of the sampling fraction for that type of dwelling), by the reciprocal of the response rate for that type, defined in terms of region, number of rooms, whether or not a certain type of rent control applies and, where it does not, distinguishing pre-1949 and post-1948 dwellings.

This adjustment does not adequately correct for the particularly high non-response rate for dwellings with new tenants who have moved in since the previous quarter. Accordingly, the weight for each such dwelling for which a rent is obtained in the current quarter is additionally multiplied by a second correction factor.

Data for the current quarter are corrected for non-response, when the rent from the previous quarter is known, by extrapolating the latter proportionately to the movement of the rent per square metre for those dwellings of the same type for which both rents were obtained. Here, the distinction between types includes a distinction between dwellings with and those without a change of tenant between the two quarters. This reflects the fact, which is important in many other countries too, that rents often rise more upon a change of tenant than they do for continuing tenancies.

Dwellings which are vacant either have to be omitted from the calculations or have a rent imputed:

(1) In the case of a dwelling vacant in the previous quarter whose current rent is known, the rent from the quarter before that is carried forward to the previous quarter. Where such earlier rent is not known, it is retrapolated from the current quarter using indices calculated from the cases where it is known, distinguishing only two

types according to whether or not a certain type of rent control applies (since the number of cases is small).

(2) In the case of a dwelling currently vacant, its previous quarter rent is carried forward, and if it remains vacant in the next quarter it is dropped from the calculation.

Finally, there is the problem of dwellings coming into the sample for the first time. Their rents for the previous quarter are retrapolated to the previous quarter, using indices calculated for six types of dwellings.

In some countries rents are lower on older dwellings, *all other things being equal*, because ageing is associated with a gradual deterioration of physical quality. When this is the case, matched rent comparisons over a succession of periods for a constant sample of dwellings will fractionally understate the quality-adjusted rise in rents. In this case, if the pure age effect can be estimated, it should be used to adjust the data. Thus, if, *all other things being equal*, rents fall by 0.7 per cent for each additional year of age, the rent indices should be divided by $.993^y$, where y is the number of years, including fractions of a year, since the rent reference period. But no adjustment is called for if the average age of the sample is held constant by regularly replacing some of the old dwellings in the sample with new ones, and if the elementary aggregate rent indices are calculated as the relatives of means for specified dwelling types (rather than as the mean of relatives from matched comparisons).

Seasonality

Seasonal adjustment

The most obvious source of seasonal patterns in the index is seasonal variation in the supplies of fruit, vegetables and sometimes other fresh foods. Seasonal variation in demand can also cause them. Furthermore, there are also institutional factors which can generate a seasonal element. They include the following:

- regular seasonal retail sales, where shops cut their prices;
- an administrative or legislative timetable which confines tax changes to a particular time in the year;
- an annual price review by public utilities;
- annual rent revisions.

User needs obviously reflect the purposes served by the consumer price index. If it, or its sub-indices, are used to deflate retail sales figures, then the unadjusted form is required. For examining inflation and for indexation, on the other hand, adjustment may be preferable, though not if it entails retrospective revisions of the index when the seasonal factors are updated. Given the variation between countries in the relative importance of different user needs, it would not appear possible to make any general recommendation.

If a seasonally adjusted index best meets the purposes served by the index, there is a choice between:

(1) seasonally adjusting the group indices or the all-items index; and

(2) seasonally adjusting the mean prices or mean price relatives for those items whose prices display strong seasonal patterns.

Alternative (1) is the easier. A standard adjustment routine is mechanically applied and the results automatically accepted. Alternative (2) forces the statistician to seek the seasonality at its root and to consider whether the adjustment method under examination yields sensible results for each separate seasonally varying item. One possible conclusion from such an examination is that seasonality is so irregular (because, for example, there are large year-to-year variations in the dates of crop harvesting) that some of the sub-indices calculated with seasonally corrected prices would still display considerable and sometimes meaningless fluctuations. It might then be preferred to include all actual fluctuations in the index by abstaining from seasonal correction. Otherwise, the logic of such an objection is that not only the regular seasonal component but also the irregular component should be removed, leaving a smoothed series. This may seem desirable, in principle, for some of the uses of an index but, in the absence of much experience with such adjustment, it is better put on the agenda for research than implemented immediately.

Seasonal availability

We now come to a problem where there seems to be no absolutely correct answer. Different methods are used in different countries, yielding dissimilar results. This is not because of differences in the purposes to be served by the consumer price index, but because of various practical approaches to a purely technical problem. This problem extends beyond seasonally varying prices, and arises when some goods or services are totally unavailable at certain times during the year, or are only available to a very limited extent when not in season, so that meaningful prices cannot be observed. The problem, a significant one, can arise with fruits, vegetables, meat, fish, sports goods, package holidays and some kinds of clothing.

The essence of the problem is that if one single set of weights is used, fictitious prices must be imputed for those months when there is no price to observe. Alternatively, if different weights are used for different months, reflecting the varying availabilities of items, the meaning of month-to-month changes in the index becomes unclear.

There is one procedure akin to seasonal adjustment which escapes both the need to impute fictitious prices and the alternative problem of interpreting month-to-month movements. This is the calculation of a 12-month centred moving average. Each month it compares the current 12-month cost of buying 12 reference-year monthly baskets with the total cost of the 12 reference-year baskets. From a practical point of view, such a moving average is not very useful, since it entails a publication delay six months longer than usual. However, it can serve as a standard for judging other methods.

Different approaches

The following argument is epitomised in figure 8. It is tempting to classify the methods used for tackling the problem in two dimensions, distinguishing the methods according to whether they use:

- one set of annual weights *or* 12 monthly sets of weights,
- one set of reference prices *or* 12 monthly sets of reference prices.

However, the second of these two classifications is best replaced by the dichotomy:

- seasonally adjusted current prices *or* unadjusted current prices.

This is because the use of monthly reference prices is equivalent to undertaking seasonal correction using the reference-year pattern of seasonal variation. For example, if the reference year is 1990, comparing a June 1994 price with a June 1990 price is the same as comparing it with:

Average 1990 price × [June 1990 price/average 1990 price]

i.e. average 1990 price multiplied by a seasonal correction factor, and this is the same as comparing the June 1994 price divided by this seasonal correction factor with the

Figure 8. Methods of dealing with seasonal availability

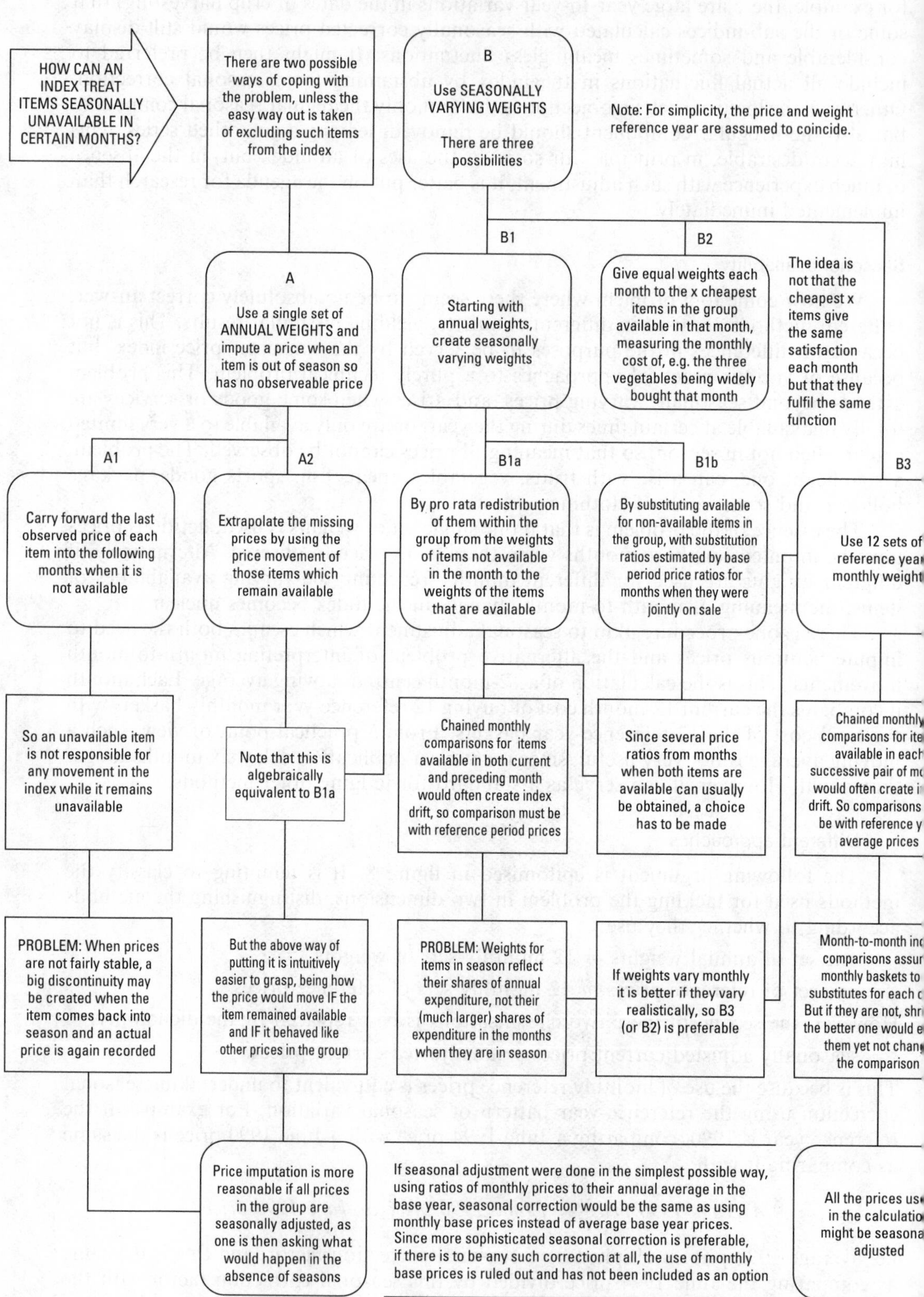

average 1990 price. In other words, it is the same as comparing a seasonally adjusted June 1994 price with a single price for the whole of the reference year, 1990.

This simple calculation of 12 seasonal correction factors, using only the monthly price data for the single reference year, provides a particularly crude seasonal adjustment of the raw price data. More complex methods of seasonal adjustment, which use data relating to more than one year, are almost certain to be preferable. Hence, simple comparisons of the current month's prices with prices in the corresponding month of the reference year may be excluded from the classification of methods, being subsumed under the methods which compare seasonally adjusted prices with average reference-year prices.

As regards the choice between annual and monthly weights, the main point, which has already been noted, is that the use of annual weights for each monthly calculation requires prices for all goods and services in the index, including those which are currently seasonally unavailable. Hence, unless seasonal goods and services are omitted altogether from the index, there will be months when fictitious prices must be attributed to non-available items. Thus, the use of annual weights necessitates either treating goods and services that are only sometimes available as though they were always available, or treating them as never available.

One way of attributing fictitious prices is to carry forward the last observed price until a price can once again be obtained. (The extremely high prices of fruits and vegetables when they first reappear may be disregarded.) Another method is to assume that, if the goods and services had remained available, their prices would have moved in the same proportion as the prices of the goods and services which did remain available. This is equivalent to giving a greater weight to these other items. Hence, the method boils down to one of changing weights between months with differing combinations of availabilities. This raises the issue of whether the method should be subsumed under the method which uses monthly weights. The answer is that, though this way of imputing fictitious prices is *algebraically* equivalent to the use of monthly weights, its implicit monthly weights do not make sense. Hence, the formal equivalence cannot be used to justify the method. Its justification must be that fictitious prices are needed and that the best way of estimating them is to suppose that, if things which are not available were available, their prices would move in parallel with other prices.

To see why the implicit monthly weights are unreasonable, consider the simple case where annual expenditures on oranges and on apples are each 40, spread evenly over the 12 months, while annual expenditure on cherries is 20, spread evenly over only the two months of July and August. Then, if cherry prices are extrapolated forward according to the movement of apple and orange prices, starting each September and continuing monthly until the following June, apples and oranges acquire effective weights of 50 per cent during these ten months. This is reasonable. In July and August, apples and oranges have weights of 40 per cent and cherries use their weight of 20 per cent. But if cherries account for 20 per cent of total annual expenditure on the three types of fruit, they must account for vastly *more* than 20 per cent of expenditure on fruit in July and August! The implicit July and August weights are, therefore, not reasonable for measuring month-to-month changes.

Finally, it should be noted that if the prices of unavailable items are extrapolated forward, the best price indicator to use for the purpose may not always be the prices of other items in the same group. Two examples that illustrate this are the use of fabric prices in the case of clothes and of admission charges for tennis in the case of football matches.

Relative merits

The above considerations explain the classificatory scheme set out in figure 8.

The easiest solution would be to avoid the problem by totally omitting all goods and services not available in all 12 months.

Methods A1 and A2 provide an index which shows how the level of consumer prices would change if certain seasonally unavailable goods and services were in fact continuously available and were being sold at the prices imputed (somewhat arbitrarily) by the compilers of the index. These methods entail the problem that there may be a discontinuity between such a fictitious price in one month and the real price obtained for the same item in the following month, when it comes back on the market. In times of marked inflation, such discontinuities will presumably be greater with A1 than with A2. Note that in some cases, for example with imported items, an even better alternative might be to extrapolate the missing prices by using other indicators than those of goods and services in the same expenditure group.

An advantage of these methods, which is not shared by methods using seasonally varying weights determined in advance, is that they can cope more easily with deviations from the normal pattern of seasonal availability. Thus, if strawberries appear on the market in sufficient quantities a month earlier than usual, their actual price can be used instead of an imputed price.

An interesting example of the application of method A2 is provided by a proposal that has been made for including package holidays in a consumer price index. The problem is not just that winter destinations differ from summer destinations; there is also the point that a week in Italy in April is different from a week in Italy in August. The proposal can be regarded as an acquisition approach, as the prices obtained will relate to holidays that can be bought in the current month (the specifications including the date of departure), which reduces the number of months for which no price is available. Some 20 package holidays will be priced, prices being collected in each month that these can be booked. In months when a particular package is not available, its last price will be extrapolated forward using the movement of those packages which remain available.

The methods B1, B2 and B3 have one drawback similar to the discontinuity problem mentioned above, with the countervailing advantage that none of these methods omits goods and services and none of them requires the statistician to impute fictitious prices. The drawback is that the index may change between two months because of a weight change, even though no price has changed and availabilities are unaltered.

It may seem unclear what an index comparison between two successive months in different seasons signifies. Is it meaningful, for example, to say that the June 1992 cost of buying the summer 1990 basket of fruit is higher than the May 1992 cost of buying the spring 1990 basket? The answer is that it is, if it can be asserted that the different seasonal reference-year baskets were of equal real value to consumers, so that if one of them currently costs more than another recently did, this group of items, which includes some seasonal substitutions, really has become more expensive.

One rough and ready way of selecting equivalent baskets would be to compose them of equal physical quantities of whatever is currently cheapest within a group of similar items. This method, B2, reflects the substitutions made by consumers but requires that in every month some items from each group are on the market. Alternatively, method B1b, to give a simplified example, implies that if, when strawberries and apples are both available, a kilo of strawberries, on average over a number of years, sells for twice as much as a kilo of apples, then when strawberries are not available, the weight of apples is increased by twice the weight given to strawberries in months when strawberries are available.

Statisticians may not like either of these two ways of selecting seasonal baskets of equal real value to the average consumer covered by the index, but it must be realised that the more mechanistic method B1a also does this, albeit implicitly. Method B3 does it too, but in a more subtle way, which requires explanation.

The point is that the comparison of the current-month cost of the month's reference basket with its reference-year cost at reference-year average prices would be unaltered if the quantities of all the items in it were changed in the same proportion. Hence, even if some of the 12 baskets were thus equiproportionally changed in such a way as to make all 12 of equal real value to consumers, the comparison of the current-month cost of each with its reference-year cost would not be altered. One can, therefore, interpret the cost comparisons for the actual baskets *as if* they were comparisons for these unknown changed baskets of equal real value.

As has already been noted, with varying weights between months, a change in the sub-index can happen even though none of the prices of the continuously available goods and services which it covers has changed. However, this may not actually happen and, even if it does, it may not show up in the more aggregative indices of which the sub-index forms a part. It could in any case be explained as being caused by a substitution of equivalent baskets which unavoidably alters costs to consumers.

Whether or not seasonal adjustment, either of the raw price data or of sub-indices, is desirable depends partly on the needs of the users and partly upon technical considerations.

A practical point already noted is that the seasonal adjustment of the raw prices of such seasonal goods as fruit and vegetables encounters the difficulty that their seasonal price behaviour can be very irregular. However, it is the effect of such seasonal adjustment upon the sub-index which matters, not the effects upon each individual series used in the calculation of that sub-index. Another practical point is that re-estimations of seasonal factors should not be applied retrospectively because of the difficulties caused by such index revisions.

Seasonal adjustment of the raw prices in methods A1 and A2 has the advantage of making the imputation of fictitious prices more defensible than it would otherwise be, since the imputation of a price which does not exist because of seasonality implies that seasonality is being disregarded.

The article "Treatment of seasonal fresh fruit and vegetables in CPI", by L. C. Clements, reprinted in Appendix 8, gives an example of Australian practice in the treatment of seasonal items.

Combining elementary aggregate indices

Aggregation

Assume that the weight reference period and the price reference period are the same. Then the group- and all-items indices are —

the sum of current to reference-period elementary aggregate indices each multiplied by its reference period expenditure, divided by the sum of those expenditures.

Since multiplication of a current-period to price-reference-period elementary aggregate index by its reference-period expenditure yields what can be termed a "revalued expenditure", an alternative description is —

the sum of revalued expenditures, divided by the sum of reference period expenditures;

and, provided that the elementary aggregate indices are not calculated as arithmetic means of price relatives and are thus transitive, i.e. possess the property that the product of a series of month-to-month indices is the same as the index directly stretching from the first to the last month, this is equivalent to:

the sum of preceding-month revalued expenditures, each multiplied by its current to preceding-month elementary aggregate index, divided by the sum of reference period expenditures.

A similar equivalence holds if weights for the weight reference period (then summing to unity) are each revalued, as shown algebraically in box 1 and demonstrated in the table in box 13.

Weight and price reference periods

The above algebraic equivalence may be convenient for computation. But there are real substantive issues too, which are quite different. Normally, the expenditure data used for calculating weights will relate to an earlier reference period than that used for prices. Then the issue arises of whether, if feasible, the expenditures of the earlier period should be adjusted by allowing for subsequent price changes in the process of calculating the weights.

This will be feasible only when elementary aggregate indices are available for the interval between the weight reference period and the "update" period. Thus, if a revised index using 1990 expenditure data is to be price-updated to a price reference period of January 1992, the update can only be made if, starting in 1990, the prices collected include those necessary to allow calculation of indices for the set of elementary aggregates used in the revised index.

If the weights are *not* adjusted, so that they remain $P_{90}Q_{90}$, then the index calculated with January 1992 as the price reference period will depart from the Laspeyres form – unless no expenditures change, i.e. unless it chances that all $P_{92}Q_{92} = P_{90}Q_{90}$. The index measures changes in the current cost of a January 1992 set of purchases with 1990 value proportions between the different components of expenditure. This corresponds to no actual basket – unless it happens that no expenditures have changed from 1990 to 1992.

If the weights *are* adjusted, by multiplying them by appropriate indices P_{92}/P_{90} to get new weights of $P_{92}Q_{90}$, then the index calculated starting in 1992 will again depart from the Laspeyres form – unless no quantities change, i.e. all $Q_{92} = Q_{90}$. The index then measures changes in the current cost of the 1990 set of purchases in relation to its January 1992 cost. This does correspond to an actual basket.

Finally, there is the most complex possibility where, for example, 1990 expenditures are updated to end of 1991 prices for the calculation of the weights but the price reference period is different, say January 1992. The index then measures changes in the current cost of a January 1992 set of purchases with what end of 1991 value proportions between the different items of expenditure would have been had 1990 purchases been made at end of 1991 prices. As in the case of the first of these three possibilities, this corresponds to no actual basket. None the less, it may provide a practical and sensible approximation to the second possibility, which does correspond to one. Calculation of the weights will have to be done *before* 1992. It can scarcely be delayed until after the January 1992 price collection, and revaluation at end of 1991 prices will normally provide very similar weights to those which a January 1992 revaluation would provide.

When an index corresponds to no actual physical basket, it is difficult to explain what is measured. On the other hand, it is still a weighted average of elementary aggregate price indices, where the weights are calculated using expenditure and price data. It may be conceptually inferior but, nevertheless, may be necessitated by the absence of certain data or justified by the high or low quality of the data that are available.

Chained indices and reweighting

Index revision and linking

When, for whatever reason, the index base period is changed, the index with the new index base can be linked to the index with the old index base. If the old base was 1980, the new base is 1990 and if the average value of the old index for 1980 was 371.4, then values of the old index can be divided by 3.714 to put them on the 1990 index base and values of the new index can be multiplied by 3.714 to put them on the 1980 index base.

Box 13. Combining elementary aggregate indices

Indices relating current to reference period prices

Composite item	Region	Outlet type	Weight	January Index	January Weight × index	February Index	February Weight × index	March Index	March Weight × index	April Index	April Weight × index
1	N	i	0.06	1.023	0.061	1.031	0.062	1.038	0.062	1.040	0.062
		ii	0.04	1.017	0.041	1.027	0.041	1.035	0.041	1.037	0.041
	S	i	0.12	1.009	0.121	1.019	0.122	1.029	0.123	1.036	0.124
		ii	0.18	1.014	0.183	1.021	0.184	1.030	0.185	1.035	0.186
2	N	i	0.08	1.005	0.080	1.111	0.089	1.130	0.090	1.183	0.095
		ii	0.07	1.007	0.070	1.126	0.079	1.198	0.084	1.200	0.084
	S	i	0.22	1.008	0.222	1.010	0.222	1.167	0.257	1.182	0.260
		ii	0.23	1.003	0.231	1.008	0.232	1.152	0.265	1.193	0.274

Calculate the indices by dividing (sum of: weight × index) by (sum of weights), i.e. by dividing (sum of revalued weights) by (sum of weights)

	Sum of weights	January Sum of: W×I	January Index	February Sum of: W×I	February Index	March Sum of: W×I	March Index	April Sum of: W×I	April Index
N region	0.25	0.253	1.012	0.271	1.083	0.278	1.112	0.283	1.130
S region	0.75	0.756	1.008	0.760	1.013	0.831	1.107	0.845	1.127
Composite item 1	0.40	0.406	1.014	0.409	1.023	0.413	1.031	0.415	1.036
Composite item 2	0.60	0.603	1.006	0.622	1.036	0.696	1.160	0.713	1.188
Whole country, all items	1.00	1.009	1.009	1.031	1.031	1.109	1.109	1.128	1.128

Indices relating current to previous period prices

Composite item	Region	Outlet type	Weight	January Index	January Re-valued weight	February Index	February Re-valued weight	March Index	March Re-valued weight	April Index	April Re-valued weight
1	N	i	0.06	1.023	0.061	1.008	0.062	1.007	0.062	1.002	0.062
		ii	0.04	1.017	0.041	1.010	0.041	1.008	0.041	1.002	0.041
	S	i	0.12	1.009	0.121	1.010	0.122	1.010	0.123	1.007	0.124
		ii	0.18	1.014	0.183	1.007	0.184	1.009	0.185	1.005	0.186
2	N	i	0.08	1.005	0.080	1.105	0.089	1.017	0.090	1.047	0.095
		ii	0.07	1.007	0.070	1.118	0.079	1.064	0.084	1.002	0.084
	S	i	0.22	1.008	0.222	1.002	0.222	1.155	0.257	1.013	0.260
		ii	0.23	1.003	0.231	1.005	0.232	1.143	0.265	1.036	0.274

Calculate the indices by dividing (sum of: revalued weight of previous period × current to previous period elementary aggregate index) by (sum of weights)

	Sum of weights	January Index	February Index	March Index	April Index
N region	0.25	1.012	1.083	1.112	1.130
S region	0.75	1.008	1.013	1.107	1.127
Composite item 1	0.40	1.014	1.023	1.031	1.036
Composite item 2	0.60	1.006	1.036	1.160	1.188
Whole country, all items	1.00	1.009	1.031	1.109	1.128

There is rarely much point in changing the index base unless the weight or price reference period has also been updated. It is tempting to discuss such a revision of the index (and the computation of a chain index) simply in terms of a change in the composition of expenditure (a new basket) and/or a change in the price reference period. However, there is more to it than this, for two reasons:

— The weights of elementary aggregates may need to be changed not only because of changes in the composition of expenditure, but also because of a reclassification of expenditures, because of a change in the relative importance of different types of outlet or because of a change in the regional distribution of expenditures.

— The opportunity should always be taken to review and update the choice of representative items and the choice of varieties. This should be done for all elementary aggregates, whether or not their weights or definitions have been altered. Wherever there are changes, new reference prices will have to be used.

The resulting revised index can be chained to the old one by the purely arithmetic operation described above, provided that there is at least one month for which prices are collected and the index computed for both of them. It does not matter if this month and the weight reference period are different. For example, in the case of an annually chained index, the new index could be started every January, using weights relating to the previous calendar year (or the year before that). The published index for February 1992 would then be the new index for February 1992 with January 1992 as price reference period and 1991 (or 1990) as weight reference period, multiplied by the published index for January 1992. This in turn would have been calculated with January 1991 as price reference period and 1990 (or 1989) as weight reference period, multiplied by the published index for January 1991.

The weighted average of linked sub-indices may be different from the linked weighted averages of sub-indices, i.e. from the all-items chain index. This can happen when some of the sub-indices have different values within some links and there are weight changes between some links. The divergence can arise because the weighted average of linked sub-indices uses only one, the most recent, set of weights, while each of the successive weighted averages of sub-indices which are chained together to produce the all-items index uses a different set of weights. It is even possible for the linked all-items index to fall outside the range of the linked component sub-indices!

Chain indices

When an index is regularly revised, the index obtained by linking the successively revised indices end-to-end is termed a chain index.

Chaining more frequently than annually is usually impracticable and in any case is undesirable. This is because a chained index usually fails the circularity test of reverting to its original value when some prices, after having changed, return to their original values, with quantities moving inversely to prices. Such oscillatory price and quantity behaviour, if it occurs at all, is most likely to be seasonal, displaying an annual pattern.

The advantage of an annually chained index is that it follows the evolution of the pattern of consumption. It is thus more representative than an index using an unchanging set of weights. (When structural changes continue in the same direction over a series of years, the spread between chained Laspeyres and Paasche indices will be less than that between fixed weight indices.) It is true that, within a fixed weight index, one outlet or variety can be substituted for another, and representative items can be respecified, but a systematic reconsideration of the choices within the framework of a review of the weights will be more thorough.

Another advantage of a chained index is that the regular revisions of weights and of outlet and item selection can be accompanied by procedural improvements. Any statistician will think up a whole series of improvements to a consumer price index as time passes. With a fixed weight index, such a series of changes in method will appear as a series of minor discontinuities, with a risk of misunderstanding and uncertainty on the part of users.

The major disadvantage of a chained index is that it costs more, both because of the cost of obtaining and using the data for each revision and because two sets of price observations have to be obtained for the overlap month if the outlets or items sampled are changed. It also has the mathematical disadvantage that, as explained with regard to linking at the end of the previous section, the average of chained sub-indices is not necessarily equal to the chained average of sub-indices. However, in practice, any divergence will often be small. A minor disadvantage is that it is more difficult to explain to the public, though this is partly offset by the fact that it can claim to be regularly updated to follow changes in expenditure and distribution patterns.

There is a considerable literature on the relationship between a chained index and a fixed weight index which demonstrates that the relation of the former to the latter is the product of a series of factors, one for each successive link. It has been shown, for a Laspeyres index, that these factors will exceed unity if there is a positive correlation between –

the price relatives with respect to the previous period,

and

the quantity relatives with respect to the reference period,

and will be larger, the greater are the coefficients of variation of these relatives.

Thus, in the short run, if quantities rise less or fall for those items whose prices have risen most, the chain index will fall below the fixed weight index. In the longer run, such inverse price-quantity relationships may well be swamped by other factors, so that the correlation between the latest price relatives and the back-to-reference-period quantity relatives will tend to be random. Thus, there is no *a priori* prediction of which index will drift above the other. Empirical investigations show that sometimes the chain and at other times the fixed weight index rises the most. But such comparisons are only possible when one set of elementary aggregate indices is common to both, the difference between them being limited to the weighting of those elementary aggregates. Thus, the comparisons can tell us nothing about the advantage of chaining a series of indices where successive indices in the series use updated breakdowns into elementary aggregates with revised specifications of representative items. *Yet it is this updating and revision which is the important argument in favour of a chained index.*

Sources of error 7

From the point of view of a user who needs an answer to Question A, a consumer price index which instead answers Question B contains errors. But this is not what is meant here.

The problem is that if one knew the extent of the errors, they would not exist. Yet one would like to know their size in order to concentrate available resources on improving those features of the index where the error reduction will be greatest in relation to the cost. Calculation of standard errors is possible only for those parts of the computation which rest upon statistical samples. Otherwise, some quantitative indications may give a useful clue, for example:

— comparison of the price movements of items for which quality adjustments have been made with the price movements of unchanged items;
— counts of the number of missing observations, classified by cause;
— comparisons with price data from other sources;
— comparisons of elementary aggregate or sub-indices before and after quality adjustments have been made over a series of years. This will provide an indication of assessed quality changes which can be judged with the aid of expert knowledge and common sense.

In the absence of adequate quantification of different errors, the only general rule which might be proposed for deciding where efforts for improvement should be concentrated might be to give special attention to errors whose effects are likely to be cumulative.

The main possible sources of error will now be discussed individually.

Coverage

A weight may be assumed to be zero, even though this is known to be wrong, because the prices for the elementary aggregate are too difficult to collect. An example might be the prices charged by pedlars and door-to-door salesmen. In such cases it is to be hoped that the correct weight would be very small. If this seems not to be the case, then extension of the field covered by the index deserves priority.

Perhaps the inadequate coverage of the prices charged for services is an important defect in many developed countries. They may be omitted because of the difficulties of specification of representative items. Omissions may include banking and insurance services, travel bureau services, legal services, some forms of entertainment and private health and educational services.

Errors in the weights

Sampling errors in a household expenditure survey can be examined, but in most cases several sources will have been combined and quantitative judgements made, to produce the weights, rendering impossible the calculation of their variance.

Errors in the weights are much less important as a source of error in the consumer price index than errors in price collection. If the errors in weights are uncorrelated with price changes they will have little effect upon the index. It is thus much more serious if, for example, furniture price changes are overestimated by 5 per cent than if furniture expenditure used for determining weights is overestimated by 5 per cent.

Estimates of weights for those elementary aggregates whose indices are likely to move differently from the average or to be subject to above-average error should be made with the greatest precision.

Errors in prices

Selection of price observations

When statistical sampling methods are used, the quality of the frame and the sampling variance can and should be investigated. The technique of pseudo-replication can be used to measure the variance of relatives or of mean prices, different combinations of two halves of the data for a stratum being compared in order to estimate the variance of the observations.

But where the choice of items, outlets and timing is purposive, the main check upon quality can only be a rigorous but commonsense review of the choices made. Perhaps the main danger is not that they will be made badly but that they will not be reviewed regularly in order to see whether updating is necessary. In recent years, newly added representative items in one country's index have included microwave ovens, various convenience foods, self-assembly furniture, video recorders and video cassettes, nursery school fees and duvets. While items such as these may not have become important in many developing countries, it is rare to find a country without changes, either through the introduction of new products or because economic conditions have deteriorated and some items are no longer available.

Measurement

Price collectors can make mistakes or even invent prices when they are too lazy to collect them. Some errors will be spotted when the price report forms are checked manually; others may emerge as outliers in machine editing. But a continuous attempt to avoid them is necessary, and training, the development of an esprit de corps and the occasional independent duplicate collection of prices by a supervisor are the remedies to be followed.

Missing observations

A large number of missing observations indicates that something is amiss and that investigation should start straight away. The questions to be asked are:

— Have the price collectors been lazy or incompetent?
— Are there problems in transmission of the data?
— Are there problems in entering the data?
— Are items temporarily or permanently out of stock?
— If items have become permanently unavailable, have the necessary substitutions been made; if not, why not? Are there, for example, problems in using the specifications?

— Have outlets been uncooperative, temporarily closed or permanently closed?
— If outlets have been permanently closed, have substitute outlets been found?

Infrequent collection of some prices

An obvious economy measure in the design of an index is to limit the frequency of collection of certain prices which are known to change infrequently. For example, rents are often collected less frequently than the prices of items sold in shops and markets. It is evident that the timing of such collections should be chosen so that they are undertaken soon after the month(s) when price changes normally occur. If such prices do change between collections, an error is introduced into the index, though it is not a cumulative one, since the matter will be put right the next time these prices are collected. The error can become large in times of rapid inflation, when prices that have hitherto been changed infrequently begin to be raised at shorter intervals. The frequency of collection must then be increased. It is unfortunately true that the cost of compiling a good index rises when the rate of price change accelerates.

Quality adjustments

Three kinds of error can arise with respect to quality change (or changes in outlets). The first occurs when a quality change is not noticed and prices continue to be collected as if there had been no quality change. This might happen either when the change does not affect any of the characteristics of the item as set out in the specification and the specification is used to identify the item, or when there is no change in model name and it is this which is used to identify the item. The collectors must be well trained and conscientious if this trap is to be avoided.

The second kind of error is the most obvious one but there is little to say about it. It is simply that a quality judgement is made and that it is wrong. A major reason for this is the intrusion of personal tastes and preferences into the quality judgement. This can happen very easily with clothes. Unfortunately, as already pointed out, quality judgements are necessary particularly frequently in the case of clothes, not only because of fashion changes but also because shops often change the lines they have on sale within a fashion season.

The more statisticians know about quality changes, and the more they obtain advance information about them, the better equipped they will be to minimise this second source of error. This means that part of their task is to follow market developments by reading trade journals and consumer magazines, studying advertisements and interviewing retailers and manufacturers or importers.

The third kind of error is that it is possible, and sometimes inevitable, to avoid quality judgements, that this is equivalent to making implicit judgements, and that these implicit judgements may be wrong.

It has been noted above in the section on linking in the chapter on computation, that substitutions may be made in cases (1a) and (1b), and (2) without making any explicit quality comparison. The same can occur on a more aggregative plane with the replacement of an old index or group-index by a new one, whether this happens annually or only intermittently. In either case, revision of the weights may be accompanied by the inclusion of new outlets and by a more up-to-date selection of goods or services than the old one. The revised index will then be chain-linked to the old one. This can be done without considering whether the newly introduced outlets and/or goods or services offer the same quality in relation to price as those replaced.

Sometimes the avoidance of explicit quality comparisons is inescapable. Where new items or new outlets possess completely different characteristics, as in the example of the advent of colour television, they can be linked into the index, but the statistician cannot possibly quantify the resulting change in the price/quality relationship experienced by consumers.

This raises the question of the likely bias that results. Do, as these procedures assume, the quality-adjusted prices of goods that experience quality changes move in parallel with the prices of similar goods that do not experience them? Do the prices paid by buyers who change from one outlet to another move in parallel with the prices of similar goods in unaltered outlets?

It has been suggested that there will often be an asymmetry between situations of rising and falling prices because, while sellers have no incentive to conceal falling prices, they may wish to conceal price increases by introducing them mainly on new varieties. Hence, the quality-adjusted prices of varieties which are replaced by substitutes may rise faster than the prices of varieties with continuing availability. The index will then be biased downwards.

With types of goods or services where technical progress is important, new goods or services which offer better value for money take over the market from similar but less complex or less powerful earlier versions. If the older models decline in price (relatively to most goods or services in the all-items index) before they disappear from the market, and if this decline is registered in the index before the substitution of the new variety for the old, then omitting a price for one month when the substitution is made will not bias the index. If, on the other hand, the old variety maintains its price, becoming a less and less attractive purchase, and finally disappears from the market, then omitting a price for one month when the substitution is made will bias the index. If the new variety is better value for money, skipping the quality judgement in this way involves omitting to record what is in effect a price reduction.

With changes in distribution channels, new outlets which offer better value for money take over the market from old-fashioned outlets. If prices in the older shops decline in price (relatively to most items in the all-items index) before these shops disappear from the market, and if this decline is registered in the index before the substitution of the new outlets for the old, then omitting a price for one month when the substitution is made will not bias the index. If, on the other hand, the old shops maintain their prices, becoming less and less attractive places for shopping, and finally disappear from the market, then omitting a price for one month when the substitution is made will bias the index.

Thus, there are sets of circumstances under which an index will be biased downwards or upwards by the avoidance of quality judgements, an avoidance which is sometimes inescapable. Whether these circumstances hold will depend upon the way the market in question functions and upon the general economic situation of the country at the time. Whether or not there is a bias caused by the avoidance of quality comparisons is therefore a question about the functioning of a country's economy rather than a technical question about the logic of index numbers. There is no general presumption that avoidance of explicit quality adjustments will necessarily bias a consumer price index in a particular direction.

If this argument is correct, one cannot offer any advice of general validity on the issue of quality bias arising from the avoidance of explicit quality judgements.

Errors of transcription and computation

The problems linked with this type of error are the same as with other types of statistics. However, month-to-month chaining of elementary aggregate indices does create cumulative error possibilities which will be avoided if current to price-reference period price comparisons are used.

Publication of the index

8

Publication

Release of the latest figures

Publication should follow a fixed timetable, determined well in advance, e.g. on the first weekday after the 14th day of each month.

Publication normally takes the form of a press release, possibly with a press conference. The usefulness of the index and the public's reaction to it will partly depend upon the way it is presented. The all-items index figure should be compared with that for the previous month and for the same month a year previously. The comparison should make it absolutely clear when index points and when percentage change are being used. In the latter case it should be clear, for comparisons over less than a year, whether the actual change or an equivalent annual rate is being used.

The major components of the change in the all-items index should be identified and their proximate causes described. The movement of any special sub-indices that are of wide interest should also be described. Where the scope of the index is limited, the public should be reminded of that fact in the course of this analysis. Throughout, the presentation should be limited to description, with no trace of approval, criticism or disappointment, so that the objectivity of the statistician's work is apparent.

Some countries, recognising that different indices may be needed to serve different purposes, publish, for example, both a general consumer price index and an index for wage regulation. The precise details of the differences are not of international interest but it is worth noting that in these countries the press and public have become used to having two indices.

Group indices

Some breakdown of the index should also be provided in the form of group indices. The System of National Accounts classification of consumers' expenditure by purpose should not necessarily be followed in detail in deciding which such indices should be published. At an aggregate level, however, either aggregation according to the eight major groups of the SNA or a classification which permits aggregation to these groups is desirable. They are:

— food, beverages and tobacco;
— clothing and footwear;
— gross rent, fuel and power;
— furniture, furnishings, and household equipment and operation;
— medical care and health expenses;
— transport and communication;
— recreation, entertainment, education and cultural services;
— miscellaneous goods and services.

A ninth group for items in the index but not in SNA household final expenditure may be created.

The extra cost of publishing such group indices is trivial. Hence, all those which are useful should be published, provided only that they do not infringe confidentiality and that they are reliable.

Although publication of an exhaustive and mutually exclusive set of group indices is logical, it will not necessarily suffice to meet all needs. Different, but partially overlapping, group indices may serve different purposes. For example, a group index of the cost of owning and running a car and a group index for energy items may both be useful, even though they would both include petrol and diesel fuel. A separate index for consumer durables has been welcomed in a number of countries by insurance companies which insure the contents of dwellings against fire or theft.

There is a particularly strong case for publishing an "all-items except housing" index. The reason is that differences between countries in the behaviour of rental markets and in the index treatment of owner-occupied dwellings are so large that they create international incomparability of indices. Thus, such an index is much more useful for international comparisons.

Frequency of publication

The effective choice is between monthly and quarterly publication. Once again, the choice to be made must depend upon the relative importance of the different purposes to be served by the consumer price index and by the availability of resources. Thus, if the main use is as an economic indicator, the frequency should match that of other major macro-economic series. For indexing, the conclusion is less obvious: when prices are rising, payers lose and payees gain from greater frequency if more frequent publication entails more frequent indexation. Lower frequency saves costs, though perhaps at the expense of the expertise of the price collectors. How much it saves depends very much upon the way collection and computation is organised. Even with a monthly index there can be slack months.

Publication of average prices

If data are not collected separately to support average price calculations, average prices for reasonably homogeneous items where the number of price observations is large and/or price variations are small can usefully be published as a by-product of the index, though their nature and limitations should be explained.

How to express the inflation rate

If, over n months, the index rises from I_1 per cent to I_2 per cent, this can be expressed as an annual rate by subtracting unity from I_1/I_2 taken to the power of $12/n$, and multiplying by 100: $[(I_1/I_2)12/n - 1] \times 100$. However, this is not necessarily a useful thing to do for just one or two months' change in the index, even if it is of an extremely high quality. One reason is that the month-to-month change may include a seasonal component. Another is that some prices change only infrequently, perhaps only once a year. Hence, a comparison with the same month a year previously is to be preferred.

How to calculate an annual average

The mean of 12 monthly all-items indices is the same as the mean of the annual averages of all the elementary aggregate indices.

Revisions

In contrast with other statistics, additional consumption price data are rarely obtained once the collection period is past. Hence, the most likely need for revision is the discovery of past errors. These may or may not affect the current index. If they do so, then at the very least they must be corrected in the next calculation, thus avoiding cumulation of errors.

In addition, retrospective correction may be necessary, though it can create difficulties for indexed contracts and indexed government payments or receipts.

Confidentiality of details

The choice of representative items for heterogeneous composite items and the choice of varieties should be confidential. If these facts were known, it might be possible for the index to be artificially lowered by subsidising or controlling the prices of the particular items whose prices are measured. On the other hand, where the choice of representative item is obvious and varieties are few, as perhaps in the case of milk or sugar, any subsidy or control will genuinely lower the cost of the composite item and should therefore be reflected in the index.

Public relations

Consumer price indices are so widely used that public confidence in them is important. This requires not only that the work of the statisticians is seen to be carried out objectively but also that it is understood.

A methodological description of the index should be published and it should be revised and reissued when the index is revised. It is easy to allow this task to be postponed. Yet public acceptance of the index depends upon public confidence in its compilers. A detailed, frank and up-to-date account of the methods used can contribute to this. It should include a discussion of which purposes can properly be served by the index and of the nature of its limitations for other purposes. In addition, the publication of a much shorter and more popular pamphlet describing the index in simple terms is a good idea.

The preparation of a comprehensive methodological description is a major task. It may be eased if existing publications from other countries as well as this manual are used as a starting-point. The description should include, among other things, a statement of the objectives and scope of the index, details of the weights and a discussion of the precision of the index.

When a new index supersedes an old one or the weighting structure of a fixed base index is changed, the new figures will normally be expressed as a continuation of the old series. But whether or not this is done, an explanation of what it entails should be made public. In addition, if an overlap between the old and the new index is feasible, both being calculated in parallel for a number of months, both should be published together with an explanation of any difference in the price trends they disclose.

Consultation with users on major issues is to be recommended. This, particularly if it is done through an advisory committee, can both provide the statisticians with help and enable them to defend their index against criticism. The people consulted or appointed to the advisory committee should include academic experts as well as representatives of users of the index, notably employer organisations, trade unions and economic journalists.

Press, radio, television and the record of legislative debates should be scanned for references to the consumer price index so that any misunderstandings which are revealed can be corrected. These misunderstandings may arise because the statisticians have explained the index badly. If so, they must accept that they have a public relations task. If, on the other hand, the criticisms are warranted, the statisticians should be grateful for them and try to improve the index.

APPENDICES

Appendix 1

Resolution concerning consumer price indices

The Fourteenth International Conference of Labour Statisticians,

Having been convened at Geneva by the Governing Body of the ILO and having met from 28 October to 6 November 1987,

Recalling the existing international standards concerning cost-of-living index numbers contained in the resolutions adopted by the Second and Sixth Conferences in 1925 and 1947 respectively, and those concerning special problems in the computation of consumer price index numbers contained in the resolution adopted by the Tenth International Conference of Labour Statisticians in 1962,

Recognising the need to revise and broaden the existing standards in order to enhance their usefulness in the provision of technical guide-lines to all countries and particularly those with less developed statistics,

Recognising the usefulness of such standards in enhancing the international comparability of the statistics,

Recognising that consumer price indices are essential to assessments of social conditions and of economic performance and potential, and,

Recognising, therefore, that such indices need to be credible to observers and users, both national and international,

Agrees that the principles and methods used in constructing a consumer price index should be selected, with consideration of the chosen objectives, from among the guide-lines and standards which are generally accepted as constituting good statistical practice, and

Adopts, this fifth day of November 1987, the following resolution which replaces those adopted in 1925, 1947 and 1962.

Terminology

1. For the purposes of this resolution, the following terms are defined:

(a) "outlet" indicates a shop, market, service establishment, or other place, where goods and/or services are sold or provided to consumers for non-business use;

(b) "consumption" indicates all goods and services (or "items") that are acquired, used or paid for, but not for business purposes and not for the accumulation of wealth;

(c) "region" indicates any geographically defined area and/or type of area within a country;

(d) "scope of the index" indicates the population groups, regions, items and outlets for which the index is established;

(e) "reference population" indicates the population that falls within the scope of the index;

(f) "elementary aggregate" indicates the most detailed level for which expenditure or quantity weights are held constant for a certain period of time;

(g) consumption expenditure can be measured in terms of "acquisition", "use" or "payment":

   (i) "acquisition" indicates that the total value of all goods and services delivered during a given period, irrespective of whether they were wholly paid for or not during the period, should be taken into account;

   (ii) "use" indicates that the total value of all goods and services actually consumed during a given period should be taken into account; and

(iii) "payment" indicates that the total payments made for goods and services during a given period, without regard to whether they were delivered or not, should be taken into account.

The nature of a consumer price index

2. The purpose of a consumer price index is to measure changes over time in the general level of prices of goods and services that a reference population acquire, use or pay for consumption. A consumer price index is estimated as a series of summary measures of the period-to-period proportional change in the prices of a fixed set of consumer goods and services of constant quantity and characteristics, acquired, used or paid for by the reference population. Each summary measure is constructed as a weighted average of a large number of elementary aggregate indices. Each of the elementary aggregate indices is estimated using a sample of prices for a defined set of goods and services obtained in, or by residents of, a specific region from a given set of outlets or other sources of consumption goods and services.

The uses of a consumer price index

3. The uses of a consumer price index and their relative importance vary from country to country. They include:

(a) general economic and social analysis and policy determination;

(b) negotiation or indexation, or both, by government (notably of taxes, social security benefits, civil service remuneration and pensions, licence fees, fines and public debt interest or principal) and in private contracts (e.g. wages, salaries, insurance premiums and service charges) and in judicial decisions (e.g. alimony payments);

(c) establishing "real" changes, or the relationship between money and the goods or services for which it can be exchanged (e.g. for the deflation of current value aggregates in the national accounts and of retail sales); and

(d) price movement comparisons done for business purposes, including inflation accounting.

Sub-indices rather than the all-items index may be suitable for some of the above uses.

Scope of the index

4. The reference population should normally be defined very widely, specifying those income groups and household or family types that are excluded.

5. The regional scope should normally be defined as widely as possible, noting any exclusions. It should also be specified whether any regional limitation or breakdown of consumption expenditure and of price collection relates to sales in a region, or to purchases by residents of a region.

6. Separate indices may be computed for different population groups or for different regions.

7. The extent to which expenditure abroad is included should be clearly indicated.

8. Ideally, the consumer price index should relate to all goods and services (including imports) acquired, used or paid for by the reference population for non-business purposes, without any omission of tobacco or other things which may be regarded as non-essential or undesirable. The range of goods and services included may, but need not, coincide with consumption expenditure as defined in a national accounts framework. Income taxes, savings, life insurance and pension fund contributions, and financial investments (as distinct from financial services) should not be included in the consumer price index.

9. If second-hand purchases are represented in the index, then the weights for second-hand goods should be calculated net of the corresponding sales including trade-ins.

10. In some cases, such as insurance, health care, second-hand goods, etc., it may not be possible to use the same methodology as in the general index. Groups of goods or services which fall within the scope of the index but which cannot be dealt with according to the general methodology, either because this methodology cannot be applied correctly for these items or because the necessary information is insufficient or lacking, may be included in or excluded from the calculations:

(a) in the case of their inclusion, special methods will need to be used;
(b) in the case of their exclusion:
— the group may be explicitly represented by another group to which the weights of the excluded items are allocated;
— the group may be purely and simply excluded from the index (price collection and weights) which assumes that its price movement is represented by the movement of the overall index.

In all the above cases, users should be informed as to the method followed.

11. The goods and services or household expenditures should follow a classification which is dependent upon the objectives of the index, previous practices, the methods of data collection, as well as upon the nature and quality of data available for the computation of weights. Nevertheless it is desirable that this classification permit aggregation according to the eight major groups of the United Nations System of National Accounts (SNA): "Food, beverages and tobacco", "Clothing and footwear", "Gross rent, fuel and power", "Furniture, furnishings, and household equipment and operation", "Medical care and health expenses", "Transport and communication", "Recreation, entertainment, education and cultural services" and "Miscellaneous goods and services". If need be, a ninth group might be created, covering items which are not included in the household final consumption expenditure of the SNA.

Acquisition, use or payment

12. Having decided the scope of the index in terms of the reference population and the goods and services to be included, it should be explicitly considered whether the objectives of the index are best satisfied by adopting the concepts of acquisition, use or payment. These issues should be examined, taking into account the theoretical index concept, acceptability to users, availability of data, and resource requirements. These issues particularly arise in dealing with own-account consumption, owner-occupied housing, consumer credit, durable goods, remuneration in kind and goods and services which are provided without charge or are subsidised by government.

13. The concepts of acquisition of payment may be chosen if the index is defined in terms of money flows. Adherence to the conventions of national accounting may be desired if the deflation of consumer expenditure as defined in the national accounts is one of the major uses to which the index is put. When the design of the index is founded upon the consistent application of consumer demand theory, the concept of use may be appropriate. This concept implies estimating the rental value of owner-occupied housing if the data permit such estimates to be made reliably. Alternatively, it would imply the explicit inclusion of all owner-occupied housing costs.

Defining elementary aggregates

14. In defining elementary aggregates (in terms of kinds of goods or services, types of outlets and regions), the following principles should be observed:

(a) related goods or services which are thought to display similar price movements should be grouped together in an elementary aggregate;
(b) goods or services whose prices might reasonably be expected to move markedly differently should not be grouped together in the same elementary aggregate;
(c) elementary aggregates should be distinguished whenever weights (including regional or outlet weights) are available or can be estimated;
(d) such regional or outlet weights should be used in calculating the index even when separate regional or outlet-type sub-indices are not required;
(e) elementary aggregates should be described so that any good or service can be unambiguously assigned to the appropriate elementary aggregate.

15. In the calculation of elementary aggregate indices, consideration should be given to the possible use of geometric means.

Weighting

16. Weights are the relative expenditure or consumption shares of the elementary aggregates estimated from available data.

17. In deriving the weights of the elementary aggregates, a household expenditure survey is usually the main source of data. As far as resources permit, such surveys should be representative of household size, income level, regional location, socio-economic group and any other factors which may have a bearing on household expenditure patterns. The period of the survey should be a normal one (or temporary abnormalities should be adjusted in determining the weighting pattern) and should preferably cover a whole year if seasonal variations in expenditure patterns are important. When inflation during the period has been rapid and/or has differed significantly between expenditure groups, either expenditure for the different subperiods should be valued at the prices of a common time subperiod or the expenditure proportions of different subperiods should be averaged over the period, in the absence of any superior method.

18. Surveys of sales in retail outlets and household surveys on point-of-purchase can provide valuable information concerning the breakdown of consumption by outlet-type and by region. In the absence of such surveys, it is sometimes preferable for statisticians to use their personal knowledge of the markets and their nature rather than to apply equal weights to the different outlets or types of outlets and/or to different regions.

19. In countries which have reliable information concerning components of the household final consumption expenditure of the national accounts, such information can sometimes be used to derive an initial aggregate weighting pattern. In centrally planned economies in particular, retail sales data may be a major source of weights. More detailed data from household expenditure surveys can be used to break down the aggregates or to adjust the figures to relate more closely to the reference population.

20. In countries where data from household expenditure surveys are not available and where the data on the components of the household final consumption expenditure of the national accounts are inadequate, data from various surveys such as of production, export and import and retail trade, and from administrative sources may have to be used to obtain an estimated consumption pattern.

21. Before any of the survey results are used to provide weights for the index, it is necessary to examine them carefully, e.g. in the light of the sampling and non-sampling errors, in order to judge whether the survey has provided reliable and representative information. Adjustments should be made, if necessary, using other available statistics.

22. Analysis of the data to show the expenditure patterns for different regions and categories of the population is useful, both to assist in revealing those categories for which the computation of separate consumer price indices may be warranted and for establishing the elementary aggregates and their weights.

23. The weights should be examined periodically, and particularly if economic circumstances have changed significantly, to ascertain whether they still reflect current expenditure or consumption patterns. The weights should be revised or adjusted if the review shows that this is not the case. In any case, they should be revised at least once every ten years.

24. Whenever the composition and/or weighting pattern of the index is changed, the new index should be linked to the old index to provide a continuous series of index numbers.

Sampling for price collection

25. Sampling of goods and services and of outlets is necessary to decide what prices should be collected and where they should be collected for each elementary aggregate (except in cases of centrally determined and uniform prices). Sample selection methods and sizes should be adequate to provide the accuracy required for the objectives of the index.

26. Efforts should be made to ensure that samples of cities, urban areas or regions, of dwelling units, of sales outlets, and of items and varieties priced are as representative as possible. Probability sampling, although involving difficult practical problems, will normally enhance the accuracy of the index and, moreover, will make possible an estimate of the sampling error.

27. Probability sampling gives every price within the scope of the index an opportunity for selection. Each price need not have an equal probability of selection. Indeed, efficient designs use probabilities that are proportional to variables that affect the precision of the estimates.

28. Implementation of probability sampling may be a gradual process. Where one begins will vary depending on the nature of the economic structure and the availability of data. Probability sampling might begin with geographic areas, or with detailed items within larger groups, or with outlets. Each stage of probability sampling makes some contribution to the quality of the indices.

29. If sufficient information or resources do not exist for constructing a probability sample which will give a good measure of price change, then the statistician should apply the best judgement and available data to select a representative sample of geographical areas, outlets, items and varieties. If, for example, resources are inadequate to establish a representative sample for the country as a whole, it might be appropriate to decide, in principle and *a priori* (that is, outside any random sampling), that certain regions, towns or urban areas where the collection of prices is less expensive represent larger groups of regions, towns or urban areas.

30. The samples of outlets and of goods and services and the specifications used for pricing should be reviewed periodically, and they should be updated if this is necessary to maintain their representativeness.

31. Particular attention should be paid to the way in which pricing is distributed in time. Price observations of the same item at the same outlet should, especially in the case of wide price variations, be made at regular intervals of, for example, about one month or three months, depending upon the frequency of the index compilation. Account should be taken of the fact that, when the index collection period is organised on the basis of weeks, there may be time discrepancies since a month or quarter is not composed of an exact number of weeks.

32. In the case of perishable goods, attention should also be paid to the time of day which is selected for price collection.

33. Rents should be obtained from a specially designed survey relating to a sample of dwellings which is periodically updated to ensure continuing representativeness and, particularly, that newly constructed units are brought into the sample.

The price data

34. The quality of the price data is the crucial determinant of the reliability of the index. Hence, great care should be taken to ensure that the prices obtained are actual transaction prices and are collected systematically at regular intervals. Standard methods for collecting and processing price data should be developed. Where centrally regulated or centrally fixed prices are collected centrally, checks should be made to ascertain whether the goods and services in question are indeed sold and whether these prices are in fact observed. Where prices are not displayed, where quantity units are poorly defined or where actual purchase prices may deviate from list or fixed prices, check purchases by the price collectors are advisable and a budget should be provided for these purchases. Where prices are subject to significant fluctuations over the month or quarter, it is desirable to collect them more than once during the month or quarter.

35. Consistent procedures should be established for dealing with missing price observations whatever the cause, including: seasonally unavailable, unable to contact, non-response, rejected observation, temporarily out of stock. Price collectors should be well trained and well supervised, and should be provided with a good manual explaining all the procedures they have to follow. The price data sent in by the price collectors should be reviewed and edited for comparability, substitutions, unusual or simply large price changes and for price conversions of goods priced in multiple units or varying quantities, where the units or quantities do not form part of the specification. There should be procedures, such as repricing in the same outlets, for checking the reliability of the price data.

36. The specifications used for pricing, including the final selection of the particular variety and size by the price collector where relevant, serve the purpose of securing comparability between successive periods and assisting selection and evaluation of substitutes. The specifications should be precise enough to identify all the characteristics that are necessary to ensure that identical goods and services are priced in successive periods in the same outlet. It should be noted that the relevant characteristics of the goods or services should include, for example, terms of payment, conditions of delivery, guarantees and type of outlet.

37. Substitutions will be necessary when priced items disappear permanently from the outlet(s) in which they are priced. An item which is no longer available in sufficient quantities or under normal sale conditions may also be considered to be unavailable. Clear and precise rules should be developed for identifying the substitute item. Precise procedures should be laid down for price adjustment with respect to the difference in characteristics when substitutions are necessary. Responsibility for such evaluation should be clearly established. Evaluations of the difference in characteristics and decisions on how to use substitute prices in the index should, to the extent possible, be based on solid, empirical evidence of the market valuation of the difference in characteristics between the original and the substitute items. A number of techniques and data sources may be used to approximate this market valuation. In the absence of a satisfactory estimate of the specific adjustment for the difference in characteristics, a choice must be made between an assumption of no change and an assumption that the price difference is simply and wholly a reflection of the difference in characteristics. Under the former assumption, the price for the substitute should be compared directly with that of the item for which it is substituted; this assumption can be made only when the items are fairly similar. Where the whole price difference is taken as a reflection of the difference in characteristics, the index should be constructed by linking the series for the substitute to that of the item for which it is substituted.

38. Substitutions made because of a decline in representativeness or disappearance of an item from an outlet might possibly require that another outlet be chosen. This might also be necessary when an outlet disappears. In these cases, rules should be established to ensure that the price collector makes a correct choice with respect to a new outlet, and that the adjustments are made, if need be, to take account of the change in outlet or the change in the nature of the outlet. The rules should be consistent with the objectives of the index and with the way in which the price collection sample has been determined.

39. Substitutions will also be necessary if all items in an elementary aggregate disappear from most or all outlets. In such cases, if a substitute item representing the elementary aggregate cannot be found and appropriate adjustments for the difference in characteristics made, it may be necessary to redistribute the weight assigned to the elementary aggregate among other elementary aggregates within the next highest level of aggregation possible.

40. The prices to be collected are the regular actual transaction prices, including indirect taxes, paid by the reference population. Prices charged for stale, shop-soiled, damaged, or otherwise imperfect goods sold at clearance prices should be excluded unless they are a permanent and widespread feature of market conditions. However, sale prices, discounts, cut prices and special offers should be included when applicable to all customers and when the goods and services are offered in their normal availability.

41. Prices should be collected in all types of markets which are important. These may include open-markets and black-markets as well as state-controlled markets. Where more than one type of market is important, an appropriately weighted average should be used in the calculation of the index.

42. In periods of price control or rationing, where limited supplies are available at prices which are held low by subsidies to the sellers, by government procurement, by price control, etc., these prices as well as those charged on unrestricted markets should be collected. They should be combined in a way which uses the best information available with respect to the actual prices paid and the relative importance of the different types of sales.

43. Countries may wish to calculate, from the data collected for their consumer price index, average prices for selected reasonably homogeneous goods or services. However, their dissemination should be accompanied by an indication of the limitations of these calculations. Countries may also wish to establish efforts to collect separate data to support average price calculations, given considerable user interest in these data.

Dissemination

44. A consumer price index should be computed and publicly released as quickly as possible according to the resources available and to the user needs, preferably at least once every three months. Rules relating to the release of the data should be established, publicly known and strictly observed.

45. In general, retrospective corrections (e.g. as a result of an error in the data or in calculation) of the publicly released indices should only be done when absolutely necessary because of the difficulties such corrections cause for indexed contracts or payments. Instead, necessary corrections might be made to the index for the subsequent period. An explanation should be provided in order to avoid misinterpretation of the short-term price movement.

46. Sub-indices should also be released, at least for such major expenditure groups as food, clothing and footwear, housing, etc. Sub-indices for different regions or socio-economic groups or for special analytical purposes (e.g. travellers' expenses, imported items) might be publicly released if they were judged to be useful and the cost warranted it. Average prices or price ranges for important and reasonably homogeneous items may be released.

47. The exclusion of shelter from the all-items index makes the rates of price change more comparable across countries, although it does not eliminate all the difficulties encountered when making such comparisons. Countries should, therefore, provide for dissemination at the international level of an index which excludes shelter, in addition to the all-items index.

48. In order to ensure public confidence in the index, a full description of the methodology and data sources should be published. The document(s) should include, among other things, details of the weights, objectives of the index, and a discussion of the precision of the index. However, the precise identities of the outlets and goods and services for which prices are obtained and any other details which, if disclosed, would adversely affect the representativeness of the index should, in general, not be revealed.

49. The agency responsible for the index should consult with representatives of users on major issues. One way of organising such consultation is through the establishment of advisory committee(s) on which users and outside experts might be represented.

Appendix 2

The measurement of liability insurance premium trends and their inclusion in the French consumer price index

Summary

As the main users of the French consumer price index are national accountants (constant price accounts) and economic analysts, it was decided to apply the concepts of household consumption in national accounts in developing this index.

With regard to liability insurance, in the "household consumption" aggregate of national accounts, account is taken only of the service provided by insurance companies, which corresponds roughly to the difference between the total of premiums collected by such companies and the total indemnities paid in compensation to households.

Accordingly, the insurance item, if included in the index, would have a very limited weighting, so that its influence on the general index would be very small. Consequently, in 1970, INSEE decided to exclude this item from the new consumer price index which it was developing.

Nevertheless, work is currently in progress on a specific index of trends in automobile insurance premium rates. The main difficulties in developing such an index stem from the fact that information is hard to come by – it is necessary to refer to actual policies, since the rates posted by insurance companies often differ significantly from those charged in practice – that the products proposed are very numerous and that to monitor a single product over a period of time is a tricky undertaking, since it presumes that the characteristics of the vehicle, the driver and the associated risks remain constant, which in reality is generally not the case.

Extension to other types of insurance and the inclusion of insurance indices in the monthly index are very long-term possibilities.

Following a preliminary survey of two companies at the end of 1984, it was decided to use a simplified methodology.

The realm of automobile insurance is divided into strata within which contract clauses can be considered homogeneous, with rates varying only slightly.

First, a random sample of companies is chosen. Secondly, it is agreed that each strata will be represented by a standard, widely used product the premium rates of which will be monitored over a period of time. As for the majority of products included in the consumer price index, it is the trends in the premium rates of the standard products that will represent the premium rate trend for the corresponding stratum.

For each standard product, the basic indicator of the premium rate trend from the base year to year x is the relationship between the average premium rates recorded in year x for policies selected at random in that year and the average of the premium rates recorded in the base year.

In order to arrive at consolidated indices of the trend in premium rates at higher levels of aggregation (by type of risk, by company, overall, etc.), the basic indices for each standard product are weighted using weighting factors proportional to the value of the premium rates paid in the base period in the strata to which the corresponding standard products belong.

A group of 72 standard cases has been contemplated. Fourteen insurance companies will be chosen to represent the French market and almost 7,200 policies and 300 rates will be examined each year.

Le problème de la mesure de l'évolution des primes d'assurance de dommages et de son introduction dans l'indice des prix à la consommation français *

Introduction: indice des prix et comptabilité nationale

A la fin des années soixante, lorsqu'on a envisagé le lancement d'un nouvel indice des prix à la consommation, une décision a dû être prise quant au choix entre l'utilisation de concepts spécifiques à l'indicateur et la référence à des concepts déjà existants.

L'examen des méthodes utilisées dans le cadre des indices antérieurs, qui avaient été définies par une démarche relativement empirique (chaque problème était résolu en fonction d'un objectif, certes précis mais non formalisé, et selon des méthodes pas forcément prévues à l'avance), avait montré qu'avec le temps on avait abouti à un système de définitions assez proche de celui utilisé par les comptables nationaux pour caractériser et prendre en compte la consommation des ménages.

Les principaux utilisateurs de l'indice des prix étant les comptables nationaux (comptes à prix constants) et les conjoncturistes, on a donc tout naturellement décidé d'abandonner la méthode empirique du choix des définitions pour se référer aux concepts de la consommation des ménages dans les comptes nationaux avec, éventuellement, certaines adaptations particulières liées soit à l'autre utilisation des indices (conjoncture), soit à des difficultés de collecte, de calcul ou de significativité de la mesure. Par exemple, on a exclu du champ du nouvel indice l'autoconsommation et les loyers fictifs.

En ce qui concerne les assurances de dommages, on ne prend en considération dans la consommation finale des ménages que le service rendu par les compagnies d'assurances pour gérer les dossiers de leurs assurés et effectuer les transferts entre les ménages payant les primes et les ménages sinistrés. En s'en tenant strictement à cette pratique — qui revient grosso modo à chiffrer ces services rendus comme étant la différence entre le montant total des primes perçues et la somme des indemnités versées — l'indice que l'on pouvait envisager avait un caractère aléatoire et peu significatif. En outre, une difficulté supplémentaire de préhension de l'information réside dans le fait qu'en France la plupart des sociétés d'assurances n'appliquent généralement pas à leurs assurés les tarifs qu'elles annoncent. On ne peut pas, comme dans certains pays étrangers, se contenter de mesurer l'évolution des prix des tarifs «affichés»; il faut donc descendre jusqu'au niveau des polices.

Compte tenu de ces difficultés pratiques de mise en œuvre et de la faible pondération de ce service, l'INSEE avait décidé, en 1970, d'exclure ce poste du nouvel indice des prix, jugeant qu'inclure celui-ci ne pourrait avoir qu'un effet très faible sur les mouvements de l'indice d'ensemble, alors que les coûts d'observation et de calcul seraient particulièrement élevés.

Dès 1973, dans un avis rendu sur l'indice des prix, le Conseil économique et social [1] avait demandé qu'un indice spécifique des primes d'assurance soit calculé sans pour autant être incorporé dans l'indice d'ensemble.

Les difficultés d'ordre méthodologique et le coût financier et humain de l'investissement initial étaient tels que l'INSEE ne put donner suite à cette demande.

En 1982, le ministre de l'Economie, des Finances et du Budget a demandé à l'INSEE que la question soit réexaminée. Aussi l'institut a-t-il soumis en juin 1983 au Conseil national de la statistique [2] un premier projet d'indice temporel des primes d'assurance de dommages.

---

* Rapport de M. A. Marret, de l'Institut national de la statistique et des études économiques de la France (INSEE), présenté au Séminaire CEE-OIT sur les statistiques des prix à la consommation.

[1] Le Conseil économique et social est une assemblée consultative composée de personnalités qualifiées dans les domaines économique, social, scientifique et culturel, et de représentants des partenaires socio-économiques. Saisi par le gouvernement ou se saisissant lui-même, il peut donner son avis sur tout projet de loi, de décret, proposition de loi ou tout problème de caractère économique et social.

Il assure ainsi la participation des différentes catégories professionnelles à la politique économique et social du gouvernement.

[2] Le Conseil national de l'information statistique dont l'INSEE assure le secrétariat, composé également de personnalités qualifiées dans le domaine de la statistique et de l'économie, et de représentants des partenaires sociaux, donne un avis sur les programmes à moyen terme d'enquêtes statistiques du secteur public et fournit un visa pour les enquêtes retenues, leur conférant ainsi un caractère obligatoire.

Sur la base de ce projet, un groupe de travail a été constitué entre l'INSEE et la Direction des assurances du ministère de l'Economie, des Finances et du Budget [1] pour mettre au point la méthodologie d'élaboration de cet indicateur.

L'objet de ce papier est de décrire l'indicateur auquel le groupage de travail a abouti. Mais avant de donner certains détails relatifs à celui-ci, il a paru utile de situer l'assurance dans le contexte général des dépenses des ménages, puis de donner un aperçu des problèmes conceptuels, méthodologiques et pratiques dont la solution a conduit à l'indicateur finalement adopté.

I. Quelques données globales

Sur les 182,5 milliards de francs de chiffre d'affaires (hors taxes) réalisés par les sociétés d'assurances en 1983, le total des primes versées par les particuliers et les entreprises a atteint 160,5 milliards (hors taxes) et 175,8 milliards (toutes taxes comprises). Sur ce total de 175,8 milliards on a estimé [2] que les primes versées par les ménages s'élevaient à 116 milliards (toutes taxes comprises), dont 69,7 milliards pour les assurances dommages (30,3 milliards pour l'automobile) et 46,3 milliards pour les assurances vie et capitalisation.

D'après le compte semi-définitif des ménages de 1983, le service rendu par les sociétés d'assurances – qui, rappelons-le, est le seul élément retenu dans la consommation des ménages – s'élevait à 22,4 milliards (soit 0,9 pour cent de la consommation totale des ménages), dont 8,5 milliards pour l'automobile (0,3 pour cent) et 4,8 milliards pour l'assurance habitation (0,19 pour cent).

Il est également possible d'évaluer la part des primes d'assurance dans l'ensemble des dépenses de consommation à partir de l'enquête sur les budgets familiaux de 1978-79: à la date de l'enquête, les montants des primes d'assurance versées représentaient 3 pour cent des dépenses de consommation des ménages, dont 1,6 pour cent pour l'assurance automobile et 0,6 pour cent pour l'assurance habitation.

II. Problèmes méthodologiques

II.1. Indice des primes et comptes nationaux

Ainsi qu'il a été mentionné plus haut, une inclusion des assurances de dommages dans l'indice mensuel des prix à la consommation impliquerait, pour rester cohérent avec les conventions de la comptabilité nationale, de ne prendre en compte que les services rendus par les sociétés d'assurances: pour le dommage, solde entre les primes versées aux sociétés et les indemnités versées par elles. Il paraît conceptuellement très difficile de définir correctement un indice de prix relatif à ce solde, surtout à un rythme infra-annuel. En fait, le partage volume-prix dans l'évolution de la valeur nominale de ces services est quasiment impossible à réaliser [3].

Il paraît en revanche plus aisé de définir un indice du prix des primes, c'est-à-dire un indice du prix des primes payées corrigé des variations des risques couverts (indice des primes «à risque constant»).

Son introduction dans l'indice mensuel nécessiterait de lui affecter un poids correspondant au montant total des primes payées par les ménages au cours d'une année (cela exigerait également, pour certains usages de l'indice, d'augmenter les ressources des ménages des indemnités perçues). Mais alors, et souvent au cours d'une même année, on compterait deux fois en dépense des ménages l'achat de certains biens et services (pièces détachées de véhicules, main-d'œuvre pour réparation), une fois dans la prime et une fois dans l'achat direct du ménage. Les indices de prix correspondant à ces produits et prestations seraient donc très fortement surpondérés dans l'indice

---

[1] La Direction des assurances est une direction du ministère de l'Economie et des Finances qui a pour mission de veiller au bon fonctionnement des sociétés d'assurances et à une rédaction correcte des conditions générales des polices d'assurance. Elle exerce notamment un contrôle sur les tarifs pratiqués par ces sociétés.

[2] Il n'existe en effet aucune statistique sur la ventilation des primes selon les différentes catégories d'agents.

[3] Le problème du changement des caractéristiques d'un bien est une des difficultés majeures auxquelles se heurte l'établissement d'un indice de prix; au changement de caractéristiques est associée une «juste» modification de valeur du bien qui ne doit pas être prise en compte comme une modification de prix. En déterminer le montant est souvent chose délicate, mais le faire dans le cas de l'assurance est particulièrement difficile. Il faut essayer de déterminer quelle aurait été l'évolution des prix des primes lorsque toutes les caractéristiques du produit «assurance» restent constantes, et notamment les risques couverts, d'où la mise sur pied d'un indicateur d'évolution des primes «à risque constant».

d'ensemble. L'inclusion des primes d'assurance dans l'indice mensuel ne pourrait donc se faire qu'au prix d'une modification des principes des comptes et, pour certains usages, de l'augmentation des revenus des ménages de certaines indemnités versées par les compagnies d'assurances.

II.2. Qu'entend-on par «risque constant»?

Un problème d'une tout autre nature peut s'opposer à l'inclusion dans l'indice mensuel: il s'agit de la définition du «risque constant» [5]. Ce «risque constant» peut se définir *ex ante*, c'est-à-dire sur la base des estimations faites pour la période à venir couverte par la prime payée; il peut se définir aussi *ex post*, c'est-à-dire sur la base des sinistres effectivement constatés au cours de la période couverte par la prime.

Cette seconde solution apparaît la meilleure pour une évaluation correcte du risque couvert, mais elle implique de longs délais pour l'obtention de l'information, sauf si étaient trouvés des indicateurs rapides permettant d'estimer à chaque instant le risque *ex post*. Cette dernière remarque n'est pour le moment, tout au moins en France, qu'une hypothèse d'école: la situation dans notre pays est telle que le risque «effectif» est connu avec un délai non compatible avec le calcul, dans des délais raisonnables, de l'indice mensuel des prix d'une période donnée.

L'indice de la prime brute d'un mois donné ne pourrait donc être corrigé pour obtenir un indice «à risque constant» qu'avec un grand retard par rapport au mois considéré, ce qui empêcherait d'inclure les primes d'assurance dans l'indice mensuel qui ne peut être révisé a posteriori (en raison notamment des clauses d'indexation figurant dans certains contrats).

Aussi a-t-il été décidé, dans un premier temps, d'élaborer deux indices spécifiques annuels, publiés à part de l'indice général des prix, en se limitant aux dépenses d'assurance automobile des ménages:

— un indicateur d'évolution du prix des primes effectivement payées par les ménages, à caractéristiques constantes des contrats souscrits;
— un indice d'évolution des primes calculé «à risque constant».

La prise en compte des autres dépenses d'assurance des ménages (habitation, vie) et l'inclusion des indices relatifs à l'assurance dans l'indice mensuel ne sont envisagés qu'à très long terme.

La limitation à l'assurance automobile s'explique par la facilité relative (par rapport aux autres types d'assurances de dommages) de définition du «risque constant».

III. Méthode retenue pour l'élaboration des indices spécifiques par le groupe de travail INSEE-Direction des assurances

Deux méthodes étaient envisageables:

— effectuer des enquêtes régulières auprès d'un échantillon représentatif des ménages détenteurs d'une assurance automobile en leur demandant de présenter à l'enquêteur leur police d'assurance et d'indiquer les primes payées l'année de l'enquête et l'année précédente;
— tirer aléatoirement des polices d'assurance automobile dans un échantillon représentatif de sociétés et relever pour chaque police tirée ses caractéristiques ainsi que celles du souscripteur et des utilisateurs du véhicule, l'évolution de ces caractéristiques d'une année sur l'autre et, bien entendu, les primes payées pour l'année en cours et l'année précédente.

La seconde méthode a été retenue car elle présente l'avantage de pouvoir être mise en œuvre plus rapidement et d'être a priori d'un coût plus faible. Elle implique cependant une coopération importante des sociétés sélectionnées avec des difficultés techniques non négligeables:

— difficultés d'accès aux polices en raison des diversités des principes de gestion et stockage (manuel ou informatique) des polices suivant les sociétés;
— difficultés pour passer de la police à l'assuré et au risque. Une police peut en effet correspondre à plusieurs véhicules (flotte) ou à plusieurs risques (automobile, habitation);
— difficultés d'appariement des polices d'une année sur l'autre.

III.1. La méthodologie de départ

Sans entrer dans le détail, on peut préciser que le tirage des polices s'effectue à deux degrés:

— 1er degré: tirage d'un échantillon représentatif de compagnies d'assurances et de mutuelles, avec des probabilités inégales, proportionnelles aux chiffres d'affaires relatifs à la branche automobile des compagnies;

— 2e degré: définition pour chaque société choisie de catégories pertinentes de strates selon des critères relatifs aux assurés, aux types de véhicules, aux types de contrats souscrits, puis tirage aléatoire, dans chaque strate ainsi définie, des polices selon un taux de sondage préalablement fixé mais pouvant être différent d'une strate à l'autre (de l'ordre de 1/1000 en moyenne).

L'indicateur d'évolution de la prime payée par les ménages (indicateur élémentaire) entre les années $n - 1$ et n est d'abord calculé au niveau de chaque strate comme le rapport entre la prime moyenne payée l'année n et la prime moyenne payée l'année $n - 1$ par les souscripteurs des polices retenues. Il faut bien entendu s'assurer auparavant, pour chaque police, que les caractéristiques relatives au souscripteur, aux utilisateurs du véhicule et aux risques couverts n'ont pas varié entre $n - 1$ et n. Si elles ont varié, il faut recalculer pour l'année n (ou pour l'année $n - 1$) la prime qu'aurait payée le souscripteur «à caractéristiques constantes» et prendre en compte cette nouvelle prime dans le calcul de l'indicateur à la place de la prime effectivement payée.

L'indicateur global d'évolution des primes payées par les ménages est alors obtenu classiquement comme moyenne pondérée des indicateurs élémentaires.

Le mode de détermination des coefficients de pondération n'est pas encore défini avec précision (il dépend en particulier de la méthode de sondage et, bien entendu, des données disponibles).

III.2. Le test de la méthodologie

Compte tenu de l'importance du travail – de 15 000 à 20 000 polices ont été retenues, afin d'obtenir suffisamment de polices dans chaque strate – et des moyens à mettre en œuvre (notamment dans les sociétés d'assurances selectionnées), il a été décidé de faire précéder l'enquête en vraie grandeur par un test à caractère monographique et documentaire auprès de trois sociétés (une compagnie nationalisée, une mutuelle [1] et une autre société avec intermédiaire). Cette préenquête a eu lieu au dernier trimestre 1984 dans deux sociétés d'assurances. Par manque de temps, on n'a pas retenu la «mutuelle».

Dans chacune de ces sociétés, deux dossiers ont été examinés dans chacune de 96 strates, préalablement définies de manière à être représentatives des principaux risques – soit environ 400 dossiers au total.

Une grille d'analyse a été mise au point pour relever toutes les informations relatives aux caractéristiques à n et $n - 1$ des contrats, des véhicules, des souscripteurs et des utilisateurs des véhicules. Ont été relevées également les primes payées les années n et $n - 1$ et calculées les primes qu'auraient payées les souscripteurs «à caractéristiques inchangées» les années n et $n - 1$. Enfin les primes réellement payées étant parfois très différentes des barèmes affichés par les sociétés, ont été également calculées les primes qu'auraient payées les souscripteurs les années n et $n - 1$ par application des barèmes affichés par les compagnies.

A l'issue de cette préenquête, achevée à fin 1984, il s'est avéré que la méthode retenue impliquait un temps important de préhension de l'information: une heure environ par police. Il fallait en effet recueillir toute l'information nécessaire pour décomposer le prix total de la prime payée l'année n en ses diverses composantes relatives aux différents types de risques et surtout reconstituer toute l'information relative à la même police pour l'année $n - 1$ de façon à conserver d'une année sur l'autre des caractéristiques et des risques assurés constants pour le véhicule ainsi que pour le souscripteur et les utilisateurs.

Par exemple, si un conducteur était conducteur novice l'année $n - 1$ (obtention du permis de conduire moins de deux ans auparavant), ce qui implique une surprime importante, et devenait conducteur «normal» l'année n, il fallait recalculer quel aurait été le coût de sa prime s'il avait été conducteur normal l'année $n - 1$.

En outre, dans beaucoup de cas, il est difficile de déterminer des principes de partage entre volume et prix dans l'évolution des primes. Lorsqu'un conducteur passe, d'une année sur l'autre, d'un bonus [2] de 10 pour cent à un bonus de 15 pour cent et si de ce fait sa prime diminue, doit-on

---

[1] En France, les sociétés d'assurances sont classées en trois groupes selon leur nature juridique. L'un de ces trois groupes est constitué des mutuelles, ayant comme caractéristiques principales d'être réservées à certaines professions (enseignants, artisans). Les tarifs pratiqués par ces mutuelles ne diffèrent pas des tarifs annoncés et sont en général moins élevés que ceux des autres groupes de sociétés.

[2] Lorsqu'un conducteur n'a pas été reconnu responsable d'un accident au cours d'une année, les sociétés d'assurances lui accordent pour l'année suivante une réduction sur sa prime appelée «bonus».

considérer cette diminution comme une baisse de prix ou comme un changement de caractéristiques du conducteur (modification de volume)?

Aussi s'est-on orienté vers une méthode simplifiée de calcul d'un indicateur spécifique d'évolution des primes d'assurance automobile «à risque constant».

III.3. La méthode finalement proposée

On divise toujours l'univers de l'assurance automobile en strates ou classes à l'intérieur desquelles les clauses des contrats peuvent être considérées comme relativement homogènes et les prix des primes sont susceptibles de présenter une relativement faible variabilité.

On choisit, toujours au hasard, dans une première étape, un échantillon représentatif de sociétés.

Mais, lors de la seconde étape, au lieu de tirer dans chaque société choisie, et dans chaque strate, un échantillon de police et de rechercher, pour chacune des polices tirées, l'information relative à l'année précédente, on convient que chaque strate sera représentée par un «produit type» de large diffusion dont le prix des primes sera suivi au cours du temps. Comme pour la majorité des produits entrant dans l'indice mensuel des prix à la consommation, ce sont les évolutions des prix des primes de ces produits types qui «représenteront» l'évolution des prix des primes des strates correspondantes. La définition de ces «produits types» devra être suffisamment précise pour que la strate soit bien représentée, les clauses soient relativement homogènes et qu'un suivi puisse être assuré au cours du temps.

Par exemple, la strate: «fonctionnaire, conducteur »normal«, assuré pour la responsabilité civile, circulant dans une grande agglomération dans une voiture de plus de huit chevaux fiscaux» pourrait être représentée par un «conducteur, salarié de la fonction publique, âgé de plus de vingt-cinq ans, ayant son permis depuis plus de deux ans, ayant 20 pour cent de bonus, circulant dans l'agglomération parisienne dans une 505 Peugeot».

Le principal avantage de cette nouvelle méthode est une beaucoup plus grande rapidité de préhension de l'information. Il suffit en effet, une fois définis «les produits types», de rechercher dans chaque société d'assurances retenue, pour chaque «produit type», un échantillon de polices répondant à sa définition et de calculer le prix moyen des primes correspondantes. En effectuant la même opération l'année suivante, on obtient un nouvel échantillon – indépendant de l'échantillon obtenu l'année précédente –, pour lequel on calcule encore le prix moyen des primes payées pour chaque produit type. Il n'y a plus alors de problèmes de comparaison à «risques et caractéristiques constants» d'une année sur l'autre puisqu'ils sont inclus dans les spécifications des produits types et que les échantillons sont renouvelés chaque année.

Pour chaque «produit type», l'indicateur élémentaire d'évolution du prix de la prime entre l'année de base et l'année *a* sera le rapport entre la moyenne des prix des primes observés l'année *a* des polices tirées au sort cette année et le prix moyen des prix des primes observés l'année de base des polices tirées au sort l'année de base. C'est cet indicateur qui représentera l'évolution des prix des primes correspondant à la strate où a été choisi le produit type.

Pour obtenir des indices synthétiques d'évolution à des niveaux d'agrégation plus élevés (par type de risque, par compagnie) on pondérera les indices élémentaires des «produits types» par des coefficients de pondération qui dépendront de la méthode de sondage; en général, ils seront proportionnels à la valeur des primes payées à la période de base dans les strates auxquelles appartiennent les «produits types» correspondants. Pour la détermination des coefficients de pondération à appliquer aux indices élémentaires, les informations fournies par les sociétés d'assurances ne seront pas suffisantes et il conviendrait de préhender cette information auprès des ménages (par exemple en adjoignant plusieurs questions spécifiques au cours d'une enquête habituelle).

Un groupe de 72 cas types a été envisagé, avec trois modalités pour les risques, deux modalités par type de véhicule, deux modalités par type d'agglomération, deux modalités par profession et trois modalités par type de conducteur. Quatorze compagnies d'assurances et mutuelles seraient choisies pour représenter le marché de l'assurance automobile français.

Pour les quatre mutuelles de cet échantillon de quatorze sociétés, il suffit de relever chaque année les tarifs correspondant à chacun des 72 cas types retenus.

Pour les dix compagnies d'assurances restantes, dix polices seront tirées aléatoirement pour chaque cas type, car les prix réellement pratiqués sont parfois très différents des tarifs affichés.

D'où un total de 7 200 polices à examiner chaque année dans les dix compagnies et 288 tarifs à relever chaque année auprès des quatre mutuelles.

Conclusion

La mise en œuvre d'un indicateur spécifique d'évolution des primes d'assurance automobile «à risque constant» se heurte à de nombreuses difficultés d'ordre méthodologique: détermination des pondérations, partage volume-prix de l'évolution des primes, prise en compte des changements de caractéristiques du conducteur, du véhicule ou des risques couverts et pratiques (difficultés de préhension de l'information, nécessité d'assurer le concours de sociétés d'assurances participant à cette opération). En outre, si de nombreuses pressions se font jour pour l'élaboration d'un tel indicateur, certains organismes se montrent réticents vis-à-vis de ce projet.

De ce fait, il n'est guère envisageable d'obtenir les premiers résultats avant fin 1987. Par la suite, si cette première expérience se révélait positive, on pourrait envisager d'étendre cet indicateur à l'assurance habitation.

Appendix 3

Adjusting the CPI for indirect taxes*

In some countries a need has been felt to adjust the consumer price index in order either to exclude indirect taxes altogether or to exclude changes in indirect taxes, so producing a "net price index". This article examines only the technical issues involved in making such adjustments and does not discuss the uses of such an adjusted index. It thus considers how such adjustment can be made, both examining the general principles involved and describing some of the details of the way it is done or proposed to be done in five countries.[1]

It turns out that there are six major combinations of ways in which such adjustment can be specified. The adjustment may exclude indirect taxes altogether resulting in a "tax-free" index, or it may exclude only the change in them since the base period thus producing a "constant tax" index. In the latter case, change and constancy may be defined either in terms of rates or in terms of amount. In either case, the adjustment may cover only the last stages in the chain of production and distribution, thus relating only to taxes on final expenditure, or alternatively it may cover all stages, thus also covering indirect taxes embodied in the prices of intermediate inputs used in the production of final consumer goods and services. These six combinations are set out below where

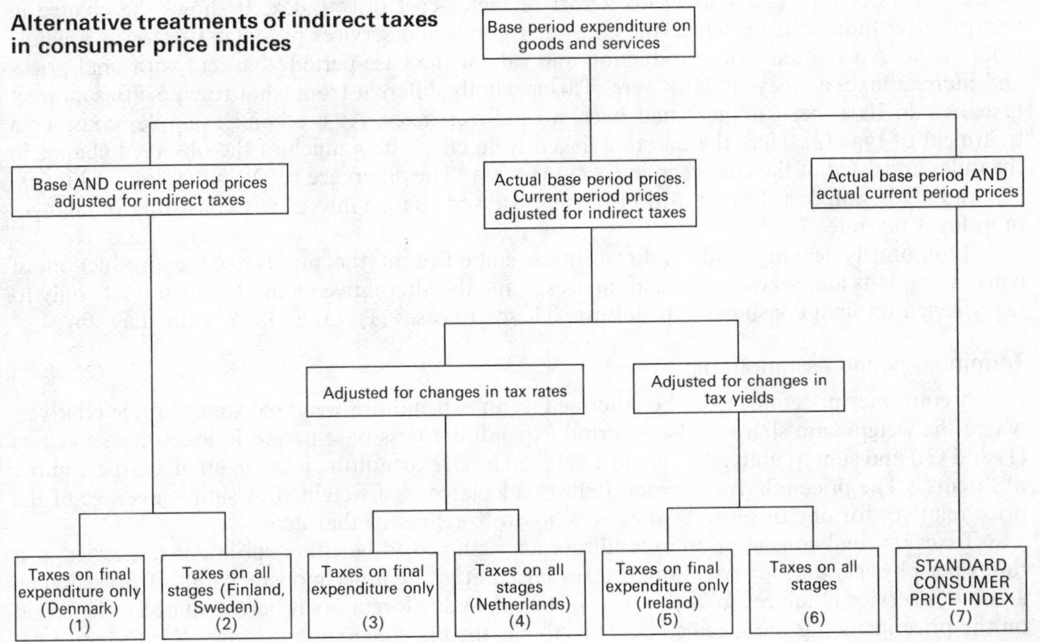

* The authors of this article are H. W. J. Donkers (Netherlands Central Bureau of Statistics), J. Bjerregaard Jensen (Danmarks Statistik), J. Hyrkkö and T. Lehtinen (Central Statistical Office of Finland), D. C. Murphy (Central Statistical Office, Ireland), G. Stolpe (Statistics Sweden) and R. Turvey (ILO, Bureau of Statistics).

[1] The five countries are Denmark, Sweden, Finland, Ireland and the Netherlands. For more detailed descriptions of the adjustments used in Finland and the Netherlands see: Hyrkkö and Lehtinen: *Net Price Index 1977*, Central Statistical Office of Finland, Studies No. 86, 1983; and Balk and Donkers: "Adjusting the consumer price index for changes of the rates of indirect taxes and subsidies", in *Statistical Journal of the United Nations*, ECE, 1 (1982), pp. 157-170.

case (7) on the right hand side of the diagram depicts the standard consumer price index without any adjustment. Note that case (3) would not differ from (5), or case (4) from (6), if all indirect taxes were specific, since in that event constant rates would mean constant yields.

In cases (1) and (2), the adjusted index equals a weighted average of the standard index (7) and an index of indirect taxes, weighted respectively by base-period expenditure and by *minus* that part of base-period expenditure consisting of indirect taxes. The indirect tax index relates the tax component of the current value of the base-period "basket" to the tax component of that basket's base period value.

Indirect taxes are taken to include subsidies as negative indirect taxes. There is no point in attempting to provide any general definition of what is covered by these terms. Which of them are in practice adjusted for in any particular country will depend upon the purposes to be served by the adjusted index, upon economic and political circumstances specific to that country and upon the availability of data. Thus customs duties with a protectionist motive have never been deducted in calculating the Danish net price index, mainly because of the practical difficulties in distinguishing between countries of origin for products when prices are being collected. But for a number of years the revenue duties on certain products supplied exclusively by import, such as wine, tea and coffee, were deducted. After the entry into a larger economic community this distinction could not be maintained, however, and today no customs duties are deducted. Finland allows for all items counted as indirect taxes or subsidies in the national accounts. Here we examine the methods of adjustment rather than their scope.

It is important to note that in speaking of methods of adjustment we are examining methods of economic accounting rather than methods of economic analysis, since nothing will be asserted about causality. What would have happened if indirect taxes had not existed or if they had not changed are questions that can only be answered, if at all, by econometric models of the whole economy. What is involved here is far less ambitious. Thus consider, for example, a treatment of indirect taxes of type (2). This yields a sort of factor-cost price index. It shows the change in receipts after indirect taxes which the consumer goods and services producing sector as a whole would have experienced from production and sale of the base-period "basket" with final prices and indirect taxes as they actually were. This is wholly different from what receipts after indirect taxes would have been if there had been no indirect taxes. As a second example, consider a treatment of type (3). Here the question asked is, in effect, how much of the observed change in the index consisted of the change in indirect tax rates? The difference between the standard index, (7), and (3) is simply a decomposition of the observed change into a part consisting of changes in indirect tax rates.

Temporarily leaving aside indirect taxes embodied in the inputs to the production of consumer goods and services, we shall first examine the alternative methods which relate only to taxes levied on final consumer expenditure. These are cases (1), (3) and (5) in the diagram.

Terminology and assumptions

A consumer price index can be described as an expenditure-weighted sum of price relatives, where the weights are shares in base period expenditure (less base period indirect taxes in cases (1) and (2)) and sum to unity. At the most detailed level, expenditure is made up of a large number of "items". The price relative for each Item is calculated as a weighted or simple average of the price relatives for one or more "varieties" chosen to represent that item.

Taxes on final consumption expenditure are assumed to be either specific taxes, levied at a rate s per physical unit, or ad valorem taxes levied at a rate a per monetary unit of price. When a good or service is subject to both forms of tax, the ad valorem tax is here assumed to be levied on the price including the specific tax. Thus if P is the price including tax, and N is the price net of tax:

$$P = (N + s)(1 + a)$$

so:

$$N = P / (1 + a) - s$$

and tax content.

$$P - N = aP / (1 + a) + s = aN + (1 + a)s$$

The tax structure may, of course, differ from these assumptions. For example, an ad valorem tax may be levied on top of the price including a general sales tax, or tax may be levied on a notional wholesale price in the case of sales directly from producers to consumers. For each such case, a different algebraic formulation will be required. The above suffices as an example, however, and no attempt will be made to formulate all possible cases.

It is assumed that for all varieties the current price, P_1, and the base period price, P_0, and current period and base period tax rates s_1, s_0, a_1 and a_0 are known.

Adjusting variety prices

Where the tax treatment of an item is uniform, the goods or services which are representative of it in terms of prices are necessarily also representative in terms of taxes. Hence the price for each variety can be adjusted to allow for taxes and the resulting price relatives averaged to provide a tax-adjusted price relative for the item. The adjustments can be made as follows.

In the case of treatment (1) it is necessary to calculate the adjusted price relative for a variety as $N_1 \int N_0$:

where $\quad N_1 = P_1 \int (1 + a_1) - s_1$

and $\quad N_0 = P_0 \int (1 + a_0) - s_0$

thus $\quad N_1 \int N_0 = [P_1 \int (1 + a_1) - s_1] \int [P_0 \int (1 + a_0) - s_0]$

For treatment (3), where current prices are to be adjusted for changes in rates of indirect tax, only P_1 has to be adjusted. The adjustment requires subtraction of any change in the tax content from P_0 to P_1 that was due to a change in tax rates. Thus the adjusted P_1 equals the current period net price plus tax at base period rates:

$$(N_1 + s_0)(1 + a_0) = [P_1 \int (1 + a_1) - s_1 + s_0](1 + a_0)$$

For treatment (5), where P_1 has to be adjusted for any change in the absolute amount of the tax yield, the adjusted P_1 is current period net price plus base period tax content:

$$N_1 + a_0 P_0 \int (1 + a_0) + s_0 = P_1 \int (1 + a_1) - s_1 + a_0 P_0 \int (1 + a_0) + s_0$$

Thus in all three cases, tax adjusted prices and price relatives can be calculated for the individual varieties using price and tax-rate data.

Calculating the direct effects

The calculations in cases (1), (3) and (5) are simple when all components of an item are taxed identically.

One method is to take a weighted sum of the adjusted item price relatives to yield the adjusted index. In cases (3) and (5) the weights, which sum to unity, will be the same as for the standard index, case (7). In case (1) the weights will be adjusted base period expenditures.

Alternatively, the adjusted index can be calculated by estimating and deducting from the standard index the contribution to it of the total tax content (in case 1) or of tax changes (in cases 3 and 5). The contribution for each item in case (3) is that part of its price relative consisting of a change in tax rates, while in case (5) it is that part consisting of a change in tax content. This approach may be suitable in practice in cases (3) and (5) if the number of taxed items is limited and tax changes are infrequent. In principle, this approach is also applicable in case (1), though it may not be appropriate if many items are subject to tax because in fact it implies calculation of an indirect tax index.

Another method, which is equivalent, is often preferred in practice. Multiplying base period expenditure for each item by the price relative calculated for the standard index for that item yields an estimate of the current value of base period purchases for each item. This current value – and each base period expenditure as well in case (1) – is adjusted for tax change or level. The current and base period expenditures are then summed over all items and their ratio taken to yield the index. This procedure is followed in the calculations made for the Danish net price index, which is of type (1). For example, in the case of an item subject to the 22 per cent sales tax, 18.03 per cent would be deducted from estimated item expenditure including tax. A similar procedure is followed for the Irish constant tax price index, which is of type (5).

Tax groups

Where tax treatment is not uniform over all the components of an item, varieties which are representative of it from the point of view of final prices may not be representative from the point of view of indirect tax rates. If in addition, weights are not available for each of these varieties, then a different approach using data relating to what may be called "tax groups" becomes necessary.

These are sets of consumer goods and/or services each of which constitutes the subject of uniform specific and/or ad valorem taxes on final expenditure. It is assumed that the tax yield obtained from a tax group is known for a past accounting period which contains the base period, so that the tax content of base period expenditure upon that tax group can be estimated. The estimate would prorate the accounting period yield according to the relative magnitudes of accounting and base period expenditure on the tax group and/or according to their relative durations, allowing for any changes in tax rates during the accounting period.

Consider first treatment (1). In Denmark, where this is the method used, special emphasis in the expenditure surveys used to obtain weights is placed on distinguishing items according to tax rates, especially for beer, wine, spirits, tobacco, etc. Hence the tax content of expenditure on each item is readily derived from the (uniform) tax content of the varieties that represent it. When, however, different tax rates apply within an item, then matters are more complicated and a tax group approach will be necessary. Summing over all goods and services in a tax group, the aim for treatment (1) is then to estimate:

$$\frac{\sum P_1 Q_0 - T_1}{\sum P_0 Q_0 - T_0}$$

where T_0 is the actual tax yield in the base period from the tax group, i.e. the tax content of $\Sigma P_0 Q_0$, and where T_1 is the tax content of $\Sigma P_1 Q_0$ at current period tax rates. If s_0 was non-zero in the base period, then ΣQ_0 can be obtained by dividing the base period specific tax yield by s. Similarly, $\Sigma P_0 Q_0$ can be calculated from the base period ad valorem tax yield.

$\Sigma P_1 Q_0$ can be estimated by multiplying $\Sigma P_0 Q_0$ by the price relative for the tax group as a whole. This can be obtained by averaging the price relatives for all the varieties representing it.

T_1 has to be obtained by multiplying T_0 by the estimated ratio of T_1 to T_0:

$$\frac{(a_1 P_1 Q_0) / (1 + a_1) + s_1 Q_0}{(a_0 P_0 Q_0) / (1 + a_0) + s_0 Q_0}$$

If a_0 and a_1 are both zero, the ratio of T_1 to T_0 reduces to the ratio of s_1 to s_0.

If we turn to the case of treatment (3), T_0 is not subtracted from $\Sigma P_0 Q_0$ and T' has to be estimated as what the tax content of $\Sigma P_1 Q_0$ would be with base period tax rates. The above ratio must therefore be calculated using a_0 and s_0 in both numerator and denominator.

In treatment (5), finally, the aim is to estimate:

$$\frac{\sum P_1 Q_0 - T_1 + T_0}{\sum P_0 Q_0}$$

so T_1 has to be estimated in the same way as in the case of treatment (1). It is to be noted that there is no need to follow this procedure in the case of the Irish adjusted index, since expenditure weights are available for the individual varieties representing each item.

In practice, in order to achieve consistency between the various parts of the calculation for a given tax group it may be preferable to multiply base period expenditure by $T_0/\Sigma P_0 Q_0$ in order to obtain an estimate of base period tax content, and to use base period expenditure instead of an estimate of $\Sigma P_0 Q_0$ founded upon tax yield and tax rates.

Indirect taxes at the wholesale level

So far, the discussion has related to indirect taxes levied on the final sale to the consumer. Before going on to consider indirect taxes levied at all the previous stages of the chain of production and distribution, consider only those indirect taxes which are levied on goods at the wholesale stage. A tax on alcoholic drinks levied on their sale to restaurants and bars will serve as an example. The drink is bought in bottles and some of it is sold by the glass, but nevertheless there is no physical transformation of the drink so that the same units of measure – litres – can be used in respect both of the wholesale purchase by the restaurant or bar and of the retail sale of the drink to the customer.

If all the varieties representing an item, e.g. various kinds of beer bought by the glass, are taxed at the same rate of specific tax, the procedure described above can be applied. It is only with an ad valorem tax, where the tax base is the wholesale price rather than the retail price, that it makes any difference whether the tax is at wholesale or at retail. Knowledge of the wholesale price paid or, which comes to the same, of the gross margin of the retailer is now necessary in order to adjust variety price relatives. Thus if the retail price, P, equals the sum of the retail margin, M, and the wholesale price, the net price:

$$N = P - (P - M)\, a / (1 + a)$$

If resort has to be made to the method of tax groups, the size of the retail margin can be treated implicitly, since what needs to be estimated is T_0 to obtain the fraction of base period expenditure consisting of tax, and T_1 / T_0. The latter in turn now requires an estimate of the ratio of current to base period wholesale rather than retail values.

In either case, therefore, adjustment for indirect taxes levied at the wholesale stage is more demanding of information than adjustment for indirect taxes levied at the retail stage as discussed in previous sections. On the other hand, input-output analysis is not required so long as the adjustment for indirect taxes is not extended to include those levied on intermediate goods and services further back in the chain than the wholesale level.

Tax levied at earlier stages

Indirect taxes that are indirectly embodied in consumption expenditure obviously do require input-output analysis. We examine what this involves upon the assumption that an input-output table exists for the year that includes the base period but not for the year that includes the current period. This means that the effects upon prices of any changes in the input coefficients have to be ignored.

Since adjustment made by the methods already described is appropriate for those indirect taxes levied at the final stage, what is wanted from the input-output analysis is only a method of adjusting for "indirect" indirect tax content. Hence two sets of coefficients are needed:

(a) Gross output at factor cost *directly and indirectly* required from each industry per unit value of base period consumption expenditure.

(b) Indirect tax on inputs per unit of gross output at factor cost for each industry.

A numerical example will make clear what these two sets of coefficients are and how they can be used to yield the "indirect" indirect tax content of base period expenditure as a whole.

Table 1 shows imaginary input-output data. Note the unusual feature that other indirect taxes are shown as being paid by the purchasing sector, not by the selling sector. Sales by the three sectors are thus given at factor cost, not market value.

The intermediate inputs in the first three rows and columns, expressed as fractions of the column totals, are:

$$\begin{matrix} .326975 & .110390 & .100000 \\ .125341 & .373377 & .080233 \\ .092643 & .165584 & .296512 \end{matrix}$$

Hence the Leontiev matrix $(I - A)$ is:

$$\begin{matrix} .673025 & -.110390 & -.100000 \\ -.125341 & .626623 & -.080233 \\ -.092643 & -.165584 & .703488 \end{matrix}$$

and the inverse of this $(I - A)^{-1}$ is:

$$\begin{matrix} 1.587539 & .349846 & .265566 \\ .355016 & 1.723679 & .247050 \\ .292627 & .451785 & 1.514610 \end{matrix}$$

The consumption of primary, manufacturing and service products expressed as fractions of total consumption, 5575, are: .358744, .206278, .152466.

Table 1. Illustrative data on input–output

	Primary	Manufacturing	Services	Consumption	Other final expenditure	Total
Primary	2 400	680	860	2 000	1 400	7 340
Manufacturing	920	2 300	690	1 150	1 100	6 160
Services	680	1 020	2 550	850	3 500	8 600
Imports	1 100	1 600	900	1 000	300	4 900
Value-added tax	—	—	—	425	—	425
Other indirect taxes	120	260	210	150	100	840
Value added	2 120	300	3 390	—	—	5 810
Total	7 340	6 160	8 600	5 575	6 400	34 075

Multiplying the inverse by this vector gives total output of each of the three sectors per unit of consumption expenditure as:

Primary: .682176
Manufacturing: .520584
Services: .429099

These are now multiplied by the indirect tax coefficients for the three sectors of: 120/7340, 260/6160 and 210/8600 respectively, and added to give .043603 as the indirect tax content per unit of consumption.

Both in order to estimate the actual "indirect" indirect tax content of current period value of base period expenditure and in order to estimate what it would have been with base period indirect tax rates, tax coefficients like those listed above will have to be used, industry by industry, preferably separately for each type of indirect tax, together with information about base and current period tax rates. In addition, information will be required about base period physical quantities where there are specific taxes and about industry price changes where there are ad valorem taxes. The estimates will be made difficult by the incompleteness of such information, especially when the sales by each industry to other industries are not all taxed at the same rate. However, much of the information gathered in order to estimate direct effects is also useful here.

In general, the input-output industry breakdown of consumption will be coarser than the breakdown by base period expenditure items. Hence there can be no question of adjusting for indirect taxes at earlier stages separately for each item. On the other hand, the input-output industries will rarely coincide with tax groups, since these are defined in terms of commodities rather than industries. (If commodity input-output tables included primary inputs, then commodity rather than industry coefficients could be used.) For these reasons the Finnish calculations for example involved extensive specific estimates, particularly for agriculture, where there are many subsidies.

The use of the set of coefficients calculated from the most recent input-output table implicitly assumes no change in physical input coefficients or in each industry's product mix.

For the alternative treatments (2), (4) and (6) distinguished in the diagram it is necessary to use this kind of analysis to estimate the "indirect" indirect tax content of the current period value of the goods and services included in base period expenditure. In all three cases this tax content has to be subtracted; in case (6) it is replaced by base period yield while in case (4) it is replaced by what it would be at base period tax rates. In practice, the Netherlands index does this by subtracting from the standard index an estimate for each tax of the indirect as well as the direct effect of any changes in it upon that standard index.

Finland uses the identity mentioned in the third paragraph of this article, taking a weighted average of the standard price index and the indirect tax index. The latter is calculated using as value weights the calculated amounts of indirect tax incorporated in the base-period expenditure weights of the standard index. This gives a weight for each indirect tax (and subsidy) which is applied to the relative of the average rate for that tax or subsidy. Note that these weights may differ from the relative total yields and costs of the different indirect taxes and subsidies because no special attention was paid to their representativeness with respect to taxes and subsidies in the choice of items and varieties for the standard index.

The general principles applied in the calculation of the Netherlands, Swedish and Finnish net price indices are thus clear. However, there are further problems which deserve mention.

One is the problem of timing. With monthly or even quarterly adjustment for "indirect" indirect taxes, the use of the estimation method just described implicitly assumes that price changes generated by changes in indirect tax (and subsidy) rates are propagated through the system very quickly. If this is not the case, some curious distortions could arise. Thus imagine that there is a sharp increase in the rate of some indirect tax whose "indirect" effects are greater than its direct effects. If the index is calculated before the "indirect" effects have in fact worked through the system, then an excessive subtraction will be made for the tax content of the current period value and the adjusted index will consequently come out too low!

Secondly, there is the point that as well as the indirect tax content of intermediate current inputs to the production and distribution of final consumer goods and services, there is also an indirect tax content of depreciation in so far as capital inputs also embody some indirect tax. The Swedish index is net of this, while the Finnish index makes no allowance for it. In principle, allowance for this element could be made by assuming the indirect tax content of depreciation to equal that of replacement investment and supposing this to be the same as the indirect tax content of final fixed capital formation in general. This would make the problem of timing in a monthly or quarterly index even more acute – unless depreciation in the input-output tables were all at replacement cost and all industries founded their pricing upon replacement costs.

Given all the difficulties in the estimation of and adjustment for "indirect" indirect taxes, it is consoling to know that they appear to be relatively unimportant in comparison with indirect taxes levied upon the final stages. This fact can be used both to justify the roughness of the methods used to include them in the calculation and to justify their exclusion from it.

Appendix 4

Reduction of errors in a consumer price index

by D. J. Sellwood, Department of Employment, United Kingdom

Introduction

Errors in consumer price indices can have serious consequences for users: an error of 0.1 per cent in the United Kingdom index could cost the Government £60 million per annum in index-linked expenditure. Such errors are, however, difficult to determine and little research appears to have been published on seeking their reduction. Index compilers have tended to collect large numbers of prices in the hope, rather than the knowledge, that this will ensure a reliable index. More analytical work is clearly necessary but some immediate steps could be taken to reduce errors and to ensure that effective use is made of resources. This article attempts to provide a basis on which such steps might be discussed.

Errors in the CPI

The overall error in a CPI derives from sampling and non-sampling errors in both price indices and weights. The magnitude of the overall error depends on the aggregate of the errors in the component price indices and on the correlations that arise through time between price changes and weights and the errors in these. Since it is common practice to use "representative" rather than random samples of prices, and to use a mixture of sample and administrative data for weights, standard statistical sampling theory does not give an accurate account of the errors. The theory may, however, provide a guide to ways in which the index compiler might seek to reduce errors. Annex A gives an algebraic description of the errors in a Laspeyres price index. It shows how errors in the weights and in the price indices combine to affect the all-items index or indices covering groups of items. It also examines the errors arising in the construction of the basic price indices, i.e. those derived from price data alone, covering "composites" of purchases of similar items made over wide geographic areas and/or from different outlet types where weighting information is not available.

In Annex B errors in the weights are ignored and errors in the prices assumed random in order to derive an optimum allocation of price collection effort for a given total cost.

Strategies for error reduction

A number of observations may be made from the results given in Annexes A and B as an indication of the sort of steps that might be taken to reduce errors.

1. Variations in the impact of errors

The requirements for accuracy in the estimates of both weights and price changes vary according to the actual development of prices. The more the price of a particular item differs from the average of price movements the more accurate the estimates of both price change and weight need to be. The index compiler may be able to respond to divergences in prices that persist by increasing the numbers of prices collected or by obtaining more or better weighting information, provided that the procedures for compiling the index are reasonably flexible. However, it would first be desirable to have some indication of the size of the errors and the cost of reducing them.

2. Reducing correlations

As a general rule, it seems desirable to reduce the correlation between price indices and their associated weights. Though negative correlations may reduce a positive overall bias and vice versa, there is often no way of knowing where the correlations will be positive and where negative.

If the total expenditure covered by the index were divided into equal parts when determining the basic composite items for which price indices should be compiled there could be no correlation involving the weights. One strategy for reducing correlations would be to attempt to sub-divide items with larger weights so as to reduce the dispersion in the magnitudes of the weights.

3. Reducing errors in item price indices

In order to reduce the error in the price indices for composite items, the items within the composite should have as similar price movements as possible. That is, the between-item "price change" variation should be maximised and the within-item variances minimised. An analysis of variance of price changes can help to identify suitable groupings for forming composites.

Increasing the numbers of prices collected does not reduce the errors in price indices for composite items where there is correlation between measured price movements and the unknown weights attaching to these. In this situation it is weighting information that is required, not additional prices.

4. Optimising price collection

The optimum allocation of price collection resources is to take sampling size for the *j*th composite item indices as:

$$n_j \propto W_j \frac{S_j}{\sqrt{C_j}}$$

Where W_j is the weight of the composite, S_j the estimated error and C_j the cost per price collected.

Comment

It is not necessary to know the errors in the weights and price indices before following these strategies. It is unlikely that a strategy would be ineffective if only rough estimates of the component errors were used. The following comments on the estimation of such errors are offered:

(a) Sample variancies for price changes may be used as a guide to error variances though these are not ideal if sampling is not random; the range of the price changes for a composite item may be used as a guide to which indices may be least reliable. Collection of additional prices, covering items not regularly priced, may be necessary for gauging the possibility of bias.

(b) Bias in price indices may be explored by reconstructing the indices using alternative sets of weights based on data from different sources. It is usually possible to improve on an implicit assumption of equal weights made in constructing price indices for composite items.

(c) In the absence of firm information about errors in either the price indices or their weights a rough assessment or ranking by the index compiler of his or her confidence in the particular estimates should be sufficient to give an indication of where action is necessary and how resources may be more effectively deployed using the results of Annexes A and B.

In attempting to reduce the overall error in the index it is not essential to tackle the whole index in one operation. Improvements can be made commodity group by commodity group or region by region.

Weights versus prices

Emphasis in practice tends to be placed on reducing errors in price indices rather than reducing those in the weights. It is not clear that this is always justified but there is a further question which is pertinent and that is "What is the optimum number of component price indices that should be used in constructing the CPI?" That is a question of the balance between detailed weighting information and additional price information. At one extreme a specific weight could be estimated for each price relative, at the other each price relative (or price) could be given the same weight. In theory, expenditure can be divided by item type, shop type and region or location and each of these may include many sub-classes. It would be possible for most countries to imagine many hundreds of strata but with a limited budget it is not likely that very large numbers of component indices would be cost effective. If international practice is a good guide, values of N of 200 to 300 are appropriate. As a general rule, sub-division that can be achieved at little cost should be adopted, e.g. if prices are collected in different regions, then constructing regional indices and combining these with approximate regional weights should improve the CPI.

How reliable should a consumer price index be?

It is clear that many economic decisions will be based on the information provided by a consumer price index. Very small differences in the change recorded by the index might affect incomes or expenditures of large numbers of individuals or businesses or of governments. Although consumer price indices require significant resources to produce, the cost of these will be very small in relation to the cost resulting from the errors in measurement. It is therefore relevant to ask "How reliable should a consumer price index be?" This section does not aim to provide an answer to this question but aims only to draw attention to the issues it raises.

The accuracy of a statistic is commonly assessed in terms of bias and error variance. There is, however, a prior consideration that is often overlooked. That is whether the statistic measures what it is desired to measure. This is the question of "validity".

Validity

In social and economic inquiry it is frequently the case that measurements are made of things that can be measured rather than that which the inquirer would ideally want to measure. This is a necessary consequence of the nature of the economic and social world but it should not be overlooked in deciding whether a particular measure can be regarded as sufficiently accurate. Does it make sense to have a consumer price index that is accurate to one part in one thousand if it grossly overstates or understates the movement of prices relevant to particular uses? There is no one answer to the question of what is it that a CPI should "ideally" measure. There are an infinite number of measures of price change that are required. Anyone who wants such a measure ideally requires a particular measure at a particular time depending on the question he or she wishes to answer. Thus someone concerned with the impact of price changes on one-parent families over the last 12 months will want one index. Whilst a government economist wishing to establish the real growth in consumption over the last three months would "ideally" like another index. These two "ideal" indices would almost certainly differ significantly in their measurement of price change over a corresponding period. More generally, it is unlikely that anyone would "ideally" want a measure of price change over the last months based on the expenditure pattern of consumers made five years before, or one year before for that matter as provided by many consumer price indices.

It is also debatable whether anyone could define the price index he or she would ideally want for any particular purpose. Given a choice between a number of idealised price indices based on particular consumption patterns and price data, each user might be able to express a preference for one particular index. But he/she is unlikely to regard the chosen index as ideal for his/her purposes. Further, many would wish to revise their choice on seeing the measurements resulting from the different indices.

All this might seem a little academic or trifling in the real world of decision-making but it is not in relation to the question of how accurate a CPI should be. The differences between the "ideal indices" are not negligible nor are the differences between the various index forms that are conventionally used, e.g. Paasche and Laspeyres chained or otherwise.

The design of a consumer price index will involve a good many compromises. Even if agreement could be made on a particular compromise index it is unlikely that such an index could be defined precisely or that whatever index is defined can be compiled with any great precision; e.g. many of the problems of quality will remain. Thus there maybe a considerable gap between what is measured by a CPI and what is required. This is not an argument for ignoring the accuracy of the CPI. It is simply a wider perspective within which to view the requirements for accuracy. Many of the problems, whether of validity or compilation, confronting the index compiler are not resolvable but they should be recognised. One way to face up to these limitations is to agree the design and construction of the index with users. This might be done by consulting users directly, e.g. by having an advisory committee on which they are represented, or by making details of the index available, e.g. in a manual, and addressing the issues raised by users.

Annex A

The analysis of errors in price indices given below uses the following standard definitions and relationships:

For random variables X and Y

Expected value of X $= E(X) = \sum_{i=1}^{k} p_i X_i =$ mean of X $= \overline{X}$

Variance of X $= V(X) = E[X - E(X)]^2 = E(X^2) - (E(X))^2$

Co-variance of X and Y $= Cov(X, Y) = E[XY - E(XY)]$
$= E(XY) - E(X)E(Y)$

For a linear function of random variables

$$E(a_0 + a_1X_1 + a_2X_2 + \ldots\ldots a_kX_k) = a_0 + a_1\ E(X_1) + \ldots\ldots + a_kE(X_k)$$

$$V(a_0 + a_1X_1 + \ldots\ldots a_kX_k) = a_1^2\ V(X_1) + \ldots\ldots + a_k^2\ V(X_k)$$
$$+ 2a_1a_2\,Cov(X_1X_2) + 2a_1a_3\,Cov(X_1X_3) + \ldots\ldots$$

When X and Y are independent

Expected value of product XY $= E(XY) = E(X)E(Y)$

Variance of product $V(XY) = \overline{Y}^2V(X) + \overline{X}^2V(Y) + V(Y)V(X)$

By definition for random samples size N

$$\text{Mean } x = \overline{x} = \frac{1}{N}\sum_{i=1}^{N} x_i$$

$$\text{Variance } X = V(x) = \frac{1}{N}\Sigma(x-\overline{x})^2 = \frac{1}{N}\Sigma x^2 - \overline{x}^2$$

$$\text{Co-variance } x, y = Cov(x, y) = \frac{1}{N}\Sigma(x-\overline{x})(y-\overline{y}) = \frac{1}{N}\Sigma xy - \frac{\Sigma x\Sigma y}{N\ \ N}$$

$$\text{From which } \Sigma xy = \frac{1}{N}\Sigma x\Sigma y + N\,Cov(x, y)$$

The Laspeyres index is defined as

$$I = \sum_{j}^{N} I_jW_j \qquad j = 1\ to\ N$$

and is estimated as

$$\hat{I} = \sum_{j}^{N}\hat{I}_j\hat{W}_j$$

The contribution of the jth composite item $I_j\hat{W}_j$ is subject to estimation errors. This may be partitioned by writing

$D_j = I_j - I$ the deviation of the jth index from I

$V_j = \hat{W}_j - W_j$ the error in estimating W_j

$e_j = \hat{I}_j - I_j$ the error in estimating I_j

Then the error in estimating the jth contribution is

$$Z_j = \hat{I}_j\hat{W}_j - I_j\ W_j = (e_j + D_j + I)\ (v_j + W_j) - I_jW_j = e_jv_j + D_jv_j + W_je_j + Iv_j$$

and the expected value of this error is

$$E(Z_j) = E(e_jv_j) + D_jE(v_j) + W_jE(e_j) + IE(v_j)$$
$$= \overline{e_jv_j} + D_j\overline{v}_j + W_j\overline{e}_j + I\overline{v}_j$$

The overall error is (NB $\sum \overline{v}_j = 0$)

$$
\begin{aligned}
E\left(\sum_j^N Z_j\right) &= \Sigma \overline{e}_j \overline{v}_j + \Sigma D_j \overline{v}_j + \Sigma W_j \overline{e}_j \\
&= \frac{1}{N} \Sigma \overline{e}_j \Sigma \overline{v}_j + NCov(\overline{e}_j, \overline{v}_j) + \frac{1}{N} \Sigma D_j \Sigma \overline{v}_j + NCov(D_j, \overline{v}_j) + \frac{1}{N} \Sigma W_j \Sigma \overline{e}_j + NCov(W_j, \overline{e}_j) \\
&= \frac{1}{N} \sum_j^W \overline{e}_j + NCov(D_j, \overline{v}_j) + NCov(W_j, \overline{e}_j) + NCov(\overline{e}_j, \overline{v}_j)
\end{aligned}
$$

The variance of the errors of the jth contribution is

$$
\begin{aligned}
V(Z_j) = V(e_j, v_j) &+ I^2{}_j V(v_j) + W^2{}_j V(e_j) + 2I_j Cov(e_j v_j, v_j) \\
&+ 2W_j Cov(e_j v_j, e_j) + 2I_j W_j Cov(v_j, e_j)
\end{aligned}
$$

However, if as seems likely the errors in the price index e_j are independent of that in the weight v_j then $Cov\ (v_j, e_j)$ is zero and

$$V(e_j v_j) = \overline{e}_j^2 V(v_j) + \overline{v}_j^2 V(e_j) + V(v_j) V(e_j)$$

Also

$$
\begin{aligned}
Cov(e_j v_j, v_j) &= E(e_j v_j^2) - E(e_j v_j) E(v_j) \\
&= E(e_j) \{(E(v_j))^2 - [E(v_j)]^2\} \\
&= E(e_j) V(v_j)
\end{aligned}
$$

and

$$Cov(e_j v_j, e_j) = E(v_j) V(e_j)$$

Therefore

$$
\begin{aligned}
V(Z_j) &= \left(I_j^2 + \overline{e}_j^2\right) V(v_j) + \left(W_j^2 + \overline{v}_j^2\right) V(e_j) + V(v_j) V(e_j) \\
&\quad + 2I_j \overline{e}_j V(v_j) + 2W_j \overline{v}_j V(e_j) \\
&= (I_j + \overline{e}_j)^2 V(v_j) + (W_j + \overline{v}_j)^2 V(e_j) + V(v_j) V(e_j)
\end{aligned}
$$

From which

$$
\begin{aligned}
V(\Sigma Z_j) = \sum_j (I_j + \overline{e}_j)^2 V(v_j) &+ \Sigma (W_j + \overline{v}_j)^2 V(e_j) + \Sigma V(v_j) V(e_j) \\
&+ \text{possible non-zero co-variance terms.}
\end{aligned}
$$

The largest contributors to this variance seem likely to be $\Sigma I_j^2 V(v_j)$ and $\Sigma W_j^2 V(e_j)$. The latter variance $V(e_j)$ depends on the variation of the price changes σ_j^2 from which the index I_j is estimated.

Thus $V(Z) \approx \Sigma I_j^2 V(v_j) + \Sigma \frac{W_j^2 \sigma_j^2}{r_j}$

where r_j is the size of sample used to estimate I_j.

Thus the overall error is a function of the errors in the component indices and of the correlations between these errors and the weights. Correlations between errors in the weights and the price changes that actually occur over the period of measurement will also affect the size of the overall error. The index compiler has little control over the correlations which may be positive or negative. Reducing the variability between the price indices would tend to reduce the co-variance of these with errors in the weights $Cov(D_j, \overline{v}_j)$ but might tend to increase the errors in estimating the price changes (e_j). Reducing the dispersion in the weights would reduce the co-variance of these with errors in the price indices $Cov(W_j, e_j)$; if the weights are all equal to $\frac{1}{N}$ then $Cov(W_j, e_j)$ is zero. However, the weights are determined by actual consumption patterns and the index compiler has only limited control. One strategy might be to increase N, the number of composite items, by breaking down those with the larger weights.

The average of the errors in the component indices $\frac{1}{N} \Sigma e_j$ will depend on the procedures followed for collecting the prices. These may give rise to biases which do not cancel; the net result may be positive or negative. It is for example common practice, for obvious reasons of economy, to collect prices of many items in a single retail outlet. The effect of this may be to impart a systematic bias unless the selection of shops is truly representative or unbiased. The cost of removing such bias, e.g. by a scientific selection procedure, may be considerable.

The variance of the overall error depends on the error variances arising from the procedures for estimating the weights and the price indices for the composite items. Weights are typically obtained from surveys of the expenditure of households covered by consumer price indices supplemented by other sources of information. Clearly increasing the size of survey samples will reduce the sampling errors in the weights but this is likely to be costly. Improving survey design, e.g. by stratification or by placing relatively more resources (questions) on items where expenditure is most variable are likely to be more cost effective. Possibilities for improving estimates in the price indices are considered below.

The above expression for the error and error variance does not show clearly how these are affected by increasing the number of composite items into which the overall index (or components thereof) are divided. Clearly errors in the weights may increase rapidly as N becomes very large. Errors in estimating the price indices will reduce as N is increased, provided the subdivision of expenditure categories produces greater homogeneity of price movement within composite items and greater variation between items. Increasing the number of composite items will have resource implications. Reallocation, e.g. of price collection may be possible within a fixed budget but there will most likely be a limit to the size of N.

Errors in price indices for composite items

The required sub-indices I_j take the same form as the overall index, i.e.

$$I_j = \sum_i W_{ij} I_{ij}$$

but in practice the weights W_{ij} are not known and the I_js are estimated from sample price data.

$$I_j = \frac{1}{nj}\Sigma\frac{P_{ti}}{P_{oi}} \quad \text{or} \quad \frac{\frac{1}{n_j}\Sigma P_{ti}}{\frac{1}{n_j}\Sigma P_{oi}}$$

From the definitions of variance and co-variance either:

$$\frac{1}{N}\Sigma\frac{P_t}{P_o} = \Sigma W_o\frac{P_t}{P_o} - NCov\left(W_o, \frac{P_t}{P_o}\right)$$

or

$$\frac{\frac{1}{N}\Sigma P_t}{\frac{1}{N}\Sigma P_o} = \frac{\Sigma P_t Q_o}{\Sigma P_o Q_o} \cdot \frac{1 - \frac{N}{\Sigma P_t Q_o} Cov(P_t, Q_o)}{1 - \frac{N}{\Sigma P_o Q_o} Cov(P_o, Q_o)}$$

Thus if there is correlation between the price relatives and the unknown weights the simple average of the price relatives provides a biased estimate of the required index. Also the ratio of average prices can give a biased estimate of the required index in certain (rather more complex) circumstances.

The bias is not reduced by increasing the sample size at random. Either weights must be found or the prices must be selected on a probability basis. Since it is common practice to collect prices for many items in each outlet it is unlikely that any biases that arise will cancel out across composite item indices.

Errors in practice

It should be noted that in practice there may be little interest in price changes measured in relation to the base period of the CPI. For the most part the CPI will be used to measure changes in prices between points in time after the base period. The price change between times $t = 1$ and $t = 2$ would be derived from the ratio of the CPI for time 2 to time for time 1, i.e.

$$I_{12} = \frac{I_{02}}{I_{01}}$$

This calculation can be written as

$$I_{12} = \frac{\Sigma W_{0j} I_{02j}}{\Sigma W_{0j} I_{01j}} = \Sigma W_{1j} I_{12j}$$

where

$$W_{1j} = \frac{W_{0j} I_{01j}}{\Sigma W_{0j} I_{01j}} = \frac{P_1 Q_0}{\Sigma P_1 Q_0}$$

$$I_{12j} = \frac{I_{02j}}{I_{01j}}$$

i.e. the W_{1j} are the base period weights revalued to time 1.

The error in I_{12} the measured price change between times 1 and 2 is thus of the same form as the ordinary Laspeyres index. It will depend on the correlations between the price changes in the composite items between times 1 and 2, estimated as I_{02j}/I_{01j} and the revalued weights W_{1j}. Any strategy that reduces errors in the CPI should reduce errors in price changes estimated from the CPI (for periods not including the base period).

Annex B

Optimisation of sample sizes for price collection

If we ignore errors in the weights, the variance of the estimate of the all-items index

$$\hat{I} = \Sigma \hat{W}_j \hat{I}_j$$

is

$$V(\hat{I}) = \Sigma \frac{W_j^2 S_j^2}{n_j}$$

where

$$S_j^2 = \frac{1}{n_j} \sum_{j=1}^{nj} r_{ij} - \left(\frac{\sum^{nj} r_{ij}}{n_j} \right)^2$$

the sample variation in the price relatives.

For a fixed total cost of price collection

$$\sum_j C_j n_j = C$$

(j = 1 to N the number of composite item indices)

the optimum allocation of the sample of relatives between composite item indices can be obtained by setting up the Lagrangian function

$$F = \Sigma W_j^2 S_j^2 / n_j + \lambda(\Sigma n_j C_j - C)$$

Where the second term represents the constraint on total cost, C_j is the average cost of obtaining the price relatives in the jth composite item index. Then

$$\frac{\delta E}{\delta n_j} = \frac{-W_j^2 S_j^2}{n_j^2} + \lambda C_j$$

setting the differential equal to zero gives

$$n_j = \frac{1}{\lambda} \frac{W_j S_j}{\sqrt{C_j}}$$

$$\Sigma n_j = n = \frac{1}{\lambda} \sum_j^N \frac{W_j S_j}{\sqrt{C_j}}$$

$$\frac{n_j}{n} = \frac{W_j S_j}{\sqrt{C_j}} \div \sum_j^N \frac{W_j S_j}{\sqrt{C_j}}$$

Appendix 5

The treatment of finance-related commodities in a consumers' price index

by Thomas J. Woodhouse and Kathleen M. Hanson, Department of Statistics, New Zealand

1. Introduction

1.1 Orthodox, Laspeyres-formula consumers' price indexes are designed to measure the changing level of prices paid by the particular set of household residents forming the index population. This is achieved by measuring the changing amount of money required to purchase the index "basket of commodities" over time and then expressing this as a ratio of the current cost over the base-period cost. If this ratio is inverted, the index then demonstrates the changing proportion of the index basket that a fixed quantity of money could purchase: i.e. it measures the changing purchasing power of money as this is experienced by the index population members.

1.2 It may therefore seem to be anomalous, or fundamentally erroneous, or both, if changes in the "value of money" are inputs into, as well as outputs of, a consumer price index. This procedure may nevertheless be a required part of the calculation methodology for some commodities within conventional Laspeyres-type consumer price indexes, if the constant-quality requirement in the index "pricing" is to be adhered to.

1.3 The use of consumer price indexes in cost-of-living escalation clauses and in related price/wage adjustments already attracts the criticism that it is a major contributor to cost-push inflation. The employment *within* an index of endogenous circular elements, therefore, supplies added weight to the claims of those same critics, by reinforcing the perception that consumer price index increases, if not directly self-generating, are, at least to some degree, self-sustaining. Hence, it may be argued that they do not merely measure inflation, they foster its continuance.

1.4 This article examines the use of sub-indexes of CPIs as inputs into consumers' price indexes with particular reference to the above criticisms and in the context of the New Zealand CPI. It proceeds by examining, in turn, selected segments of the index where such techniques are currently in use, or are being considered for use in the future. These index areas are as follows:

Loan services
- property mortgages and hire-purchase agreements;
- generalised credit schemes (credit cards);

Insurance services
- goods (vehicles/appliances/homes) cover;
- medical cover;
- mortgage repayment (life) cover;

Gambling services

Note: Similar techniques are also used in the measurement of price change for property conveyancing and real estate agents' fees. These are not detailed here to avoid repetition.

1.5 Within each topic heading, the following are discussed:

- the techniques being used (or those being considered for use);
- the appropriateness and validity of such techniques in isolation from their incorporation into the general, overall index.

1.6 Finally, the article directly addresses the question of the existence and legitimacy of any self-sustaining circularity of price movements and whether these are the proper concern of index statisticians.

Note: The merits and demerits of including such commodities as loans, insurances and gambling services in a consumers' price index are not debated here. In order to focus on the technical discussion, it is assumed that their inclusion is accepted as conceptually correct.

2. Loan services

2.1 The availability of consumer credit has mushroomed in the past two decades and with it the expenditure by private households on debt servicing. In the past decade we have also witnessed the credit card explosion. As a consequence, debt servicing, in one form or another, now constitutes a significant part of the budget of most households in New Zealand, and index statisticians face the problem of incorporating into consumer price indexes the cost of such services.

The two-component price-change approach

2.2 For any item in a conventional Laspeyres-type consumers' price index, the aim is to measure the changing cost of purchasing a fixed quantity and quality of the good or service over time. This may be a relatively straightforward exercise in the case of a can of peas, a commodity which is unambiguously specified and whose quality is capable of objective assessment. In general, there exists common agreement that the utility of peas lies in their edibility and the quality in their size, numbers and weight. Hence, if edibility and combined pea-weight are held constant, either in fact or by statistical manipulation, then the price series will satisfactorily measure "pure" price change.

2.3 For other commodities in the index the measurement of pure price change requires the employment of more precise definitions. The key to the simplicity of the canned peas example is the near universal agreement on the commodity's use. The quality control of the item, i.e. adjustment of the price series for the degree to which the different samples of the product surveyed in each pricing period will perform the same function, derives directly from this. If, by contrast, the commodity has a multiplicity of functions, then any specification must include sufficient detail to define unambiguously what is being purchased. For example, if the commodity is the services of a doctor, and such a person may not work for an undifferentiated hourly charge-out rate, then the precise service being purchased must be nominated. If this is not done, then, to nominate an extreme example, the cost of obtaining a repeat prescription for medication in one period might be inadvertently compared to the cost of triple-bypass heart surgery in the next. In summary, where precise functional utility is not implicit in the commodity's name, then it must be made explicit in the specification.

2.4 This embodiment of function in an index commodity's specification achieves its greatest level of difficulty when the commodity concerned is not merely multifunctional, but also beyond quality specification in itself. This is the case with, for example, loan services. The service of lending money can only be properly specified, in terms of being an index commodity, as the borrowing of sufficient funds to purchase a fixed quantity and quality of specified goods and services.

2.5 There are two alternative approaches to pricing credit using the above concept:

(a) associating the loan with the commodity or commodities, for which the finance has, at least ostensibly, been raised; or

(b) regarding the loan as a means of increasing the borrower's immediately available disposable income and hence applicable to the full range of commodities being purchased at that time.

Associating the loan with specific commodities

2.6 The following hypothetical example illustrates this pricing method by calculating the changing cost of financing the partial hire purchase of a television set over one year:

	Base period	*Period 2*
TV cash price less 50% deposit	$1 000 $500	$1 200 $600
Hire purchase advance Current interest rate One year's interest charge	$500 10% $50	$600 12% $72 (44% increase)

The calculation for the index is as follows:

$$\frac{\text{Period 2 price}}{\text{Base period price}} \times \frac{\text{Period 2 interest rate}}{\text{Base period interest rate}} = \frac{600}{500} \times \frac{12}{10}$$

$= 1.2 \times 1.2$ (20% increase in each)

$= 1.44$ (a 44% compounded increase in interest charges)

2.7 In New Zealand this technique is applied not only to hire purchase cost changes, but also to the changing cost of servicing mortgages for owner-occupied housing. The price-change indicator in this latter case is the compounded product of interest rate changes on all currently outstanding mortgages and the changing price of residential property itself.

2.8 Quality change in respect of the mortgage agreements as such is exercised primarily through holding constant the mix of surveyed housing loans in terms of the length of time remaining for repayment of the principal, on the grounds that the utility of a loan depends on the amount and the period over which the use of the loan is available before repayment. For mortgages with less than five years to run, the mix of first to subsequent mortgages is also held constant. This technique is predicated on the following concepts:

(a) Loans could be analysed by a diversity of characteristics, such as loan type, lender, initial term, year taken out, "rank", type of security, etc. However, the data base used for the New Zealand CPI's mortgage interest change measure would not support such a structure and the rigour of that approach is considered unnecessary. It was decided that the most important "quality" factor by far was the length of time remaining before the currently outstanding debt must be repaid.

(b) The "rank" (whether the loan is a first, second or third mortgage) represents different degrees of risk to the lender. Hence, although this "quality" factor is more from the point of view of the price-giver than the price-taker, quality control, in the form of maintaining a fixed weight for first versus subsequent loans, is employed for mortgages with five years or less to run. In New Zealand the majority of subsequent mortgages are for terms of five years or less.

2.9 Quality change in respect of property price changes is achieved by a statistical technique which removes from the measurement the influence of any overall movement in the qualitative mix of the residential properties within age-of-dwelling categories. This is made possible by the five-yearly revaluation of all New Zealand residential properties by an ad hoc government agency. By assuming that there is no overall change in the quality mix of properties between those government valuations, any increase or decrease in the government valuations can be interpreted as sampling error and the methodology discounts this to isolate the "real" price change.

Pricing interest charges as a distinct commodity

2.10 The commodity which acts as security for the loan need not necessarily be the commodity whose purchase is being wholly or partly financed by the loan. For example, second or third mortgages may be raised on a dwelling in order to finance the purchase of a motor vehicle or an overseas holiday. Further, if a loan is raised to purchase a television set, it could be because the buyer prefers neither to draw on his/her savings, nor to forgo some other general or specific purchases. Any loan can thus be seen as relating to the purchase of those items whose acquisition would otherwise have been forgone, rather than, or in addition to, the purchase of the commodity for which the loan was nominally raised.

2.11 Loans are essentially a means of increasing the immediate disposable income of the borrower and it is not possible to identify which dollars pay for which commodities from the aggregate of the borrower's purchases. Bringing forward in time the receipt of loan money increases its value due to its capacity to earn interest in the interim and the avoidance of the devaluing effects of inflation. For this reason the lender is able to charge for the loan service. In some cases the lender's charges are such that the borrower is paying more in real terms than if he/she had waited and saved. The discrepancy can be viewed as the price paid for instant, rather than delayed, gratification. This supports the contention that loan charges are not simply related to the acquisition of the item concerned.

2.12 It can therefore be argued that credit services should be treated as a distinct commodity, divorced from any specific goods or services for which, or on which, the loans were nominally raised. On conceptual grounds this approach argues that there is essentially no distinction between the interest paid on mortgages for housing, interest on loans to purchase motor vehicles, hire-purchase charges, and credit card charges, etc. In each case the purchaser is paying to borrow money, the precise purpose of which is somewhat illusory. To price credit under this concept would involve combining the movements of two components:

(i) changes in the average interest rates on hire purchases and loans; and

(ii) changes in the purchasing power of the borrowed dollar using all or most of the consumer price index as an indicator.

2.13 The use of a substantial subset of the CPI for the purposes of maintaining constant the purchasing power of borrowed funds, when calculating the real price of credit, would result in the index partly generating its own increases.

Mathematically, if

P = full CPI
P' = the CPI with the interest item excluded
I = the measured CPI interest item, viz. the price of borrowing a specific real or constant value amount of money
i = effective interest rate

then $\Delta P = K\Delta P' + (1 - k)\Delta I.$
where $\Delta I = \Delta P'\Delta i$

2.14 Using the full, or nearly full, subset of the CPI as an input into its own calculations is not fundamentally different from combining interest rate changes with the changes in the price of more specific goods and services; it is merely a more general application of the same concept. Accordingly, despite its self-evident circularity it would be a legitimate and necessary component of the methodology.

2.15 However, in the New Zealand CPI the above approach has not yet been applied. There is, however, one obvious case where the technique of using either the full index, or a substantial proportion of it, as a component of the price change has been endorsed. This is in respect of "generalised" credit schemes; specifically the cost of using credit cards.

2.16 The consumer's perception of a loan being tied to a particular good or service does not generally apply to credit cards. Many and varied items are purchased directly, or indirectly via cash advances, on credit cards. Often the variety of items purchased and the erratic timing and overlapping of payment periods for such purchases make it difficult to associate the credit charges with specific commodities. Therefore, the only practicable method of calculating price changes for credit charges would involve the product of two separate indicators, namely:

(i) changes in the average rate of interest and other charges being levied on credit cards, etc.; and

(ii) changes in the prices of a substantial subset of the commodities in the regimen of the CPI, if not the entire index itself. In addition to everyday purchases, cash advances on credit cards can be used for such seemingly unlikely purposes as paying dwelling rentals, putting deposits on houses and vehicles, etc.

It may therefore be, in this area of the index, that we are first likely to see the use of a significant subset of the New Zealand CPI as an input into its own calculations.

3. Insurance services

3.1 Insurance schemes are essentially risk-sharing mechanisms in which individuals, or groups of individuals, contribute to a pool of funds which its members may draw on in the event of specific misfortunes occurring. Contributions to the fund cover:

(i) expected claims by members (payouts),

(ii) costs incurred to operate and administer the schemes, less any independent (non-premium) incomes derived from fund activities such as investment.

3.2 It can be argued that, as the drawings are generally spent on the replacement of goods or services, then the index expenditure weights of those commodities should include such expenditure, as well as that incurred directly by index population members on those same commodities. This would mean that the ratio of the consumed income of the insurance company (premiums minus payouts) to the premiums themselves could be used as the nominal "price" paid for the insurance company's services. Measuring changes in this "retained" percentage of total premiums would provide a single-element price-change indicator.

3.3 In practice the above approach is not practicable, as identification and separation out of the "service" component from the premium for weighting purposes, let alone for surveying its "price" changes, is fraught with innumerable difficulties. Fortunately there is a viable alternative.

3.4 The alternative approach, and the one employed in New Zealand's CPI, is to specify the insurance service in terms of purchasing insurance cover for specific quantities and qualities of goods and/or services under certain fixed conditions. The expenditure weight thus becomes the sum of total premiums paid for that type of insurance by the index population. The price-change indicator is more complex for, to maintain the quality of the priced service, the value of cover must be maintained in real terms.

3.5 Regimen items for insurance on dwellings and their contents are specified for the price survey in terms of providing a "real" value of cover. This is achieved by adjusting the nominal value of that cover in line with price changes of the insured commodities. In effect this is before-the-fact quality control of the surveyed prices, and elements of the index, measuring price changes in dwellings, furniture, furnishings and appliances, are "re-cycled" for this purpose. The adjustment of the value of cover may be done by the statistical agency concerned or, as happens in some cases in the New Zealand CPI's price survey, by the respondent insurance company itself. It is of ironic interest to note that many insurance companies offering "replacement value" policies proved upon investigation to be adjusting the dollar value of the policy's cover and the associated premiums by applying the change in the full consumer price index. *De facto*, therefore, some procedures already discussed in this article have been introduced into the index, not by the conscious decision by the Department of Statistics, but by the practices of part of the insurance industry.

3.6 In the case of motor vehicle insurance, the cost of insuring a range of vehicles specified in terms of age, make, quality and relevant driver characteristics is surveyed. The value of cover is adjusted by quality-controlled sub-indexes for new and used cars. No satisfactory means of adjusting the resultant price series for changes in "excesses" has yet been developed.

3.7 For medical insurances, the cost of premiums providing fixed cover for actual quantities and qualities of services and goods is surveyed, these being generally amenable to precise specification. As the insurance companies themselves adjust the premiums for cost changes there is no need for action in that respect by the survey. Any changes in the terms and conditions of the policies are adjusted for in terms of "normal" quality-control procedures. It is acknowledged, however, that intangibles such as improvements in the likelihood of a cure or of successful treatment due to technical improvements in medical care are beyond quantification and therefore cannot be accounted for.

3.8 In the New Zealand CPI only one form of life insurance is included, this being "mortgage repayment" insurance. There is no savings element in this type of insurance as it only provides for repayment of loans upon the policy-holder's death. Accordingly, although the nominally insured "item" is the death of the mortgagor, the value of the policy is not determined in terms of the "value" of the insured individual, but rather in terms of the level of unpaid debt. Accordingly the value of cover specified in the price survey is adjusted by changes in residential property values. In essence the technique is identical to that used for mortgage interest, except that, in this instance, the quality controlling value-adjustment takes place before the "rate" portion of the price change is surveyed.

4. Gambling and betting services

4.1 Consideration is currently being given to the inclusion of some gambling and betting services in the New Zealand CPI at the forthcoming 1988 index revision. Their past exclusion has been in part due to anticipated public reluctance to accept gambling and betting services as valid index items but has also been due to practical difficulties in weighting and pricing.

4.2 The weight for gambling and betting in a CPI is properly the net outlay on the service being provided, i.e. winnings netted against outlays. There can be considerable problems in obtaining such data for some forms of gambling, but not in the case of New Zealand's state-controlled "Golden Kiwi" lottery and "totalisator" horse-race and greyhound betting. It is these services which are being considered for inclusion in the index.

4.3 The pricing of gambling services would involve combining the movements of two factors:

(i) changes in the percentage "take" of the organiser(s), including tax; and

(ii) changes in the cost of maintaining the value of a "bet" at the same level of perceived satisfaction as a "bet" in the base period.

4.4 To maintain the "value of the bet" the most suitable indicator is considered to be the consumer price index in its entirety. The logic of this is that as inflation rises, incomes rise and average bets tend to rise in response to the same underlying forces. If the utility of gambling is the money value of the "win", then this devalues with inflation and to maintain its "value" the CPI is the appropriate measure.

4.5 It can therefore be seen that, in using the entire CPI as an element of price change for gambling services, the technique of using changes in subsets of the index as inputs into present or future indexes reaches its most generalised application. There is, however, no difference in principle between using the full index in this way and in using part of it – as is done to measure real price changes for hire-purchase agreements. It is simply a question of scale.

5. Conclusion

5.1 Techniques employed in the New Zealand consumers' price index in which measurements of price change incorporate changes in the level of other prices as measured by other elements of the index may at first appear to be double counting the price changes and/or leading to circular self-generating increases and hence be considered invalid. However, closer examination reveals that, in each instance, measurement of a fixed quantity and quality of services such as lending, insurance and gambling require incorporation of factors which reflect the changing purchasing power of the dollar in respect of relevant goods and services in order to impose relevant and proper quality control on the calculated price series.

5.2 By employing the discussed techniques in consumer price indexes, index statisticians may be perceived by critics to be internalising within their series escalation-clause-type adjustments. Inevitably this may lead to criticisms that the index is feeding inflationary forces rather than merely quantifying them. Arguably this is not the case. The double application of price changes in a commodity for both the item itself and for loans taken out to purchase that item is entirely legitimate and essential and does not necessarily involve any endogenous circular mechanism. Circularity only occurs where the output of a subset of the index is an input to a member of that subset. In practice this can be avoided by excluding that member to which the compound factor is to be applied.

5.3 Price escalation formulae and similar inflation-adjustment processes are major applications of a consumers' price index and testimony to public confidence in the series. Any suggestion that the index reflects less than the totality of price change must be firmly rejected. The exclusion by index statisticians of purchasing power adjustments for some classes of services would weaken the validity of that index in that a critical quality-control element would be omitted from measurement of "pure" price change.

Appendix 6

Pricing of new vehicles in the Australian consumer price index

Adjusting for quality change

by L. C. Clements, D. N. Allen, and T. C. Travers, Australian Bureau of Statistics

The general approach

1. The concept of "quality" used by the Australian Bureau of Statistics in the consumer price index is based on the notion of consumer utility. Questions relating to quality changes in durable goods such as motor vehicles are in general decided by reference to the notion of "value to the consumer" of the changes. It is not possible to conform strictly to this notion but it is used as the principal guide in making decisions on how to quantify quality changes.

2. Prices of new motor vehicles are obtained from a sample of dealers. The prices used in compiling the CPI are the actual prices paid by consumers; that is, prices net of discounts or "over allowances" (i.e. higher than normal prices paid) for used vehicles traded in.

3. Prices are collected in respect of a selection of about a dozen motor vehicle models; appropriate representation is given to various sizes of vehicle, to imported and locally produced vehicles, and to the various makes of cars which predominate in the market. The introduction of new models within the selection is the main indication that quality changes have occurred. However, minor changes are sometimes made in between model changes and often these are not publicly announced. Regular contacts with the manufacturers and importers concerned enable us to identify such changes and to take account of them.

4. Whenever changes are detected, comprehensive and quite detailed information is obtained from the manufacturer or importer concerning the nature of the changes, the reasons for the changes, and other technical and cost information to assist in assessing whether the changes do in fact involve changes in "quality" (in terms of "value to the consumer") and, if so, in evaluating those changes. When a model change occurs a study is also made of assessments of the new model by motoring organisations and in road tests published in motoring journals and newspapers. A decision is then taken as to what, if any, changes will be treated as quality changes and an estimated dollar value is placed on each of the changes separately. Consideration is always given to quality changes in both directions (that is, both improvements and degradations). For example, if an improvement in fuel economy is obtained at the expense of reduced engine power the latter adjustment would be deducted from the former, and the final adjustment would reflect net quality change. The price for the new model used in the index is the average selling price (net of discounts, etc.) less the estimated net value of improvements in quality.

5. The actual method used to determine the value to be placed on a change depends on the nature of the change and the amount of relevant data available. These changes tend to fall into one of the following four categories:

(a) Changes which involve the addition, deletion or substitution of equipment which is also sold separately in the market place; for example, replacement of cross-ply tyres by radial tyres. Both types of tyres are sold in substantial numbers in a very competitive market and the relative merits of each type of tyre are considered to be fairly well known to consumers. In such circumstances it seems reasonable to believe that the difference in retail prices between the two types of tyres is a reliable measure of the value to consumers of the difference in tyre qualities.

(b) Changes which involve fitting, as "standard equipment", features previously available as optional equipment, where the feature is not sold separately in the market place: an example of such a change is the fitting of automatic transmission as standard equipment in place of manual transmission. In these cases account is taken of the previous price of the feature when purchased as an option, and the proportion of buyers previously purchasing the option. If

a high proportion of buyers previously purchased the option the former option price would normally be regarded as a reliable measure of the value consumers place on that feature.

(c) Changes for which no market price is available but for which it is reasonable to consider that the change in manufacturing cost (marked up to retail value by application of an appropriate margin) provides a basis for assessing the value to the consumer of the change: an example of such a change is the use of a higher grade of material in covering the car's seats.

(d) Changes for which no actual data exist to assist in determining the monetary value to consumers of the change: such changes generally involve design changes which affect the basic characteristics of the vehicle, such as changes to body design which have the effect of increasing passenger space; or changes to suspension design which lead to substantial improvements in handling. In these cases the decision as to the monetary value to be placed on the change is necessarily subjective. However, by examination of information such as road test reports and costs and performance data provided by manufacturers it is usually possible to establish the significance of the changes and to determine a relatively narrow range within which the assessment of value to the consumer must fall.

6. Many changes associated with lower or higher production costs of course involve negligible, or no, quality changes. For example, a change from expensive to inexpensive production materials for certain components may not involve quality deterioration (provided they do not affect the durability or performance of that component). On the other hand, some changes which result in increased production costs are regarded purely as "styling" changes and are not regarded as quality improvements.

7. Occasionally, model changes occur which are of such a radical nature that the general approach used for evaluating and aggregating specific quality changes is unworkable and it becomes impossible to separate price changes and quality changes. Where the old and new models of a particular vehicle have been available for a lengthy overlap period, the difference in the value of the vehicles at a certain point in that period can be regarded as being equivalent to their quality difference and the price of the new model spliced into the index. However, it has rarely been possible to use this approach in the Australian CPI and it would not be regarded as a satisfactory approach unless both models were sold side by side in the same market, and in significant quantities, for a considerable period of time.

Quality adjustments for changes in fuel consumption

8. Up until comparatively recently no quality adjustments were made to reported retail prices of new motor cars in respect of changes in fuel consumption (measured in terms of litres per 100 kilometres). This practice could be justified on the grounds that fuel economy had not been generally regarded by the community as a major factor when comparing two consecutive models of a car. By contrast, such things as increased engine capacity and improved suspension have been regarded as quality improvements, in line with Australian community attitudes.

9. With steeply rising fuel prices in the past two or three years, it has become clear that fuel economy has now become a much more important factor in car purchase decisions. Manufacturers' advertising now gives considerable emphasis to fuel economy and the shift towards purchases of smaller new cars is indicative of changed community attitudes. (This shift of course is treated as a weight change in the CPI; that is, new combining weights are spliced into the index at intervals. However this is a different issue which is not discussed in the article.) As a further indication of changed community attitudes large cars have been subject to considerably larger declines in trade-in values than have smaller cars.

10. Because of the significance, over the life of the car, of savings resulting from reduced fuel consumption and because of strong evidence of changed community attitudes with regard to fuel consumption it was decided that allowance should be made for quality improvement resulting from this factor. Accordingly, since mid-1979 allowance has been made for such improvements on a number of occasions.

11. In quantifying the value to the consumer of the savings resulting from reduced fuel consumption the following steps are taken:

(a) the amount of savings in fuel is calculated on an annual basis, in terms of current quarter fuel prices; this involves using data from authenticated reports of reductions in fuel consumption, and making assumptions about:

(i) the number of years new car buyers will, on average, retain their cars before selling or trading in;

(ii) the average annual distance travelled for private purposes for the average retention period;

(iii) future fuel price movements over the average retention period.

(b) an estimate is made of the difference in re-sale (or market) value attributable to the differential fuel consumption at the end of the average retention period;

(c) the present capital value of the future savings resulting from the reduced fuel consumption is calculated; the formula used in this calculation requires an assumption to be made about future interest rates.

12. This method involves making a number of assumptions about the future. At present it is assumed that new car buyers, on average, retain their cars for five years before selling or trading in. Forecasts are also made of fuel price movements and interest rates over the ensuing five years. It is particularly difficult to estimate the difference in resale value attributable to the differential fuel consumption at the end of five years because there are as yet no firm data available on which to base an estimate. The value used in the calculation is therefore largely a subjective estimate.

13. The formula used to calculate the value to the consumer of reduced fuel consumption is:

$$PV = \frac{(ax_1)}{(1 + \frac{r}{2})} + \frac{(ax_1)(x_2)}{(1 + \frac{r}{2})(1 + r)}$$

$$+ \frac{(ax_1)(x_2)(x_3)}{(1 + \frac{r}{2})(1 + r)^2} + \frac{(ax_1)(x_2)(x_3)(x_4)}{(1 + \frac{r}{2})(1 + r)^3}$$

$$+ \frac{(ax_1)(x_2)(x_3)(x_4)(x_5)}{(1 + \frac{r}{2})(1 + r)^4} + \frac{b}{(1 + r)^5}$$

where PV = present capital value of the savings stream

a = estimated annual saving in fuel cost in terms of current quarter prices

x_n = estimated increase in fuel prices between current quarter and average for year n

r = estimated rate of interest payable in each full year

$\frac{r}{2}$ = estimated rate of interest payable between current quarter and the average of year 1

b = estimated difference in resale values, between the two models in five years' time, which is attributable to the differential fuel consumption.

Appendix 7

Price indices below the basic aggregation level *

by Bohdan J. Szulc, Central Research Section, Prices Division, Statistics Canada

1. Basic aggregation level

1.1. Notion of the basic aggregation level

Consumer price indices published by national statistical agencies, including Statistics Canada, are mostly described as measures of price change obtained by comparing, through time, the cost of a fixed set of commodities. Prevalence of this *fixed-basket approach* (fixed-quantities approach) in the computation of consumer price indices over the period between links is a matter of fact, whether the approach is being adopted for its own conceptual merits or to approximate a constant-utility price index series.

As a result, consumer price indices are usually represented by some variant of the following aggregative formula:

$$(1) \qquad \frac{\sum_{i=1}^{N} p_t^i q_c^i}{\sum_{i=1}^{N} p_b^i q_c^i}$$

where p_t^i and p_b^i

are prices of the *i*-th individual commodity in the observation (given) time *t* and in the base time *b*, respectively

q_c^i

is its fixed quantity, drawn from the basket reference time *c*, and

N

is the number of all individual commodities covered by the given index

or by one of the numerous equivalent formulae, expressed as a weighted arithmetic mean of price relatives, such as, for example:

$$(2) \qquad \frac{\sum_{i=1}^{N} p_{t/b}^i w^i}{\sum_{i=1}^{N} w^i}$$

where $p_{t/b}^i = p_t^i \div p_b^i$

is a price relative for the *i*th individual commodity, and

$w^i = p_b^i \times q_c^i$

is a "hybrid-value" weight assigned to it.

Caution, however, is necessary in interpreting these popular formulae. If read literally, they oversimplify both the underlying concept and the computation procedure of contemporary consumer price indices. The latter are not generated by comparing, through time, the cost of all individual consumer goods deemed to be represented by a given index. It is commonly stated that consumer price indices cannot be calculated, strictly speaking, by means of formula (1) or (2) because of the impossibility of collecting prices or monitoring price change for all individual commodities. While this is true, the volatility of the purchase and consumption of individual goods

* The article explicitly deals with consumer price indices. *Mutatis mutandis*, however, most of its reasoning and conclusions also apply to other price index series being currently produced by national statistical agencies.

is another reason not to do so. Indeed, an index series based on the assumption of fixed quantitative proportions among all individual goods, if only between link times,[1] could be deceptive and subject to odd variations.

Nowadays, most consumer price indices are constructed in a stepwise fashion, following the fixed-basket concept in spirit rather than to the letter. The all-items index reflects, then, fixed quantitative proportions, but only among composite commodities at a certain aggregation level, hereafter referred to as the *basic aggregation level.*[2] Indices for aggregates between the basic and the all-items levels, referred to as *macro-indices*, enjoy the same properties. On the other hand, indices below the basic level are initially derived by sample estimation of *micro-indices*, which may be combined in a flexible way, using various assumptions and techniques.

1.2. Role of basic aggregates

By definition, basic aggregates play a strategic role in the index structure. They serve as strata in price sampling and provide primary blocks to build up indices at higher aggregation levels consistent with the fixed-basket approach. Under these circumstances, macro-indices can be interpreted as weighted arithmetic means of indices for basic aggregates, so that the latter also predetermine how one can decompose and analyse price movement at macro-levels. It follows that a very careful designation of basic aggregates is necessary to assure their optimal functioning in all capacities.

Furthermore, it is highly desirable to inform users about the aggregates designated as basic in the above sense, although this is not a standard procedure in publications about consumer price indices.[3] Such precision is useful not just to satisfy the curiosity of users but also to help them in reproducing index calculations similar to those in the official series. In addition, the information about basic aggregates could be useful when different price index series are compared to each other, as illustrated by the following example.

Statistical agencies and researchers occasionally analyse divergences between the corresponding series of Laspeyres and Paasche price indices, in order to assess the formula bias.[4] Assuming a negative correlation of quantity shifts with price changes among consumer goods, one expects Laspeyres indices to be definitely higher than the respective Paasche indices. In practice, the divergences often turn out to be rather small and, sometimes, even of the opposite sign to what is expected.[5] It is then tempting to consider the purported correlation and, therefore, also the formula bias as immaterial. However, such a statement would not be conclusive. The bifurcation into Laspeyres and Paasche indices only starts at the basic aggregation level, whatever its designation. Indices below this level are common to both series, hence the quantity shifts that actually took place among consumer goods below the basic level have no impact on the observed divergences between the corresponding Laspeyres and Paasche indices. Yet, the price-induced substitution of goods and the resulting negative correlation of quantity shifts with price changes are more likely to happen among goods that are directly substitutable than among broad categories of consumer commodities. It follows that one can observe paradoxical or negligible divergences between the two price index series just because the basic aggregation level has been set relatively high. It is possible that the expected formula bias would be evident over the same

---

[1] According to the present Canadian practice, consumer baskets are changed and index series are linked every four years.

[2] Statistics Canada explicitly introduced the notion of basic aggregates (in the above sense, though initially under the term of "elementary commodity groups") for the first time in the Reference Paper for its consumer price index series based on 1974 expenditures. Their functions were described in a more comprehensive way in the Reference Paper for the series based on 1978 expenditures, while the term "basic" was first used in the Reference Paper for the series based on 1982 expenditures. See Statistics Canada (1978), p. 18 (1982), p. 28 and (1985), p. 34. Incidentally, J. D. Sellwood (1986) uses the term "(basic) composite item" in a similar sense.

[3] In *Statistical Sources and Methods*, Vol. 1, Consumer Price Indices, published by the ILO in 1984, two levels of commodity aggregations were mentioned in descriptions of national indices. They were termed "major groups" and "items", the latter meaning the smallest grouping for which a weight is used. However, in some cases, countries providing the information diverged from this definition. The 1987 edition seeks to clarify the matter.

[4] In this article, the term "Laspeyres index" is used only in the strict sense.

[5] See Généreux (1983) and Statistics Canada (1985), pp. 104-105.

time period, if basic aggregates were designated closer to individual commodities. In any case, an explicit reference to the basic aggregation level, its functions and actual designation could help users in understanding this comparative analysis.

1.3. Actual computation of macro-indices

As stated before, macro-indices are supposed to reflect fixed quantitative proportions among basic aggregates. Theoretically, this could be achieved in two ways, either by imitating the aggregative formula (1), as follows:

$$(3)\qquad \frac{\sum_{j=1}^{M} P_t^j Q_c^j}{\sum_{j=1}^{M} P_b^j Q_c^j}$$

where Q_c^j

is the fixed "quantity" of a given composite commodity that is designated as the j-th basic aggregate, estimated as of the basket reference time c

P_t^j and P_b^j

are "prices" of this composite commodity, estimated as of the observation time t and the base time b, respectively, and

M is the number of basic aggregates contained in the given macro-aggregate,

or the weighted arithmetic mean formula (2), as follows:

$$(4)\qquad \frac{\sum_{j=1}^{M} P_{t/b}^j W^j}{\sum_{j=1}^{M} W^j}$$

where $W^j = V_c^j \div P_{c/b}^j$

is a "hybrid-value" weight assigned to the j-th basic aggregate and estimated assuming price levels as of the base time b and quantity levels as of the basket reference time c.

$P_{t/b}^j$ and $P_{c/b}^j$

are indices for this aggregate that estimate price change from the base time b till the observation time t and the basket reference time c, respectively and

V_c^j

is the actual value of (the actual expenditure on) the j-th basic aggregate as of the basket reference time c.

Generally, the weighted arithmetic mean formula (4) is much more suitable for practical purposes than the aggregative formula (3). Firstly, the very notions of "quantity" and "price" become obscure when applied to basic aggregates, which are sometimes composed of quite heterogeneous commodity groupings. This is not the case with notions of "value" (expenditure) and "price change", which are perfectly applicable to basic aggregates, however heterogeneous they may be. Secondly, even if it was conceptually acceptable to consider some kind of "total quantity" or "average price" in certain circumstances, a serious problem would remain concerning their estimation. Again, this is much less a problem with "total value" or "average price change". While aggregate values (expenditures) are among the most available macro-economic data, aggregate quantities are not. Still more complicated is the estimation of "average prices" for basic aggregates from samples of individual commodities. Not only does their universe typically exhibit a large price dispersion but, due to a lack of appropriate stratification criteria, it is impractical to create commodity groupings that would be relatively homogeneous from the point of view of price levels. On the other hand, it is feasible to stratify the universe of individual commodities into groupings which are relatively homogeneous from the point of view of price change, so greatly easing the estimation of average price changes. In particular, the criteria used for analytical considerations to designate basic aggregates (such as end-use of commodities, their main component materials or production methods) bear little, if any, correlation with price levels but are strongly correlated with price changes. For this reason, basic aggregates automatically become natural strata from the point of view of price changes, while they are not proper strata from the point of view of price levels.

There are good reasons to present the weighted arithmetic mean formula (4), or an equivalent one, in documents describing consumer price indices, and not only as information about the algorithm actually applied in the construction of published index series. In fact, formula (4) is also instrumental in reconstructing (constructing) macro-indices consistent with the official methodology and in analysing (decomposing) them, tasks often performed by users of consumer price index series. In order to make this information fully beneficial, however, price indices and weights at the basic aggregation level should be made available as well, together with comments on how to simulate the published index series. In this context, the users need to be advised that the weights applied for averaging basic price indices have to be expressed (re-expressed) to reflect price levels as of the base time of these indices and that no averaging may be done across link times in the published series.[1]

On the other hand, if just formula (4) was shown, the index concept would be concealed from the users behind its mechanics. It is expedient, therefore, to present at least the idea given by the aggregative formula (3), i.e. the idea that macro-indices reflect fixed quantitative proportions among basic aggregates, drawn from the basket reference time. In any case, the users should be warned that neither formula (4) nor (3) applies across the link times.

1.4. Derivation of indices for basic aggregates

It follows from the previous section that price indices are needed for all basic aggregates. While some of them may be imputed, most are derived from sample price data, explicitly collected to represent the "pure" price movement of commodities contained in a given basic aggregate.

Sample price data may be used directly in estimating an index for the given basic aggregate or may be first used to estimate indices for its sub-aggregates. In the latter case, a weighted arithmetic mean formula is normally applied to combine them into the basic aggregate index. In statistical terms, this is a stratified sampling procedure, recommended when reasonable stratification criteria and strata weights are available. In such cases, the quantitative proportions among the sub-aggregates are kept fixed in the basic aggregate index, though not necessarily during the entire period between the consecutive link times designated for the macro-indices. This offers a certain flexibility in the index-making process and provides a clear distinction between the basic aggregation level and the lower-level commodity strata.[2] The stratification procedure may be applied more than once before the index for the given basic aggregate is calculated. Whatever the number of the intermediate steps, there is always the first step, when a price index for a certain commodity is directly derived from the sample price data. Such indices, referred to as *micro-indices*, are the main topic of this article.

There is an abundant literature, both theoretical and descriptive, on the computation of consumer price indices above the basic aggregation level, but little is written about their derivation below that level. In this respect, the index makers resemble those chefs who only allow their dishes

[1] Take as an example the Canadian consumer price index series with the 1974 basket, which was linked to the previous series as of September 1978. The corresponding reference paper (see Statistics Canada 1978) contained only one set of weights, specifically the 1974 family expenditure data, without much insistence on how they could be used in the index calculation. Many users tried to apply these data for averaging all kinds of indices, such as those on the 1971 base (which were chain indices) or those with the previous year as their base, and were surprised to receive index numbers different from those published. In fact, the expenditure data, as released, cannot be used to simulate the calculation of official indices at all. Although they relate to 1974, they do not apply to the 1974-based indices, which, if calculated, would be of a chain form. They do not apply, either, to indices on a September 1978 base, because they should be first price-updated to September 1978 before being used as weights.

[2] In addition, a different source of weight data is frequently used for the basic aggregates and for their sub-aggregates.

to be presented to patrons at a certain stage of preparation, without showing how they have been mixed and simmered in the kitchen. The reserve in explaining these details does not imply that the meals are unhealthy or tasteless, and a similar conclusion holds for price indices. On the other hand, the early stages of preparation do impact on final results and are of interest, at least to some specialists.

Many reasons may contribute to this relative silence on indices below the basic aggregation level. Such indices are derived by using a great variety of techniques, whose exhaustive description might be too long and boring for the general public. Many of these techniques are quite empirical, often based on compromises and ad hoc decisions. This might be considered not sufficiently attractive, or even not sufficiently orthodox, to be presented to theoreticians. In fact, there is not much in index theory to comfort practitioners working in this area. Only a few authors paid attention to the topic of deriving price indices up to the basic aggregation level, in particular, R. G. D. Allen (1975) and A. G. Carruthers, D. J. Sellwood, P. Ward (1980).

This article is not meant to fill all the gaps in the literature, but, rather to tackle some aspects of the problem. In particular, various formulae are subsequently discussed in the context of deriving micro-indices from sample price data.

2. Formulae for micro-indices

2.1. Introductory considerations

The universe of prices for a given commodity in a particular time is composed of all price quotations for each and every unit [1] purchased in that time. In order to compute a micro-index, price samples are drawn in the observation and base times, either randomly or by an arbitrary selection of individual commodities whose prices are taken into account. The micro-index, approximating collective price change for the given commodity, can then be computed using one of the following two approaches:

I sample mean prices are first calculated for the observation and base times and their ratio is considered as the micro-index, or

II price relatives are first calculated for the corresponding individual commodities in both samples and their mean is considered as the micro-index.

Several concrete solutions are conceivable within each of the two approaches. First of all, various kinds of means could be used for averaging prices or price relatives. Among them, the arithmetic, harmonic and geometric means are best known.

Furthermore, it is possible to envisage *a priori* that these means could be calculated either with or without specific weights attached to particular prices or price relatives. The weights, however, would not make much sense if they just reflected the importance of those individual commodities that happen to fall into the sample. This becomes particularly obvious when one realises how small price samples usually are and how they are actually drawn from the universe. On the other hand, while weights reflecting the importance of larger commodity groups with presumably similar price behaviour, if available, would make sense, this procedure would simply create another stratification step, and, as described in the previous section, there still would be a need for further micro-indices to represent price movement of these groups. In conclusion, micro-indices considered in this article are assumed to use equiweighted ("unweighted") means.

The following list contains some of the micro-index formulae, ordered by the approach and kind of mean:

1. First approach:

A. Arithmetic mean

$$P_{t/b}^{IA} = \frac{\sum_{i=1}^{n} p_t^i}{n} \div \frac{\sum_{i=1}^{n} p_b^i}{n};$$

[1] These are standard physical units, to which prices of the given commodity generally refer.

H. Harmonic mean

$$P_{t/b}^{IH} = \frac{n}{\sum_{i=1}^{n} \frac{1}{p_t^i}} \div \frac{n}{\sum_{i=1}^{n} \frac{1}{p_b^i}};$$

G. Geometric mean

$$P_{t/b}^{IG} = \left[\prod_{i=1}^{n} p_t^i\right]^{1/n} \div \left[\prod_{i=1}^{n} p_b^i\right]^{1/n}.$$

II. Second approach:

A. Arithmetic mean

$$P_{t/b}^{IIA} = \frac{\sum_{i=1}^{n} p_{t/b}^i}{n};$$

H. Harmonic mean

$$P_{t/b}^{IIH} = \frac{n}{\sum_{i=1}^{n} \frac{1}{p_{t/b}^i}};$$

G. Geometric mean

$$P_{t/b}^{IIG} = \left[\prod_{i=1}^{n} p_{t/b}^i\right]^{1/n}$$

where

$i = 1, 2, \ldots, n$ are individual commodities in the sample.

Of all listed formulae, only the two using geometric means provide the same result in both approaches, regardless of price data. In all other cases, the two approaches generally lead to different results and the differences may be quite large. This is so for the most popular formulae — those which use arithmetic means. It will be proven in the subsequent sections that at least some of the discrepancies do not result from a mere combination of circumstances, but are systematic.

2.2. Comparisons of selected micro-index formulae

The micro-index formulae using arithmetic and harmonic means are shown in the Annex in three forms, after an algebraic transformation whenever applicable:

— as ratios of arithmetic mean prices (with explicit or implicit quantity weights),
— as arithmetic means of price relatives (with explicit or implicit value weights), and
— as aggregative price indices (with explicit or implicit fixed quantities).

Several comparisons of formulae are now possible due to their transformation to identical forms.

It follows from the comparison of indices in the ratio-of-arithmetic-mean-prices form, that the explicit or implicit quantity weights attached to particular individual commodities from the sample are:

— equal to each other when formula P^{IA} is applied,
— inversely proportional to prices in each time when formula P^{IH} is applied (i.e. commodities with lower prices in any given time have more impact on the mean prices in that time than other commodities),
— inversely proportional to prices in the base time when formula P^{IIA} is applied (i.e. commodities with lower prices in the base time have more impact on the mean prices in both times than other commodities), and
— inversely proportional to prices in the observation time when formula P^{IIH} is applied (i.e. commodities with lower prices in the observation time have more impact on the mean prices in both times than other commodities).

By comparing indices in the arithmetic-mean-of-price-relatives form, one can conclude that the explicit or implicit value weights attached to particular individual commodities from the sample are:

— equal to each other when formula P^{IIA} is applied,
— proportional to prices in the base time when formula P^{IA} is applied (i.e. commodities with higher prices in the base time have more impact on the mean price relative than other commodities),
— inversely proportional to prices in the observation time when formula P^{IH} is applied (i.e. commodities with lower prices in the observation time have more impact on the mean price relative than other commodities), and
— inversely proportional to price relatives when formula P^{IIH} is applied (i.e. commodities with lower price relatives have more impact in the mean price relative than other commodities).

Finally, by comparing indices in the aggregative-price-index form, one can conclude that the explicit or implicit fixed quantities attached to particular individual commodities from the sample are:

— equal to each other when formula P^{IA} is applied,
— inversely proportional to prices in the base time when formula P^{IIA} is applied (i.e. commodities with lower prices in the base time have more impact on the aggregative index than other commodities),
— inversely proportional to prices in the observation time when formula P^{IIH} is applied (i.e. commodities with lower prices in the observation time have more impact on the aggregative index than other commodities), and
— inversely proportional to both prices in the base and the observation time when formula P^{IH} is applied (i.e. commodities with lower prices in the observation and in the base times have more impact on the aggregative index than other commodities).

The above findings, although interesting in many respects, do not lead to any direct and firm conclusion about the actual merits or demerits of particular index formulae. The situation would be different if we knew which individual commodities should have more impact on the index and in which way. Normally, however, there are no comparative data on expenditures made and/or quantities purchased for particular commodities in the sample and, even if such data were available, it would be wrong to treat individual commodities in the sample as strata, since their selection is not made with this purpose in mind.

Theoreticians may object to this pessimistic note. It is indeed possible, at least ideally, to design price samples in such a way that prices related to each unit of the commodity would have the same chance of being selected for the sample, and in this case formula P^{IA} would be a strong favourite. On the other hand, a design in which every dollar spent on the commodity had an equal chance of selection would argue for the use of formula P^{IIA}. Yet, no sample design can in practice provide this kind of assurance in both the base and observation times, particularly because of the principle of "matched samples", which will be discussed in subsequent sections. Therefore, other premises should be taken into account in evaluating the choice of the micro-index formulae.

2.3. Relationships between selected micro-index formulae

There are some unconditional and some conditional relations between micro-index formulae. The following two belong to the former category:

(i)
$$P^{IG}_{t/b} = P^{IIG}_{t/b}$$

which can be directly deduced from the formulae definitions shown in section 2.1, and

(ii)
$$P^{IIH}_{t/b} \leqslant P^{IIG}_{t/b} \leqslant P^{IIA}_{t/b}$$

which results from a more general relationship between the arithmetic, harmonic and geometric means for the same set of values.

In order to find further relationships, a reasoning similar to that invented by L. Bortkiewicz with respect to the discrepancy between the corresponding Paasche and Laspeyres price indices will be used.[1] For this purpose, compare micro-index formulae in their arithmetic-mean-of-price-relatives form, as presented in the Annex. All of them are arithmetic means of the same set of values (price relatives) but with different weights, whether explicit or implicit. The correlation of price relatives with ratios of alternative weights decides which of the respective micro-indices will yield higher numerical results. This way, the following conditional relationships can be found:

$P^{IIA}_{t/b} > P^{IA}_{t/b}$ and $P^{IIH}_{t/b} < P^{IH}_{t/b}$ — when there is a negative correlation of price relatives $p^i_{t/b}$ with the base-time prices p^i_b, which is likely to be a preponderant situation (because commodities with relatively low base-time prices tend to exhibit relatively high price increase),

$P^{IIH}_{t/b} < P^{IA}_{t/b}$ and $P^{IIA}_{t/b} > P^{IH}_{t/b}$ — when there is a positive correlation of price relatives $p^i_{t/b}$ with the observation-time prices p^i_t, which is likely to be a quite frequent situation (because commodities with relatively high observation-time prices have a good chance to be among those that exhibited relatively high price increases), and

$P^{IA}_{t/b} > P^{IH}_{t/b}$ — when there is a positive correlation of price relatives $p^i_{t/b}$ with the product of the base-time and the observation-time prices $p^i_b \cdot p^i_t$, which may or may not happen (because nothing in the market behaviour favours either situation).

The above analysis has proven that some micro-index formulae tend to yield higher numerical results than some other formulae, but it failed to provide sufficient arguments to call any formula downward-biased or upward-biased. Indeed, the formulae have been compared to each other and not to the only valid benchmark, which would be a known, correct measure of the pure price change for a given commodity. Again, to find such a measure, other premises should be taken into account – in particular, the actual price sampling techniques.

2.4. Problem of "matched samples" and linking of micro-indices

If the given commodity was homogeneous in quality and all its units represented the same quantity, the universe mean price would be a meaningful parameter and the ratio of such parameters from the observation and base times would be an ideal indicator of the pure price change for this commodity. The task of computing the corresponding micro-index would then be reduced to a sample estimation of both universe mean prices, which could be best achieved using the arithmetic mean prices from random samples of a sufficient size. Indeed, according to the theory of estimation, a sample mean is an unbiased, consistent and, under normality conditions, most efficient estimator of the respective universe mean.

In reality, micro-indices are computed, not for perfectly homogeneous individual commodities, but rather for ones that are heterogeneous.[2] As a result, ratios of the universe mean prices may become biased as indicators of the pure price change if the given commodity exhibits trends towards higher or lower quality. If samples are drawn independently from the universe each time, the ratios of their means may be additionally impaired by erratic variations in the quality mix among the selected individual commodities. The risk is very real with samples of a small size, which is often the case. For this reason, the principle of "matched samples" is applied in most practical situations, by which only pairs of identical or equivalent individual commodities are taken into account in any two directly compared (divided by each other) sample mean prices.

The use of matched samples reduces the representativity of the samples with the passage of time, whether they have been initially selected at random or by an arbitrary decision.[3] In order

[1] L. Bortkiewicz (1922, 1924) first published his analysis in 1922, but it is reproduced in many contemporary textbooks and papers, among others by R. G. D. Allen (1975, pp. 62-63). A generalised version has been shown, for example, by B. J. Szulc (1983, pp. 563-564).

[2] In fact, commodities are not simply homogeneous or heterogeneous but, rather, they exhibit a certain degree of heterogeneity. The assessment of this degree may depend on one's point of view.

[3] The use of matched samples also implies that there cannot be true independent random price samples in both the base and the observation times.

to minimise the effect of this drawback, samples have to be periodically or occasionally updated and, in such a case, two different samples are established each time – one for comparisons with the matched sample from the preceding time and another for comparisons with the matched sample in the subsequent time. The two resulting ratios of sample mean prices are then linked to each other, which is not without its own dangers. In fact, in specific situations, linking of indices may result in a systematic bias.[1]

Considering the impact of linking, index formulae can be classified into two categories, namely transitive, which include ratios of equiweighted mean prices (whether arithmetic, harmonic or geometric), and non-transitive, which include the equiweighted and harmonic means of price relatives.[2] The former provide the same result by a direct index as from linking in any link time, while the non-transitive formulae do not have this property. The fact that a chain index diverges from its direct counterpart is not, *per se*, symptomatic of the unsuitability of a given index formula for linking. An index formula, however, may be considered not suitable for linking when linking tends to aggravate the otherwise known bias of the corresponding direct index.

Take as an example the equiweighted arithmetic mean of price relatives P^{IIA}, also referred to as the Sauerbeck formula, one of the favourites in the computation of micro-indices. In this formula, the base-time value weights are implicitly assumed to be equal for each commodity and, consequently, the implicit base-time quantities assigned to particular commodities are inversely proportional to their base-time prices. Such assumptions are justified if the commodity sample has been drawn in the base time with equal probability given to every dollar spent. The Sauerbeck index, though, like the Laspeyres index, has a tendency to overstate price increases and to understate price decreases compared to the corresponding fixed-utility price index.[3] Moreover, if relative prices tend to "bounce" and if linking is undertaken within the bouncing cycle, a chain Sauerbeck index becomes definitely higher than its direct counterpart, hence also definitely more biased than the latter. The size of the bias depends on the periodicity of linking, combined with the periodicity of price bouncing.[4] In other words, some upward bias is to be expected when micro-indices are calculated in a direct mode as equiweighted arithmetic means of price relatives, but the bias may become very large when this formula is applied in a chain mode.

In the Canadian practice, an automated system of linking micro-indices every month is in service, operating whether there is a change in the sample or not. The system has many advantages, assuring a flexible updating of samples and providing the opportunity to monitor price changes on an ongoing basis, but it virtually rules out the use of the Sauerbeck formula for all those commodities that exhibit frequent price bouncing. Since the system calculates micro-indices using both, the equiweighted arithmetic means of price relatives and the ratios of equiweighted arithmetic mean prices, the magnitude of divergence is readily available and it is often quite spectacular when the two formulae are applied in a chain mode with monthly linking to commodities subject to sales with special prices.

The additional bias, resulting from linking micro-indices, can be avoided when transitive index formulae are used. In Canada, most micro-indices are calculated using the ratio of equiweighted arithmetic mean prices P^{IA}, which has a long tradition and is considered to be more easily understood by the general public than other transitive index formulae, such as the ratios of equiweighted harmonic or geometric mean prices. The reasons for using this particular transitive micro-index formula are not that strong, though, and in future discussions other factors might be taken into account as well. If a broader use of random or quasi-random sampling techniques were contemplated in the future for example, a re-examination of the issue in question would certainly be justified.

---

[1] For a comprehensive discussion on the bias of linking, see Szulc (1983).

[2] The equiweighted geometric mean of price relatives is transitive, because it is equal to the transitive ratio of equiweighted geometric mean prices.

[3] When the equiweighted arithmetic mean of price relatives is expressed in the aggregative form (see the Annex), it becomes clear that the Sauerbeck index implicitly uses the fixed quantitative proportions among commodities as they have been in the base time (i.e. proportions inverse to the base-time prices) and by this feature it resembles the Laspeyres index. Both of them do not allow for price-induced substitutions between commodities (or, as a matter of fact, for any substitutions), hence they tend to give higher results than the corresponding cost-of-living price index assuming fixed base-time utility.

[4] See Szulc (1983), pp. 552-554.

2.5. Role of outlets in the computation of micro-indices

There is no sample frame embodying all individual commodities purchased by the population, not to speak of information on the quantities and values of transactions. For this reason, outlets (markets) are normally the first stage of sample selection, whether random or purposive, and the commodities whose prices are the actual subject of the surveys are selected within the sample outlets. In theory, the price sample could be stratified according to the type of outlet, but in practice there is not enough knowledge about the pricing behaviour and the importance of specific outlet types with respect to particular commodity groups to justify such a stratification on a large scale.

Without stratification by outlets, price quotations from all outlets are put together with the same weight in the process of computation of micro-indices. In fact, outlets represent clusters of the actually purchased single units of the given commodity (and of transactions made with respect to this commodity), but they are clusters with a peculiar feature. Their size is, indeed, correlated with the surveyed variable, i.e. with the price. Normally, one expects that outlets with lower prices would attract more customers, sell more and have larger transactions. When the sample is being established, it is possible to take into account the actual volume of transactions at that time and to offer a higher probability of selection to outlets with a larger volume of transactions, whether the sampling is done at random or by an arbitrary decision (in Canada, purposive sampling prevails in the area of consumer goods, with priority given to outlets and commodities that make larger sales). The sample, however, remains unchanged for some time (because of the principle of matched samples) and, subsequently, may not reflect the redistribution of sales, which is to some degree a function of price changes. As a result, outlets offering reduced prices are likely to become under-represented, while those with increased prices become over-represented.

In the described conditions, the equiweighted arithmetic mean of sample prices has an upward bias. This is not so with the equiweighted harmonic mean of sample prices, which automatically assigns to each quotation an implicit quantity weight inversely proportional to the price quoted. The former is based on a tacit assumption that the same number of units of the given commodity corresponds to each price, while the latter is based on the assumption that the same expenditure corresponds to each price. This property of the equiweighted harmonic mean of sample prices may offer a convenient solution in the case of commodities relatively homogeneous by quality, but with frequent "price wars", special prices, etc.

2.6. Micro-indices for commodities heterogeneous by quality

The use of equiweighted harmonic means of sample prices (and their ratios as micro-indices) is probably less advisable in the case of commodities that are heterogeneous from the point of view of quality and, consequently, also from the point of view of price levels. When the same or similar goods are sold at different prices, the assumption that their purchase, in quantitative terms, is inversely proportionate to those price levels is rough but consistent with normally perceived consumer behaviour. On the other hand, when very different goods are sold at very different prices, such an assumption would be problematic, at best.

Moreover, in the case of heterogeneous commodities, even the use of ratios of equiweighted arithmetic mean prices may be considered questionable. This index formula particularly emphasises commodities with high base-time prices, which is quite obvious when the formula is expressed as an arithmetic mean of price relatives (see the Annex), where the base-time prices appear as weights attached to particular price relatives. Then, there is the risk that micro-indices using the formula in question could be subjected to an undue influence exerted by a few expensive commodities, which entered the sample because of arbitrary decisions taken by price surveyors or other specialists (the risk is particularl y real when samples are small, which is quite often the case).

There is no perfect solution to this problem. It is impossible to make all commodities at the micro-level very homogeneous. This would mean very narrow specifications in the entire spectrum of commodities, common to all outlets and, maybe, regions. For many commodity groups, it would make the selected varieties very difficult to find in the market, much less representative and sometimes truly marginal. In conclusion, there will always be commodities at micro-level that are very heterogeneous by quality.

If the commodity is heterogeneous to the point that the use of ratios of equiweighted arithmetic mean prices as micro-indices become questionable, then the problem of linking has to be seriously examined. The equiweighted arithmetic and harmonic means of price relatives are not transitive and often biased, when used in a chain mode. One of the solutions could be a limitation of the frequency of linking, e.g. from monthly to yearly, which is acceptable for some commodities that do not require very frequent sample updatings. Another solution could be the use of price-updated weights, derived from the initial equal weights, to be assigned to particular price relatives. In both cases, however, the continuity of the series of price relatives should be assured, which creates new problems.

Finally, other kinds of micro-indices could be envisaged. One obvious candidate is the equiweighted geometric means of price relatives, which is transitive, equal to the ratio of equiweighted geometric mean prices and has no tendency to exhibit extreme results. Curiously, this formula does not seem to be very popular, except for the International Comparison Project. The reason for this lack of popularity may be the fear that the formula is not sufficiently intelligible for the general public, a fear which is not necessarily justified. In any case, the geometric means should at least be considered in the discussions on the future development of consumer price indices.

References

Allen, R. G. D.: *Index numbers in theory and practice*, Chicago, Aldine Publishing Co., 1975.

Bortkiewicz, L.: "Zweck und Struktur einer Preisindexzahl", Parts 1 and 2 in *Nordisk Statistik Tidskrift*, Stockholm, Vol. 1, 1922, Vol. 3, 1924.

Carruthers A. G., Sellwood, D. J., Ward, P.: "Recent developments in the Retail Prices Index", in *The Statistician*, Vol. 29, No. 1, London, Mar. 1980.

Généreux, P. A.: "Impact of the choice of formulae on the Canadian Consumer Price Index", in *Price level measurement: Proceedings from a conference sponsored by Statistics Canada*, Ottawa, Nov. 1983.

International Labour Office: *Statistical Sources and Methods*, Vol. 1, Consumer Price Indices, Geneva, 1980.

Sellwood, D. J.: "Reduction of errors in a consumer price index", in *Bulletin of Labour Statistics*, ILO, 1987-1.

Statistics Canada: *The Consumer Price Index Reference Paper, concepts and procedures, updating based on 1978 expenditures*, Catalogue No. 62-546, Occasional, Ottawa, Nov. 1978.

ibid., Catalogue No. 62-553, Occasional, Ottawa, May 1982.

The Consumer Price Index Reference Paper, updating based on 1982 expenditures, Catalogue No. 62-553, Occasional, Ottawa, Feb. 1985.

Szulc, B. J.: "Linking price index numbers", in *Price level measurement: Proceedings from a conference sponsored by Statistics Canada*, Ottawa, Nov. 1983.

Annex

Micro-index	Ratio of arithmetic mean prices	Arithmetic mean of price relatives	Aggregative price index
$P^{IA}_{t/b}$	$\frac{\sum_{i=1}^{n} p^i_t \cdot 1}{\sum_{i=1}^{n} 1} \div \frac{\sum_{i=1}^{n} p^i_b \cdot 1}{\sum_{i=1}^{n} 1}$	$\frac{\sum_{i=1}^{n} p^i_{t/b} \cdot p^i_b}{\sum_{i=1}^{n} p^i_b}$	$\frac{\sum_{i=1}^{n} p^i_t \cdot 1}{\sum_{i=1}^{n} p^i_b \cdot 1}$
$P^{IH}_{t/b}$	$\frac{\sum_{i=1}^{n} p^i_t \cdot \frac{1}{p^i_t}}{\sum_{i=1}^{n} \frac{1}{p^i_t}} \div \frac{\sum_{i=1}^{n} p^i_b \cdot \frac{1}{p^i_b}}{\sum_{i=1}^{n} \frac{1}{p^i_b}}$	$\frac{\sum_{i=1}^{n} p^i_{t/b} \cdot \frac{1}{p^i_t}}{\sum_{i=1}^{n} \frac{1}{p^i_t}}$	$\frac{\sum_{i=1}^{n} p^i_t \cdot \frac{1}{p^i_b p^i_t}}{\sum_{i=1}^{n} p^i_b \cdot \frac{1}{p^i_b p^i_t}}$
$P^{IIA}_{t/b}$	$\frac{\sum_{i=1}^{n} p^i_t \cdot \frac{1}{p^i_b}}{\sum_{i=1}^{n} \frac{1}{p^i_b}} \div \frac{\sum_{i=1}^{n} p^i_b \cdot \frac{1}{p^i_b}}{\sum_{i=1}^{n} \frac{1}{p^i_b}}$	$\frac{\sum_{i=1}^{n} p^i_{t/b} \cdot 1}{\sum_{i=1}^{n} 1}$	$\frac{\sum_{i=1}^{n} p^i_t \cdot \frac{1}{p^i_b}}{\sum_{i=1}^{n} p^i_b \frac{1}{p^i_b}}$
$P^{IIH}_{t/b}$	$\frac{\sum_{i=1}^{n} p^i_t \cdot \frac{1}{p^i_t}}{\sum_{i=1}^{n} \frac{1}{p^i_t}} \div \frac{\sum_{i=1}^{n} p^i_b \cdot \frac{1}{p^i_t}}{\sum_{i=1}^{n} \frac{1}{p^i_t}}$	$\frac{\sum_{i=1}^{n} p^i_{t/b} \cdot \frac{p^i_b}{p^i_t}}{\sum_{i=1}^{n} \frac{p^i_b}{p^i_t}}$	$\frac{\sum_{i=1}^{n} p^i_t \cdot \frac{1}{p^i_t}}{\sum_{i=1}^{n} p^i_b \cdot \frac{1}{p^i_t}}$

Superscripts $i = 1,2, \ldots n$ indicate individual commodities in the sample.

Appendix 8

Treatment of seasonal fresh fruit and vegetables in CPI

by L. C. Clements, Prices Branch, Australian Bureau of Statistics

Introduction

1. This note outlines briefly the results of recent work in the Prices Branch of the Australian Bureau of Statistics relating to the future treatment of "seasonal" (i.e. available for only part of each year) fresh fruit and vegetables in the CPI. It does not attempt to canvass the theoretical implications of the various options considered or to argue the case for or against particular approaches in detail. Rather, it records the process of elimination we went through in attempting to find a practical solution consistent with the data we have available and with the need for the treatment adopted to be readily explainable to CPI users and broadly in line with users' expectations of how the CPI should behave.

2. We are indebted to Dr. Ralph Turvey of the ILO for making available various draft working papers on this topic. In reaching our own conclusions about the merits and demerits of alternative methodologies we have found Dr. Turvey's papers invaluable in helping to point up advantages and weaknesses in particular procedures and in suggesting different ways of looking at things.

Present practice

3. Up to now fresh fruit and vegetables included in the Australian CPI have been restricted to items available throughout the year. Because of the country's temperate and tropical climate and well-developed facilities for long-distance transport, storage and marketing of produce, a substantial range of fresh fruit and vegetables is available year round in the capital cities. The 13 items already included in the CPI account for something like 70 per cent of total household expenditure on fresh fruit and vegetables by the CPI population group. In common with other items in the CPI, each of these items has a fixed weight representing base year expenditure.

Practical investigations undertaken

4. In recent years, as part of a general move to expand the coverage of the CPI, investigations have been made into the possibility of extending the list of fresh fruit and vegetable items to cover some of the important items that are available for only part of each year. The term "seasonal items" is used to describe these in the rest of this article.

5. The investigations concentrated initially on developing experimental price collections for a dozen or so important seasonal items which, if included, would raise coverage in the CPI to approximately 85 per cent of total household expenditure on fresh fruit and vegetables. Since fresh fruit and vegetables account for close to 2 per cent of the total CPI, an improvement of this kind is worth making if it is practicable. The new price collections were set up in order to:

(a) test the practicability of maintaining reliable price series over time;

(b) examine the behaviour of prices over a number of years; and

(c) assess whether any form of seasonal adjustment of prices would be useful for CPI purposes.

6. Monthly consumption (sales) data were also examined in order to assess the patterns of availability of different items. The relationship of prices and quantities for both existing CPI items and prospective new items was examined so that consideration could be given to the introduction of varying monthly weights.

Alternative methodologies considered

7. In parallel with this practical work a study was made of the various alternative methodologies for incorporating seasonal items in a CPI, taking as a starting-point the information on national practices gathered by Dr. Turvey following the joint ECE/ILO meeting in 1978.

8. Selecting the most appropriate methodology for measuring price changes for items not available throughout the year, and for which prices and quantities consumed vary substantially, involves making judgements on a number of separate issues, e.g.:

(a) whether to use varying monthly base prices or fixed base year prices;
(b) whether to use variable monthly weights or fixed weights throughout the year;
(c) if variable monthly weights are used, whether to use chain linking between successive months;
(d) if fixed annual weights are used, how to deal with missing prices in months when particular items are not available;
(e) whether original prices or seasonally adjusted prices should be used.

Monthly or annual base prices

9. At an early stage we rejected the use of varying monthly base prices on the ground that this is in effect a crude form of seasonal adjustment in which the pattern of prices in the base year is assumed to be representative of subsequent years. From our observations of monthly price movements over several years we could see no evidence that any single year could be regarded as reflecting representative patterns of prices. Consequently we took the view that if seasonal adjustment of prices was required it would be preferable to use standard seasonal adjustment techniques, which can accommodate changing seasonality, to adjust current price series first and then to compare these with annual base year prices.

Varying monthly weights

10. Next we considered the relative merits of using varying monthly weights without chain linking and with chain linking. The use of varying monthly weights without chain linking was rejected, principally on the ground that it would be impossible to explain satisfactorily the causes of short-term movements in the index. Between successive months, changes in the index could occur as a result of changes in the composition and weighting as well as (or even without any) changes in prices. We concluded that a paramount requirement of the CPI is that it should not show change unless prices can be seen to have changed (or readily shown to have changed, if masked by quality change) and that an index not meeting these requirements would not be acceptable to users.

Chain linking

11. The use of varying monthly weights with chain linking from each month to the next was considered as a possible means of overcoming the problem of the index moving in response to composition and weighting changes, since in a chain-linked index the changing basket or changing weights themselves cannot cause movement in the index. However, while this technique results in the index showing "correct" month-to-month movements it would not necessarily reflect "correct" long-term movements, for two reasons. First, our investigations showed that such indexes seem to have an inherent downward bias because prices of new items entering the measure tend to be spliced in at relatively high (new season) prices and spliced out at lower prices (or at least this seems to happen far more frequently than the reverse). Second, there is the problem that a chain-linked index tends to drift away from the "true level" because items enter and leave the index regimen at different weights. This means that even if all prices return to the original level the overall index may not return to its original level. As a result the chain-linking approach was also rejected.

Fixed weights and annual base prices

12. Having rejected methods involving use of varying monthly weights and/or varying monthly base prices, we were left with methods using fixed weights and annual base year prices. In this kind of approach the key problem is how to treat items other than year-round items in those

months when they are not available. Leaving aside the fallback option of continuing to exclude all such items altogether there are two possibilities:

(a) to impute prices in some way on the basis of price movements for items that are available; or

(b) to repeat the last observed price of each available item until that item becomes available again.

13. The idea of repeating prices for unavailable items on a consistent, planned basis did not appeal. First, it arbitrarily assigns too much importance to the last monthly price when the "season" finishes and distorts the annual average. Second, to record no change throughout the period of unavailability and hence dampen the movements in the index seems incompatible with the basic objective. The alternative of imputing prices of missing items on the basis of movements in prices of items that are available (which is really just a mechanical device – the actual effect achieved is redistribution of the weights of the missing items amongst the available items each month) seems more in keeping with representing price movements of as many items as possible even though not all are available all the time. Under this procedure any item enters directly into the price measure whenever it is available (in sufficient quantities for prices to be considered representative) and has no effect on the measure when it is not available.

Seasonal adjustment of prices

14. We also considered whether prices of fresh fruit and vegetable items ought to be seasonally adjusted before being incorporated in the CPI measure, in the light of a suggestion by Dr. Turvey that seasonally adjusted prices of available items might be used to impute seasonally adjusted prices of missing items. However, we saw two problems in using seasonally adjusted prices.

15. First, the data we had available on prices suggested that there were substantial variations from year to year in the seasonal pattern of prices – depending on climatic variations which have considerable influence on when supplies of seasonal items begin, when peak supplies are available and when supplies cease. This applies to a number of year-round items as well as to those available for only limited periods. Given this irregular behaviour from year to year of the prices of many items the application of standard seasonal adjustment techniques may have limited value inasmuch as removal of a recurring (systematic) seasonal component is likely to leave behind a substantial irregular component (including what is attributable to varying climatic conditions) which may or may not have relevance to the non-available items. It would also open up the possibility of, or at least fears of, "incorrect" movements being reflected in the CPI as a result of an unrepresentative seasonal pattern built into the adjustment process.

16. Second, if the seasonal pattern changed over time there could be practical difficulties in publishing authoritative index numbers, because the average pattern adopted for the purpose of seasonally adjusting price series would be liable to change significantly when regular re-estimation of seasonal factors is carried out. This could lead to retrospective revisions in seasonally adjusted price series which in turn would raise the question of revising CPI numbers. Given the many critical institutional uses of CPI figures, e.g. in adjustment of wages, pensions, tax rates, etc., and in a wide range of contractual arrangements (which usually occur soon after each figure is issued), we considered that the practical difficulties created by revising index numbers, even marginally, at later dates would make the practice unacceptable. On the other hand, to use seasonally adjusted prices but to deliberately not follow through the implications of re-estimation of seasonal patterns would seem to deny a basic feature of the practice of seasonal adjustment. Consequently it was considered that the use of seasonally adjusted prices in the CPI would lead to undesirable complications and should be rejected.

Conclusion

17. The end result of this process of progressively eliminating options because of one unsatisfactory feature or another led to the conclusion that the most acceptable technique for representing unavailable seasonal items is simple imputation of prices on the basis of price changes recorded for a range of related items which are available in the particular period. This technique has the advantage of being simple to explain and can be seen to reflect "correct" short-term movements (i.e. the index changes only when actual prices change) and "correct" long-term movements (i.e. if all prices return to the original level the index returns to its original level).

Index